T0324739

Enacting Research Methods in Information Systems:
Volume 3

Enacting Research Methods in Information Systems: Volume 3

Edited by

Leslie P. Willcocks
London School of Economics and Political Science, UK

Chris Sauer
Oxford University, UK

and

Mary C. Lacity
University of Missouri-St Louis, USA

Editors
Leslie P. Willcocks
London School of Economics and
Political Science, London, UK

Chris Sauer
Oxford University
Oxford, UK

Mary C. Lacity
University of Missouri-St Louis
St Louis, Missouri, USA

ISBN: 978-3-319-29271-7 (hardback)   ISBN: 978-3-319-29272-4 (eBook)
DOI: 10.1007/978-3-319-29272-4

Printed on acid-free paper

This Palgrave Macmillan imprint is published by Springer Nature
The registered company is Springer International Publishing AG Switzerland

Contents

List of Figures and Tables

Figures

Tables

Introduction

Leslie P. Willcocks, Chris Sauer and Mary C. Lacity

Overview

Research methods is a term open to multiple construals. For graduate programmes of study it often means one or more core courses that introduce the student to different research tools and their likely applicability. Often there is an implicit linearity: identify an important and not fully understood topic, formulate your research question, and then decide which methods to apply. There is little discussion of what to do if you find that there are no adequate methods to answer the research question other than go back to the start and find a new topic and question. Yet, in practice there can be an interplay as methods and question are iteratively adjusted and refined.

There can also be fashions in research (Baskerville and Myers 2009). Structural equation modelling and meta-analysis are two methods much in vogue. When new techniques are invented and promoted, it is reasonable that researchers should try them out and stretch them to their limits and, when those limits are discovered, move on to something new if that takes us nearer to answering the big questions. In this volume, we see researchers engaging with the Design Science approach – they kick the tyres and road test it to see how robust it is. But we also see other researchers, Yasmin Merali and Melanie Wilson, exploring other avenues – complexity theory and gendered approaches respectively.

Five of the articles that follow explore the possibilities of Design Science. While often seen as less scientifically reputable than more traditional hypothesis testing based on surveys or experiments, Design Science seeks to develop knowledge through doing something practical. It is the design work that is the contribution to knowledge, and the evaluation of the design in practice helps validate that knowledge.

Of course, it is not radically new in the Information Systems field to seek knowledge through practice. As we have seen in the first two volumes, Action Research aims to do just that (Wood-Harper et al. 1985). While in this they are similar, there are other differences. In what we might describe as its high church form Design Science mines existing knowledge to synthesise for a new idea in the form of a product or system design. The knowledge base provides a justification for the design that is on a par with a literature review motivating a research question and hypotheses. The idea is validated through practice. By contrast, Action Research will use a knowledge base to formulate an intervention which may take the form of an IT artefact or of a social/organisational intervention related to a technology artefact. So, in this its scope extends beyond Design Science. Where it differs more obviously is in its focus on what happens when academic knowledge in the form of the proposed intervention meets practice in a given context. Then Action Research encourages reflective modification to improve the efficacy of the intervention and revise our understanding. So Design Science is different while pursuing the theme of building knowledge through practice. In Section VI, we see what happens when a variety of researchers kick its tyres.

Introduction to Section VI: Design Science

Section VI includes five chapters on the Design Science approach to research.

Chapter 19 sees McKay, Marshall, and Hirschheim start with the question of what is design such that it can form the basis of a research method. They turn to other disciplines which have accorded design greater respect – engineering, architecture, and management. They argue that these disciplines have a more liberal interpretation of design than those who promote high church Design Science in Information Systems. For them, the outputs of a design process can be more than a product or a blueprint. In addition, design can be plans, models, and intentions. Not surprisingly, therefore, with such a liberal interpretation they charge Hevner and other proponents of Design Science (Hevner et al. 2004) with promoting a dysfunctional separation between design research and behavioural research. Surely, they argue, behavioural theory needs to be integrated with design if practice is to be effective. Supposing that a product can be designed and then behavioural knowledge be applied as a separate layer unrealistically simplifies the relationship between design and use.

In **Chapter 20**, we hear from Arnott and Pervan who have worked in and tracked developments in Decision Support Systems (DSS) research for decades. The term DSS is somewhat dated as other terms such as Business Intelligence (BI) and Business Analytics have grown in currency, but for simplicity we follow the usage of the authors of this chapter. They detect a growing trend to Design Science-based research in DSS. They see it as improving in quality slowly but having the potential to influence the whole field of IS. For the academic purist, one of the potential strengths of Design Science in DSS is that system functionality could in principle be designed according to academic decision theory and the results evaluated in neat and constrained ways. This would be closer to the high church view that McKay and colleagues challenged, and would be very different from the enterprise systems applications where the technology is highly complex and the use and outcomes diffuse. However, Arnott and Pervan stop short of making this argument. Why? This is a question for debate. If they were of the view that even DSS is not sufficiently constrained to permit the ready application of academic theory in practice, then what limitations does this imply for the application of Design Science to the rest of the field.

In **Chapter 21** Hanseth and Lyytinen identify problems in the design of what they define as information infrastructures and develop a design theory to fit. They focus on the tension between the bootstrap problem and the adaptability problem as a distinctive design problem. The bootstrap problem is that an information infrastructure has to deliver early value otherwise it will not retain and grow its user base. The adaptability problem is that as time passes, as needs develop, as technology enables new capabilities so the infrastructure must adapt accordingly. The core tension that these authors identify is that the solution to the bootstrap problem is adopted without knowledge of the adaptability needs. This may well hamstring the designers of solutions to the adaptability problem. Conversely, if the early design focuses on adaptability for unknown needs it may fail to address the bootstrap problem. You can think of Hanseth and Lyytinen as designing a design theory thereby exemplifying a way of doing so in a systematic way. They also surface an issue for Design Science which is that technology designs are not static. They evolve. So testing may not be readily undertaken just at the moment of immediate application of the technology. It may be years before facets of a design show their worth. Here the authors make a distinctive methodological choice. They examine their design theory against historical observations, that is, ex post facto rather than in the moment, thus sidestepping the problem of not being able to observe lagged effects. On a final note for the aficionado of good research practice, their comments on the insufficiency/limitations of their theory are a salutary example.

Chapter 22 follows a route of examining intellectual history to try to understand the place of design-based research in the broader, academic, intellectual context. Heinrich and Riedl examine the design roots and current flowering of research in German-speaking countries. They provide a story that is plausible but they duck the question of why German-speaking research has gone the design route and US research the behavioural route (only recently re-discovering design). Implicitly, they suggest that the norms of academia have been different with top journals being influential. At their most challenging, they speculate on whether there is any evidence to support the practical value of behavioural research allied with design or whether we might not do better leaving design to the instincts and intuition of designers, a view quite contrary to that expressed by McKay et al. in Chapter 19. If this speculation were correct, it would open up some interesting questions as to what the purpose of IS research is and should be, and then what its topics of interest would be.

Finally, in Chapter 23, Salmela uses action research to design and evaluate a process for an under-considered problem – analysis of the business cost of risks. This article could readily have fitted under the action research section, but its approach to action research is not novel. Rather it illustrates the relationship between action research as a method and Design Science research. It highlights the distinction that action research can be about design but is not necessarily so. In this case it is a means to achieving and examining a design with the benefit of learning about the designed process at the same time, that is, it surfaces the sensitisation of technical staff to the business impact of risks attendant on their work/mistakes.

Introduction to Section VII: Alternative Approaches

In Chapter 24 Price and Shanks report on an approach to framework development that is driven by theory. Academic authors often find it convenient to encapsulate their contribution to knowledge in a framework. We shall see this in the final article in this collection by Melanie Wilson. A conceptual framework can be a genuine contribution, but can also be somewhat ad hoc as a means of summarising a set of findings. Here, the potential value of Price and Shanks' work is its applicability beyond its immediate target which is information quality.

Their approach to framework development has five parts: definition of the theoretical concepts or categories, stipulation of the derivation method for assessment criteria based on the definitions in the first part, criteria for objective assessment, criteria for subjective assessment, and refinement through feedback. It is noteworthy that their use of theory only extends so far and that they take a more pragmatic literature based view as they extend into what they term subjective assessments of quality.

So they offer a systematic approach to framework development based on theory. But, they alert the reader to the fact that it is not so simple. There is a question as to whether the semiotic theory they use really is a theory or whether it is merely a commonsense set of interrelated definitions. Then, we are stimulated to ask, "can you trust a theoretically derived framework especially if some of it is not theoretical?" Price and Shanks seek to get around this through empirical study using focus groups.

They conclude that some aspects of their framework need development and it does not meet every need. In fact, it is an interesting indication of why we cannot rely on theory alone for framework development. Where theory meets practice, practice should dominate – this returns to the earlier discussion of behavioural theory versus design. If any theory does not contribute to better design then practitioners are going to question its worth.

In **Chapter 25** Merali makes the case for and offers a tutorial about the application of complexity theory to Information Systems research. Complexity theory is a set of concepts drawn from physics and mathematics that seek to render tractable highly complex phenomena, often based upon network structures and dynamics. She uses interest in the application of complexity theory to organisational studies as a bridge to the legitimising of its application to Information Systems (Anderson et al. 1999, McKelvey 1997). At the heart of her approach to Information Systems research, as too to its application more generally to organisations, is a fundamental problem. The phenomena that make up Information Systems and their use in context are highly complex (i.e. interrelated) and they interact dynamically. We have seen this graphically in developments such as the internet and social networking. Consequently, no linear theorising nor research methods that seek to test linear ideas can adequately represent and cast light on the phenomena in which IS researchers are interested. What is needed she argues is a toolkit that uses different language and can be applied to inherently complex phenomena. She talks us through the concepts of chaos and complexity, of self-organisation, of emergence, of co-evolution and co-adaptation and introduces us to a variety of attractors. The methods question is how usable these concepts are. One answer is to be found in agent-based modelling in Merali's own paper. Another is to be found in Hanseth and Lyytinen's paper in Chapter 21 where they employ concepts drawn from complexity theory to describe and elucidate the development of the internet as a major information infrastructure.

Chapter 26 has Wilson considering how to research gender questions in IS and what kinds of questions should be studied. She doubly embodies alternativeness by seeking inspiration in social studies of science and in taking a gendered approach to research questions. Her analysis focuses principally on the world of work and to that extent is a product of the time at which it was written. Most of the questions she asks remain relevant. Where the paper would be different if written today is that it would reflect the advent of social networking systems. An important element of her work is the recognition that gender and IS cannot be studied separately from the gendered nature of organisation. Nor indeed can any focus on feminist analysis progress without the counterpoint of an analysis of the masculine. Where Wilson contributes to the study of methods is in highlighting the importance of adopting methods that recognise the issue of power and gender. In particular she notes that social constructionist and Actor-Network approaches are deficient in this regard. This is particularly challenging as they are typically viewed as some of the more advanced/progressive approaches to researching IS.

Concluding remarks

There is no one right way to study IS phenomena. There are many ways. The art is to select the methods most appropriate to the research question. If their use will contribute to getting us closer to understanding a problem because it will deliver valid results then that should be enough. What we have seen in this volume in particular, but in the preceding two volumes also, is experienced researchers reflecting on their attempts to advance our ability to use new and established research methods. They usually identify promise but recognise limitations. If the articles in these three volumes help the reader understand the balance to be struck between the promise and the limitations then they will have served their purpose.

References

Anderson, P., Meyer, A., Eisenhardt, K., Carley, K. and Pettigrew, A. 1999. Introduction to the Special Issue: Applications of Complexity Theory to Organization Science, *Organization Science*, 10: 233–236.

Baskerville, Richard L. and Myers, M.D. 2009. Fashion Waves in Information Systems Research and Practice, *MIS Quarterly*, 33(4): 647–662.

Hevner, A.R., March, S.T. and Park, J. 2004. Design Science in Information Systems Research, *MIS Quarterly*, 28(1): 75–105.

McKelvey, B. (1997). Quasi-Natural Organization Science, *Organization Science*, 8: 351–381.

Wood-Harper, A.T., Antill, L. and Avison, D.E. *(1985)*. *Information Systems Definition: The Multiview Approach.* Blackwell Scientific, Oxford

Section VI
Design Science

19
The Design Construct in Information Systems Design Science

Judy McKay
Faculty of Information & Communication Technologies, Swinburne University of Technology, Australia

Peter Marshall
School of Computing and Information Systems, Faculty of Science, Engineering and Technology, University of Tasmania, Australia

Rudy Hirschheim
Department of Information Systems and Decision Sciences, E.J. Ourso College of Business, Louisiana State University, USA

Introduction

The concept of what constitutes design is *in flux, and constantly expanding* (Stewart, 2011: 515). The industrial revolution is argued to have given rise to design-based disciplines, such as engineering and architecture, and during the 19th and 20th centuries, design emerged as being concerned with the conceptualization and actualization of material things and the shaping of material and artificial environments. The 21st century has, however, seen the proliferation of new design contexts and practices, largely driven by digital information technologies and the globalization that such technologies support. Information systems (IS) design and organizational design are but two examples, important as they represent a fundamental shift from design of the material to the immaterial, with more concern for abstract and animate entities than were the interest of engineering and architectural designers of previous centuries (van Aken *et al.*, 2007). Thus, emerging areas of design are not just focusing on traditional notions of production and functionality,

Reprinted from "The design construct in information systems design science," by J. McKay, P. Marshall and R. Hirschheim in *Journal of Information Technology*, 27, 2012, pp. 125–139. With kind permission from the Association for Information Technology Trust. All rights reserved.

11

but on more immaterial notions such as systems, processes, organizations, user experiences, on-going interactions, relationships and the situated meaning of things (Stewart, 2011), all important concepts in the broad spectrum of IS research. The concept of design is thus critical in IS, with IS design research needing to accommodate both the material and immaterial foci of design. Given these developments, reconceptualizing design becomes important, as does developing a science of design that encompasses the new notions and perspectives.

The concept of design, and of design science (DS), has gained prominence in IS as evidenced by the attention to the work of Hevner *et al.* (2004).[1] Building from earlier work of Walls *et al.* (1992), March and Smith (1995) and Markus *et al.* (2002), Hevner and colleagues established a basis for DS in IS (Kuechler and Vaishnavi, 2008). However, Carlsson (2006, 2007), McKay and Marshall (2005, 2007), Niehaves and Becker (2006), and Niehaves (2007a, b) have questioned some of the perspectives adopted and promoted by Hevner and others, and offer alternative views. Thus emerge two DS communities: the mainstream, organized around the Hevner *et al.* (2004) perspective, and a more pluralistic community. The mainstream DS community adopts a prescriptive, rather constrained definition of design, DS and DS research. The pluralistic community promotes a variety of perspectives around design (e.g., Carlsson, 2007; McKay and Marshall, 2007; Niehaves, 2007a,b; Avital *et al.*, 2009).

The argument advanced here builds from Jones (2003) and Campbell (1977) (writing about organizational studies and organizational effectiveness), to articulate why it is neither possible nor wise to have a single all-encompassing definition of either IS or of design in IS. Particular conceptualizations of design in IS may only be useful in certain circumstances, and thus must be located within a theoretical framework or context which reveals a perspective of IS in which we make sense of that conceptualization of design. This builds on the notions articulated by El Sawy (2003) who noted that any single perspective is just that: a single view among many possible views of 'reality.' El Sawy (2003) noted that each perspective both highlights and backgrounds different elements: different perspectives are not right or wrong: they offer differing views and insights. Building from this, we assert the different design communities in IS focus on different aspects of DS and that multiple perspectives are important for building a broader-based DS in IS.

We argue for multiple conceptualizations of design to be accepted within the field of IS, and thus the production of new knowledge of design in IS, the very basis of building a science of design in IS, can progress along a much broader front. Research needs to progress our understanding of both the material and the immaterial facets of design. Further, we argue that in addition to the important work already undertaken by Hevner *et al.* (2004), Walls *et al.* (1992), Markus *et al.* (2002), Peffers *et al.* (2008) and many others in starting to articulate what we here label as a construction-centered DS in IS, knowledge needs also to be built in a human-centered DS in IS (Roth, 1999; Avital *et al.*, 2009).

This paper is a conceptual study based on a substantial review of the design literature in both IS and non-IS disciplines, and is advanced in five main sections. In the next section, the Hevner view on DS is discussed, and from that we argue that this view of DS stems from a particular view of IS. The paper then examines the ways in which design is framed and conceptualized in many non-IS disciplines, and reveals a number of different conceptualizations of the design construct. In the section that then follows, these conceptualizations are compared with and contrasted with the narrower ways in which design is conceptualized in the current IS DS literature. This is important for if we accept Campbell's (1977) argument, the science of design that is built will be constrained by the conceptualizations we have of design. A number of important issues and concerns arising from the ways in which design in IS is currently conceptualized are then discussed, and other ways of thinking about design in IS are then proposed. The paper concludes by arguing that this inclusiveness is instrumental to build an overarching theory of design embracing all aspects of design relevant to IS. The conclusion also considers some of the theoretical and practical implications of rethinking the design construct in IS.

An exploration of the Hevner position

In drawing on the work of Hevner *et al.* (2004) as the basis of our discussion, we are not implying that this is the only view of DS in IS. We support Kuechler and Vaishnavi (2008), who suggest that despite other somewhat different positions being articulated most notably by scholars from Europe, the Hevner perspective has *been widely promulgated to the entire academic IS design community* (p. 7). Kuechler and Vaishnavi (2008) add that it has *become so widely adopted by design researchers in IS that it dominates the field* (p. 4), and is the view which they argue is *currently held by the majority of those practicising in the field* (p. 5). Thus, we use the Hevner position as one widely accepted and adopted within the IS academic community and one which typifies most research on IS DS at the current time.

Hevner *et al.* (2004) delineate IS knowledge as falling within two paradigms: the behavioral science and the DS paradigms. Essentially, they argue that DS in IS is about the design of *new and innovative artifacts* (p. 75), IT artifacts, which are then implemented or instantiated in particular situations to solve problems identified within organizational contexts. In contrast, the behavioral paradigm is seen as seeking to explain and predict *organizational and human phenomena* **surrounding** [bold added] *the analysis, design, implementation, management, and the use of information systems* (p. 76). In Figure 19.1 from Hevner *et al.* (2004: 79), the relationships between business and IT strategies and infrastructures are depicted, and the interplay between these four elements is seen as rightly falling within the interests of IS researchers. However, while Hevner *et al.* (2004) recognize that there are many design activities involved in realizing alignment between IS and organizational strategies, their interest in DS in IS is limited to the design activities associated with the building of an IS infrastructure (circled in Figure 19.1). To quote, Hevner *et al.* (2004: 78) write that: *Our subsequent discussion of design science will be limited to the activities of building the IS infrastructure within the business organization. Issues of strategy, alignment, and organizational infrastructure are outside the scope of this paper.* This, and subsequent statements in their paper, such as *we do not include people or elements of organization in our definition* [of the IT artifact], *nor do we explicitly include the process by which such artifacts evolve* (Hevner *et al.*, 2004: 82) and *artifacts constructed in design science research are rarely full-grown information*

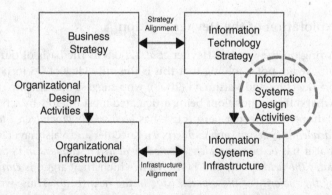

Figure 19.1 The focus of design interest in IS according to Hevner *et al.* (2004: 79)

systems that are used in practice (Hevner *et al.*, 2004: 83) seem to reveal worldviews on both 'design' within an IS context and 'information systems' which serve to delimit their subsequent argumentation.

Carlsson (2007) argues that in the writings of Hevner *et al.* (2004), and other key authors, design and the DS paradigm in IS are arguably presented as being about the IT artifact. That is, about elements of the innovative combination of hardware and software, and the means by which these may be developed and realized. Hevner *et al.* (2004: 78) note the dichotomy that design is about both the product, the artifact itself and attendant methods and models, for example, and the process, the set of activities by which such innovative products are produced. They argue that other interests fall within the behavioral science para-digm in IS – the social, cultural, political and human dimensions asso-ciated with the implementation, use, acceptance and exploitation of the technical artifact in an organizational context. This then suggests a particular view of design and IS, as illustrated in Figure 19.2.

The DS interest in the IT artifact in Figure 19.2 is viewed as consisting of the new innovations described by Hevner *et al.* (2004), which may be combinations of innovative software and hardware (instantiations), or constructs, models and methods, and the like. This IT artifact is of inter-est to the DS researcher who, through building and evaluating such arti-facts builds knowledge in the DS paradigm. The knowledge, insights and skills revealed by a DS researcher collectively build a science of design, a *construction-centered DS*. The IT artifact may then be implemented into an organizational (socio-technical) context, and hence these artifacts in the organization may become of interest to the IS researcher working

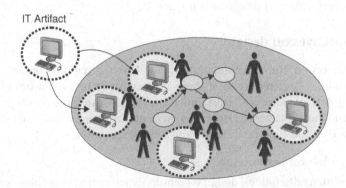

Figure 19.2   The IT artifact 'surrounded' by the organizational context

in the behavioral science paradigm. Note that such artifacts are seen as 'surrounded' by human and organizational phenomena, as being able to be split out from the organizational context in which they are implemented. The Hevner *et al.* (2004) conception of IS thus would seem to embrace a bounding of the IT artifact from other constituent elements of an organizational context. There appear to be similarities between this and what El Sawy (2003: 591) described as the connection view of IS, in which IT is *a separate artifact that can be connected to people's work actions and behaviors*. The effect of this, however, is to paradigmatically separate the building and developing activities from the social, cultural and political aspects in organizational contexts.

Separating design activities into two paradigms potentially causes fragmentation: the recognition of the building of a science of design in IS is shared broadly across the IS academic community, but the position adopted by Hevner *et al.* (2004) would appear to result in a split between two different spheres of design knowledge.[2] We argue that such a view is not held in non-IS disciplines in which design is of considerable interest. We thus support the views of Kuechler and Vaishnavi (2008: 8), who express concern *that the pressure for (short-term) relevance and the understandable desire for definitional closure for the area are prematurely narrowing the perception of ISDR; focusing it exclusively on the constructivist methodology and on prescriptive design theories (models) for low level artifacts (IT mechanisms) rather than allowing it to have the breadth it has achieved in other design fields*. By focusing on the IT artifact, and conceptualizing IS as separable from the organizational context, it is inevitable DS in IS is limited to design of the IT artifact. The question to be considered is whether a different and broader conceptualization of design in IS might be helpful in building new and insightful knowledge and practices about design as it impacts IS.

Perspectives on design

In this section, the conceptualization of design in disciplines other than IS will be considered to see if there are insights to be gained from the way others construe, and thus understand and research the construct of design. These different perspectives on design are briefly summarized in Table 19.1 and then discussed in the following section.

Design as problem solving

Across many disciplines, design is commonly referred to as problem solving, a way of defining problems (Buchanan, 1992; Boland *et al.*, 2008),

Table 19.1 Differing perspectives of design from non-IS disciplines

Design as ...	Brief description
Problem solving	Transforming and improving the material environment, solution-oriented, finding solutions to field problems and implementing those solutions
Product	Objects, entities, artifacts that arise and are imbued with meaning within those contexts, designer inextricably linked to the designed product
Process	Processes and actions that lead to the realization and implementation of an artifact in a particular context, design involves action taking and change
Intention	Deliberate thought processes that enable the designer and user to see connections between problem and possible solutions, the intent driving the design activity and the impacts this has on the realized artifact
Planning	Working hypothesis (or plan, model, etc.) that captures and formalizes the designer's intentions
Communication	Conceptual characteristics (form and content) of artifacts that resonate with users, the ways meaning is reconstructed by users
User experience	The range of experiences (both manifest and latent) created for and received by the user of an artifact, the meanings and experiences a user constructs with an artifact over time
Value	The value (often symbolic and/or social) placed on the artifact and the experiences of that artifact by a user, and how this changes over time
Professional practice	The broad responsibilities and activities of designers who inevitably change the world through their actions, an attitude towards a 'problem,' consideration of the knowledge and skills required by designers
Service	Day-to-day problem solving, ability to understand and help others resolve or ameliorate problems, mindful of contextual forces and constraints

and it is argued that this rational problem solving view of design has become dominant and normalized in conceptualizing design in many disciplines (Dorst, 2006). When viewed as problem solving, design is often characterized as a *means of ordering the world* (Dilnot, 1982: 144), of meeting needs, making desired improvements, of transforming and improving the material environment (Willem, 1990; Friedman, 2003). Emphasis is often placed on design involving careful analysis and definition of the problem, and on gathering adequate information about the problem before seeking solutions (Kruger and Cross, 2006). However, in some conceptualizations of design as problem solving, the emphasis is placed on design as being the solution to the problem. In this way, the conceptualization of design shifts slightly to generating solutions, and to redefining the problem in light of these emerging solutions (Kruger and Cross, 2006). Design is thus argued to solve problems by being solution-oriented, as designing or developing solutions to situations regarded as problematic by stakeholders (Romme, 2003; Keys, 2007; van Aken, 2007). These problems are of certain types, however, with van Aken (2007) distinguishing between knowledge problems (which arise through limitations in knowledge) and field problems (which arise from a recognition or desire to realize a better social reality). Design is seen as solving field problems, and the problem solving activity involves not only designing a solution but also realizing or implementing that solution in some material or social reality (van Aken and Romme, 2009).

Design as problem solving can be understood as the obscurity that surrounds requirements or goals, the practicality of envisageable 'provisions' (a term used by Archer, 1979 to refer to possible emergent solutions or designs), and the misfit that may occur between requirements as perceived and articulated provisions. The solution that emerges is ultimately the provision that offers an acceptably small residual misfit, and an acceptably small degree of residual obscurity of requirements. Thus, design as problem solvsing is conceptualized as an oscillating conceptual and practical activity, with thinking and activity swinging between clarifying requirements (reducing obscurity) and articulating provisions that match the requirements to varying degrees, until a solution that satisfies the problem owner emerges (Archer, 1979) (see Figure 19.3). In viewing design as problem solving, activities involved are people- and solution-oriented, and the implemented solution is to a problem experienced within a particular context (a field problem) (van Aken, 2007).

Design as product

In conceptualizing design as product, artifacts arise within particular social and historical contexts and are imbued with meaning within those contexts (Dilnot, 1982). There is often reference to the importance of design's involvement in giving material form to a problem solution, of the artifact meeting some perceived need, or solving some sort of organizational, technical or human problem (Willem, 1990). The role of the designer is often mentioned and always assumed, in the sense that the designer is seen as adding characteristics of desirability and/or utility to the object of interest (Dilnot, 1984a).

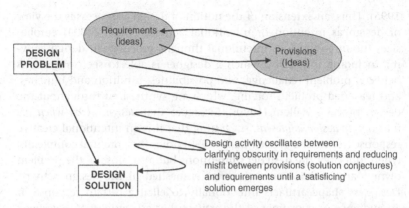

Figure 19.3 The oscillating nature of design problem solving

Design as process

The limitations of the product view of design arguably stem from the fact that the activity or process involved in materializing a problem solution is marginalized, and thus definitions of the product view of design cause angst in some circles, where there is a tension perceived between the *product* of creation and the *activity* of creation. For example, Miller (2004) asserts that the product or result of creation is an entity, an output of design, but is not design itself. In contradistinction to the product view is the process view of design: design is a series of thoughts and activities by which an artifact is created and realized (Andreasen *et al.*, 2002). The concept of problem solving is often retained in definitions of these types, where design is seen as the activity involved in moving from a vague, possibly ill-defined problem to a clear and creative response, and in these activities shaped by context lies the essence of design (Ryan, 1997). The goal of design from this perspective is thus to take action and to produce change in human contexts (Willem, 1990). Galle (1999) further expands this notion of design such that it embraces all human activities dedicated to both realizing an artifact and in embedding that artifact in a context of use in which it is met with approval and use (or not).

Design as intention

In the philosophy literature, the aspect of design that is emphasized is the fact that it results from intentional activity (Dipert, 1995; Hilpinen,

1995). Thus, an extension of the notion of design as process is the view of design as intention or intentional activity. Miller (2004) emphasizes the importance of intentional thought processes in design activity, including insight by which a designer is able to see connections between problem (challenge) and possibilities, intuition and hunches, and reasoned problem solving, which are synthesized throughout the design process. Willem (1990: 45) argues that *design occurs when the intention to design is present,* suggesting that it is an intentional creative response to external events. Galle (1999) notes the potential complexity when, not only the designer's intentions but also those of the problem owners and solution users become enmeshed in the design activity. Designers shape artifacts intentionally to elicit a certain response in an audience or consumer of the artifact, but as *consumers ... encounter artifacts, their interpretations may correspond with those that were intended, but might also differ from those intentions in many varied ways* (Crilly *et al.*, 2008a: 15). In constructing meanings, the consumer may not have access to or knowledge of design intentions. Thus, the designed artifact that is experienced by the user may or may not align well with the intentions of the designer (Crilly *et al.*, 2008b).

Design as planning

Furthering the view of design as intention, Buchanan (1992: 8) argues that design can be regarded as a plan or *working hypothesis* which constitutes or formalizes the designer's intention. Similarly, Dilnot (1984b) suggests that design can be thought of as a conscious attempt to plan and build patterns, which will then shape the emergence of an artifact from a conceptualization of the designer. The task of a designer could be argued to involve the planning and representation of forms, which aim to reconcile the many competing and possibly conflicting views and constraints with the intention of the designer, those of the intended user(s), and organizational factors viewed as constraints on the planning and representational activity (Crilly *et al.*, 2009). Wieringa and Heerkens (2007) agree, arguing that design involves specifying what you intend to do before you actually do it, and thus is fundamentally concerned with conceiving and planning something in one's mind. Galle (1999: 65) refers to this as the problem of the *absent artifact*, the challenge of conceptualizing, planning and realizing something that does not currently exist.

Dilnot (1984a) notes that before the Industrial Revolution, designing, planning and making artifacts were conceived of as one construct, whereas afterwards, the planning and designing of artifacts has typically been separated from the making of artifacts. Galle (1999) is sympathetic to this view, as he argues there are several stages of planning involved in the process of realizing an artifact and embedding it in its context of use. Thus, in moving from conception of a solution to realized artifact, there are stages of design representation or plans. Van Aken (2005a) argues that such plans are themselves designs: the plans and sketches of a house, for example, are the design of the house. According to the conceptualization of van Aken (2005a), following the design is another stage of planning, constituted by the plans of action and activities involved in the realization of the physical artifact, in which the design representations are transformed into an artifact of utility.

Design as communication

Designers either knowingly or unknowingly enshrine human values and opinions in their designs, based on their own worldview, and on their understanding of the audience for which the design is intended. A design resonates with an audience when it appeals to their interests, values and attitudes, for example, and in this way communicates with its audience (Buchanan, 1989; Lunenfeld, 2003). Kazmierczak (2003) argues that design is the process by which the meanings intended by the designer are communicated to an audience, and received as intended, or as reconstructed by the audience given their context, values and the like. This perspective of design is thus quite different from many of those presented above. It moves from notions of objects or artifacts, and the processes by which the artifact is realized, and focuses on the conceptual characteristics embodied in objects that serve to communicate with an audience. Kazmierczak (2003: 45) writes that it *redefines designs from finite, fixed objects of aesthetic and practical consideration to semiotic interfaces enabling the reconstruction of meaning by receivers.* Design thus becomes associated with form and content, with emphasis placed not just on the role of the designer in shaping form, but also on an essential role of the designer in shaping communicative content with the aim of encouraging particular interpretations, which is evidenced through the meaning or interpretations or thoughts design induces in an audience (Redstrom, 2008; Crilly, 2011). The role of the artifact as mediating communication between designer and audience thus becomes paramount (Crilly et al., 2008b). Design, thus conceived, becomes linked to a designer using the 'right' language to express his/her intentions in a way that can be accurately comprehended and responded to by the recipient audience (Krippendorff, 1996; Redstrom, 2006). The success of a design is thus dependent on the successful comprehension of the design by its intended audience (Kazmierczak, 2003).

Design as user experience

The notion of design as communication is extended by Redstrom (2006), who suggests that design is better conceived of as the user's experience of an object. The focus shifts from communicative elements to the experiences, which the design creates and enables for its audience. The audience thus becomes the subject of design, through their dynamic and multisensory experiences of an artifact (Redstrom, 2006: 126). This represents a substantial shift away from the material object or artifact, and the processes surrounding the conceptualization of the object and its physical realization. Design thus becomes concerned with the immaterial, how one designs user experiences, not just in terms of utility or usability, but also in terms of communication, interpretation, understanding and experience (Kazmierczak, 2003; Redstrom, 2006; Boztepe, 2007). Norman (2009) argues that a product is better viewed as *a cohesive, integrated set of experiences* (p. 54), and views design as concerned with thinking systemically about the full gamut of user experiences, ranging from *discovery, purchase, anticipation ... first usage ... continued usage, learning, the need for assistance, updating, maintenance, supplies, and eventual renewal ...* (p. 52).[3] This focus on user experience in design seeks to appreciate and understand both manifest functions of artifacts (that the artifact satisfies the needs and objectives for which it was designed), and also potential latent functions (the uses to which an artifact is actually put, or the purposes it actually serves). Further, user experience is argued to be shaped by the users' anticipation and perceptions of the designers' intentions and actions, impacting both the user experience of, and on-going interactions with the artifact (Crilly, 2011). In this way, the creativity and innovation associated with design are shared among designers and individual and collective agency arising from user experience.

Design as value

The value of design is linked to the value a consumer (user) places on the range of user experiences noted above (Norman, 2009). Other writers note that design itself has become associated with value, often not an intrinsic part of the artifact itself, but as some sort of iconic status that becomes associated with a particular object. In this sense, we get expressions such as 'designer jeans,' designer labels' and the like, where value becomes associated with the significance attached to an object rather than the object itself (Dilnot, 1984a,b). Thus, design becomes associated with heightened social status, or reaffirmation of belonging to a particular sub-culture, for example (Almquist and Lupton, 2010). In this sense, design achieves something akin to cult status for the consumption of the general public in which value, sentiment and enjoyment is attached to that status as much as to the product or object itself (Schneider, 2007). Boztepe (2007) furthers the social and cultural aspects of value, arguing that design can be ascribed symbolic and social value. Value is added (or not) as designs communicate messages independent of their use, thus taking on a symbolic and signaling value. Understanding how designs *are made sense of ... what range of social ends they provide to users* (Boztepe, 2007: 57) thus becomes an important consideration when considering design as value. The value concept is a dynamic one: value may change pre- and post-acquisition, from first-time to short-term to long-term use and so on, suggesting that value changes as user experiences change (Boztepe, 2007).

An alternative position is to consider the value(s) that are both designed into artifacts and services, and that may emerge through the implementation and use of such artifacts. These emergent values may or may not reflect the designer's intentions, and may have impacts (positive and negative) both on direct consumers of the artifact and indirect stakeholders (Friedman, 2008). Being mindful and proactive regarding the values embedded in artifacts, and of potential impacts of these designs through intended use and also possible unintended uses is emphasized from this perspective.

Design as professional practice

Many definitions of design include close consideration of the designer, and some come to argue that design is *what designers do* (Dilnot, 1984b). Thus, design starts to be seen more as professional practice, with identified responsibilities to clients, fellow designers, the public, and broader social and environmental responsibilities (http://www. aiga.org). Wolford-Ulrich (2004: 2) argues that *framing design as practice recognizes the interactive and iterative pattern of designers acting in the world, changing the world, being changed by the world, and experiencing change in themselves through the process of changing the world.* Design as a professional practice can be viewed as a way of thinking and an attitude toward a design task (Wangelin, 2007), as a practice delimited by the design task (Hooker, 2004), or engagement directly in a specific design activity (Fallman, 2003). This view of design emphasizes the situatedness of the designer in a real-world context involving uncertainty, ambiguity and value conflict (Fallman, 2003). Louridas (1999) and Wangelin (2007) argue that design is bricolage, an attitude toward a problem in which previous knowledge and experiences, tools and resources, can be intuitively adapted and applied to a current challenge. This view of design serves to emphasize the subjective nature of interpretation and value judgments made about the problem at hand, the intended audience and so on. Considering design as a professional practice implies a need to think much more closely about the knowledge, skills and attributes required of designers as they conceptualize and realize artifacts intended to improve problem situations (Friedman, 2003; Keys, 2007). Hence, there is a need to retain a *sense of design as a pluralistic and multiple activity, a synthesis of heterogeneous activities defined not by the separate activities, but by their integration* (Dilnot, 1982: 141).

Design as service

In post-industrial societies, most design activity is centered on service provision, described as *non-esthetically motivated service* (Dilnot, 1984b: 4), rather than heroism, the highly creative, innovative and bold heroic individual, who manages to turn design of a product with various aesthetic values into an outlet for personal expression (Lundgren, 1978). Design as service arguably needs more attention than has historically been the case in much of the design discourse (Secomandi and Snelders, 2011). Lundgren (1978: 20) writes that *design activity ... has so much more to do with sustained service, an anonymously methodical day-in, day-out solving of problems, than with the constant ferment of creative choices exercised by the loner hero-artist.* The design as a service view encapsulates the ability to understand the problem as experienced by these problem owners and their objectives in seeking a resolution of that problem. The context in which the problem is embedded is thus critical to successful design, with service in this sense being *enacted in the relations between diverse actors, rather than as a specific kind of object to be designed* (Kimbell, 2011: 42).

This list of differing conceptualizations of and nuances associated with the design construct from non-IS fields is not intended to be exhaustive, nor are these mutually exclusive. There are clearly overlaps and close relationships between the differing perspectives of design discussed here. However, it illustrates some of the ways in which design is understood and researched in a range of non-IS fields. Willem (1990) notes that it may be 'disconcerting' to take such a broad view of a range of possible activities and entities that are considered under the rubric of design. However, to not do so, is to arbitrarily assign the label of design to a subset of these activities, which Willem (1990) argues may seem somewhat capricious. Willem (1990: 45) goes on to note that *the recognition of a large host of coherent activities as design may provide a richness of experience that is presently missing*. He notes that science accommodates a large range of disciplines and activities within its fold without having a detrimental effect on any of them: design can do likewise. Further, this broader conceptualization of design helps make sense of a statement made in the introduction, based on the arguments of Campbell (1977), where it was argued that no single all-encompassing definition of design could be established. Rather, any particular definition of design delimits a worldview of design, and thus locates design within a particular frame or context. Knowledge production is then also located within that context, and offers important insights about that particular worldview, but is also limited in not offering insights into the many other possible worldviews that may be entertained.

The conceptualization of design in IS

The tables below offer a comparison of the ways in which design is conceptualized in non-IS areas (Table 19.2) as opposed to IS (Table 19.3), and thus offer insights into the ways in which design in IS may be thought of. To construct Table 19.2, the authors independently read the papers listed, identifying the ways in which design was conceptualized. These independent assessments were then discussed and consolidated. Where there were disagreements, each individual identified those parts of the paper that had led to a particular classification. This was discussed, compared with other instances of similar classification, and a consensus reached. In nearly all cases, this led to agreement that additional conceptualizations were evident in a particular paper. A cross (x) in any particular column means that the authors agreed that in the paper of interest, there had been substantive discussion of design from a particular perspective and that a discussion, justification and/or compelling argument of some length was built around the view of design adopted and promoted. In disciplines other than IS, we see a very broad understanding of design. When compared with IS publications, the contrast is quite stark. There are currently four predominant conceptualizations in IS: design as problem solving, as product or artifact, as process (often referred to as building and evaluating), and as planning, modeling and representing.

The narrower conceptualization of design in IS DS research limits what gets legitimized as a researchable conception of design, what might fall

Table 19.2 Conceptualizations of design in non-IS literature

Non-IS papers		Conceptualization of design									
Author(s)	Year	Problem solving	Product, artifact	Process	Intention	Planning	Communication	User experience	Value	Professional practice	Service
Andreasen et al.	2002			x							
Boland et al.	2008	x							x		
Boztepe	2007							x			x
Buchanan	1989						x				
Buchanan	1992	x				x		x		x	
Crilly	2011						x				
Crilly et al.	2008a				x		x	x			
Crilly et al.	2008b				x		x	x		x	
Crilly et al.	2009				x		x	x			
Dilnot	1992	x	x			x					
Dilnot	1984a		x			x			x		
Dilnot	1984b					x			x		
Dipert	1995										
Dorst	2006				x						
Fallman	2003										
Friedman	2008									x	
Friedman	2003									x	
Galle	1999		x		x	x					
Hilpinen	1995				x						
Hooker	2004									x	
Kazmierczak	2003						x	x			
Keys	2007	x								x	x
Kimbell	2011										x
Krippendorff	1996						x				
Kruger and Cross	2006	x									

Louridas	1999
Lundgren	1978
Lunenfeld	2003
Marxt and Hacklin	2005
Miller	2004
Redstrom	2006
Redstrom	2008
Romme	2003
Ryan	1997
Secomandi and Snelders	2011
van Aken	2004
van Aken	2005a
van Aken	2007
Wangelin	2007
Wieringa and Heerkens	2007
Willem	1990
Wolford-Ulrich	2004

Table 19.3 Conceptualizations of design in IS literature

Non-IS papers											
					Conceptualization of design						
Author(s)	Year	Problem solving	Product, artifact	Process	Intention	Planning	Communication	User experience	Value	Professional practice	Service
Abbasi and Chen	2008		x	x							
Adams and Courtney	2004		x	x							
Adomavicius et al.	2008	x	x								
Arnott	2006		x	x							
Au	2001		x	x							
Cao et al.	2006	x	x	x							
Choi et al.	2010		x	x							
D'Aubeterre et al.	2008		x	x							
Germonprez et al.	2007	x	x	x							
Gregor and Jones	2007		x	x							
Hevner et al.	2004	x	x	x							
Iivari	2007		x	x	x						
Jones et al.	2003	x	x	x							
Kolfschoten and De Vreede	2009		x	x							
Lee et al.	2008		x	x							
March and Smith	1995		x	x							
Markus et al.	2002			x							
Mittleman	2009		x			x		x			
Niehaves	2007b	x	x	x							
Parsons and Wand	2008	x	x								
Siponen et al.	2006		x	x							
Storey et al.	2008		x	x							
Umapathy et al.	2008		x								
Walls et al.	1992		x	x							
Walls et al.	2004		x	x							
Wastell	2010	x	x	x							

under the rubric of design research, and what might constitute design knowledge or a science of design. We support the view of Hatchuel (2001) that a theory of design should not be limited to problem solving, product and process. This narrow conceptualization raises a number of important issues, which will be explored in the following section.

Issues in current conceptualizations of DS in IS

Thinking about the notion of design in IS requires us to be mindful of the reasons why we design. There are obviously economic imperatives, for greater efficiency and remaining competitive in a complex and uncertain global marketplace. A design imperative in IS must surely be to help organizations manage these forces and to achieve sustainability in such environments. But there are also cultural, social and ethical imperatives that revolve around thinking about designing ISs that utilize IT to help humans enrich their experience of organization, of work, of society, of education, to add meaning and value to what they do (Buchanan, 1996). If we accept both sociocultural as well as economic imperatives, then it could be argued that we need to build a DS in IS that, in addition to the construction-centered design knowledge, builds knowledge in our designers (and so creates knowledge, capabilities and a culture among our IS professionals) so that they know how to achieve both imperatives through their range of design activities in organizations. What they know will limit and shape what they can do – thus a construction-centered conceptualization of design will potentially perpetuate construction-centered solutions being proffered as solutions to design problems.

The worldview that apparently underpins Hevner *et al.*'s conceptualization of IS is well suited to the articulation of design knowledge relating to the IT artifact as they define it. It is, however, not sufficient to support the breadth of research activity that could take place under the rubric of design within an IS context if some of the conceptualizations of design from non-IS disciplines were adopted within IS. Opponents to this stance may assert that in the Hevner *et al.* (2004) view, many of the broader conceptualizations of design and the associated research problems would certainly remain within the interests of IS research, but would be seen as belonging to the behavioral science paradigm. That is certainly one way of dealing with this problem. However, we know of no other discipline where such a separation has been made. In engineering (Marxt and Hacklin, 2005), management (Friedman, 2003; Boland, 2004; Boland *et al.*, 2008), organizational development (Romme, 2003;

van Aken, 2004, 2005a, b; van Aken and Romme, 2009), industrial design (Cross, 2001; Crilly *et al.*, 2008a,b, 2009), education (Brown, 1992; Edelson, 2002), and in the arts and humanities (Lunenfeld, 2003), for example, design and design knowledge are not viewed as being split across two paradigms, but multiple conceptualizations embraced within a DS. Other worldviews are possible and important, and need to be considered in gaining a new perspective of what the construct design might mean in IS. Figure 19.4 depicts one other possibility.

The worldview captured in Figure 19.4 takes a socio-technical view of IS, adopting a philosophical position of trying for joint optimization between technology and the individuals who must use that technology. According to Mumford (1983: 10), socio-technical systems design involves 'making the best use of people ... the best use of technology.' This view emphasizes the 'situatedness' of the technology within an organizational context. An IS emerges from the relationships and behaviors that result in organizational contexts that involve people, activities, information, technology, culture, politics, history and the like (Mumford, 2000). It is not divisible. Viewed in this way, IS are not *surrounded* by organizational and human phenomena as suggested by Hevner *et al.* (2004) but are part of that phenomena, are socially constructed by designers (IS practitioners and users) and society shaping (Hughes, 1987), and hence shape and are shaped by the context of use. In this regard, we support the view of Kroes (2001) who argues that technical objects cannot be separated from the context of their intended use,

Figure 19.4   A socio-technical view of IS situated in context: the IS artifact as the '*ultimate particular*'

and that it is within this context that the function of the IT artifact is socially constructed. Thus, IT artifacts are components of IS, as are people, activities, communication, information and so on. But the *IS artifact* emerges from the interactions and interdependencies that result from looking at the whole, rather than constituent elements. This view seems more in harmony with the fusion view defined by El Sawy (2003), where IS design occurs in shaping organizational contexts by changing the way information is communicated, stored, created, shared and used, the way work is done, the way people interact, the way organizations are structured, the way in which cultural and power relationships are played out (Boland *et al.*, 2008; Avital *et al.*, 2009), and in reshaping the technology over time. Stolterman (2008: 59) argues that the IS artifact thus conceived is an example of the *ultimate particular*, the unique outcome of an intentional design process which evokes particular emergent properties through the interactions between technical, human and organizational elements. Such design activity must be cognizant of the culture, politics, sociology and history of that context. Thus, the IS artifact, its utilization and evolution over time within a particular wider socio-technical organizational context becomes the object of both design activity and research interest. These designed IS artifacts form part of the improvement of the problem space or situation. For IS researchers and practitioners, this emphasizes the need for broad conceptualization and interest in design, and the need also to recognize, understand and elucidate practices with respect to transforming situations (by the responsible application of IT artifacts) into more desired states, taking account of context and the uses for which people may appropriate such systems. Human-centered design knowledge and construction-centered design knowledge should both be recognized as falling legitimately within a DS in IS.

Considering the differences between worldviews, a much more complex view of design starts to emerge (see Figure 19.5). Taking the construction-centered view of design, the focus is on the IT artifact (Purao, 2002; Carlsson, 2007) and the resultant form that it is given as a result of design activity. Through research and reflection, the body of knowledge about construction-centered design is built and accumulated over time. When that artifact is implemented within an organizational context, users interact with that artifact, and endow it with meaning within that particular context of use. Knowledge of design within organizational contexts (human-centered design knowledge) is likewise built and accumulated over time. Such knowledge bases form part of our knowledge of design, and hence our knowledge of the world. Designers

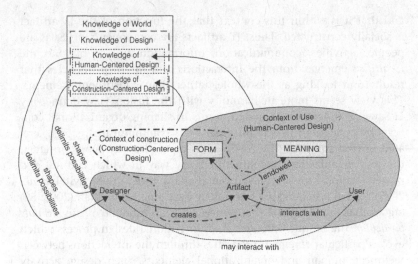

Figure 19.5   Components of IS design science
Source: Based on Krippendorff (1996) and Galle (1999).

are inevitably shaped and limited by their knowledge of design in both senses. The Hevner perspective, widely adopted in IS (Kuechler and Vaishnavi, 2008), focuses primarily on construction-centered design and building a DS based on the knowledge accumulated in the construction of the artifact. The additional worldview articulated in this paper focuses primarily on human-centered design and has argued that a DS can be built from knowledge accumulated in the context of use. The various perspectives of design can also be interpreted against this diagram, and an argument put forward to suggest that broadening our current conceptualization of design can lead to much richer and broader understanding of design in IS, and hence of the types of research into design that can, indeed should, be pursued. It is also the contention of this paper that IS as a discipline is better served and greater coherence in the discipline achieved if these potentially two DSs are seen as one.

Implications for IS research

Table 19.4 provides an outline of how our view of DS could be applied to the IS domain. In addition to the research activity currently being undertaken in the construction-centered DS space, we have argued for a broader conceptualization of the design construct, opening the

Table 19.4 Developing a research agenda for human-centered design science in IS

Design as ...	Potential research interests
Problem solving	How does a design solution emerge from the multiple perspectives of what constitutes the field problem? How do designers and users co-construct a new (changed) social–technical reality to resolve this problem? How does a generic solution to a problem type encapsulated in a software package morph into a designed and implemented solution that has the characteristics of utility and desirability and meets a range of economic, social, cultural, political and organizational objectives?
Product	How do stakeholders seek alignment between the problem and solution as evidenced in the package software and the problem(s) and possible solutions as perceived by organizational members? How does the social, cultural, political and historic organizational context shape and influence the implemented realization of the previously designed packaged software?
Process, action	How does co-design evolve? Are there particular practices and processes that are more conducive to 'good' co-design? If analysts adopt a design attitude rather than a decision attitude throughout the process of both realizing and implementing a solution, can better outcomes be achieved? How might a design attitude change the processes and activities involved in managing an IS implementation process?
Intention	How do IS designers' intentions become evident to relevant stakeholders, through discourse, models, plans and other representations (design artifacts)? How do the intentions and requirements of the users become evident to IS designer? How do these then shape and impact the work of the IS designer? Will an IS be used as intended if the meanings ascribed to the IT artifact are in accordance with the intentions of the designers and the relevant stakeholders?
Planning	What is the process by that ideas generated can be captured as plans, models, sketches, and how does the design of the desired future state emerge and co-evolve from these interactions? How well do emergent plans and models align with the intentions of IS designers and relevant stakeholders, and how might it be possible to achieve and ensure greater shared understanding and alignment of those models?
Communication	How can IS designers ensure that the realized artifact communicates with stakeholders as intended? How do stakeholders reconstruct meanings, and how can an IS designer ensure that these reconstructed meanings are in accordance with their intentions?

(continued)

34

Table 19.4 Continued

Design as ...	Potential research interests
	Do claims from stakeholders that an IS does not meet their requirements result from a lack of correspondence between the IS designers' intentions, and constructed meanings of stakeholders as mediated via the IT artifact? How do IS designers influence the interpretations of stakeholders? How are their intentions communicated via IT and IS artifacts to stakeholders?
User experience	How can we explicate notions of user experience in the context of an IS, before, throughout and following the organizational implementation of this software and attendant organizational changes? In what ways could IS designers ensure that the user experience becomes more satisfying, intelligent and meaningful through their design activity? How do stakeholders respond to cues, features and functionality embedded in a software system, and thus how close is the match between the manifest functions, the appropriation of the software, and hence the latent meanings ascribed by users within a particular context?
Value	What contextual factors might contribute to different perceptions of value being ascribed to an IT artifact? Are there predictive events, triggers or trajectories that lead to positive or negative value being ascribed to the implemented IT artifact? Is there symmetry between the value ascribed by the designers and project team, and that ascribed by the users, and stakeholders? How does the value ascribed by users change over time as their experience of using the IT artifact increases?
Professional practice	How do good designers engage both with the perceived problem or need? How do they engage successfully with users; how do they come to appreciate the perceptions and experiences of users; and how do they come to appreciate the economic, cultural, political and ethical aspects of social forces operating in the design context? How do they manage the resultant value conflicts and ambiguity? What changes to professional practice would ensue if IS designers were to view relevant stakeholder groups as co-designers of their organizational contexts?
Service	How do support teams go about understanding the problems as experienced by users and their objectives in seeking resolutions so that the service desired by users can effectively be designed and delivered? How are on-going modifications and enhancements consonant with the original intentions of IS designers and stakeholders and with perceptions of the value associated with the IS implementation?

possibility for knowledge creation in a unified broad science of design in IS. DSs (such as engineering, medicine, law) are geared toward improving the human condition through finding solutions to field problems (Jelinek *et al.*, 2008). Design is ultimately seen as involving both the design of a solution and the realization and implementation of a solution in *material or social reality* (Van Aken, 2007). DS is thus geared more toward intervening in contexts to make improvements and ensuring that change works well. It is thus oriented toward the future, not just describing and understanding what is. There is a clear precedence in other fields to view DS as falling within one paradigm where the unifying feature is providing solutions to problems or challenges/opportunities of interest, and particularizing the implementation of those solutions and innovations. This is relevant also in IS. 'Problems' in the IS discipline can arise in the technology space, and finding solutions to those essentially technical challenges/opportunities is thus catered for well already in the construction-centered DS articulated by the followers of the Hevner perspective. But IS academics and practitioners also face problems and opportunities in the field, within organizations and communities, where a raft of behavioral, social, cultural and political elements interact and are interlocked with the technical. Designing solutions in these contexts requires the human-centered DS as proposed in this paper, in addition to the construction-centered view. Design is not just about process, product and problem solving, but can be construed from much broader lenses, resulting in increased, deepened understandings of how to intervene in general in design-related problems. This knowledge could then be particularized by IS practitioners, cognizant of the context in which they are intervening. A broad, encompassing and integrated IS DS is required for our socio-technical discipline (see Figure 19.6).

Conclusion

In the context of the emergence of new design fields and practices, we have demonstrated that it is both possible and important in IS to broaden our conceptualization of what constitutes design. Doing so brings a much richer and broader understanding of design, and hence of the types of research into design that should be pursued. Given the many possible lenses on design, we argue that IS DS would be enhanced if, as IS researchers, we developed research agendas, and hence knowledge, about all facets of design and design thinking. A DS that incorporates the human-centered perspective, and hence expands its

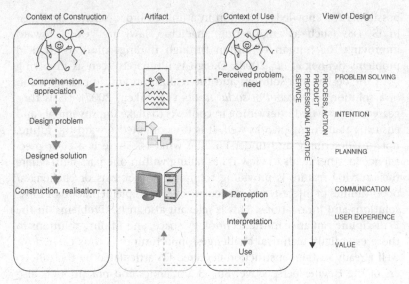

Figure 19.6 Embracing multiple conceptualizations of design
Source: Based on Crilly and Clarkson (2007).

perspective and vision to include the above types of knowledge, would be richer and more generally applicable than one that is restricted to the construction-centered perspective of the dominant view in the extant IS literature. Building on Bayazit (2004), design research in IS could be conducted, and hence knowledge of design in IS accumulated through:

• Conducting research, not only into both IT artifacts and how they work, but into IS artifacts, how they enable the performance of tasks in work systems (Alter, 2006), how they improve management systems in organizational contexts, how they solve perceived field problems (or take advantage of opportunities), and the effects they have on the contexts of use;
• Conducting research into the processes of realizing and deploying IT and IS artifacts in organizational contexts, the nature of IS design as intentional human activity, how IS designers think and work, how they carry out design activity, the impact of the designer on realized IT and IS artifacts and on the contexts in which they operate; and
• Conducting research into the artifact resulting from purposeful design activity, how IT and IS artifacts appear to users, what they

mean to users, how they communicate to users, the nature of the user experience with the artifact, the value ascribed to designed artifacts within contexts of use by users.

IS DS would be better served if both the construction-centered and the human-centered approaches were adopted, and the conceptualization of the design construct broadened.

Acknowledgement

We would like to thank Matt Levy for assistance with Table 19.2 of the paper.

Notes

1. For brevity hereafter, we will simply refer to this perspective as the Hevner view or perspective.
2. The position adopted by Hevner *et al.* (2004) regarding the IT artifact seems consistent with the Benbasat and Zmud (2003) call for making the IT artifact the core of IS research. This position is not necessarily shared by the rest of the IS community, however (Hirschheim and Klein, 2003).
3. This view is commonly shared by the ACM HCI community, some of whom are actively engaged in research of this type that would be of interest to design researchers. See http://www.sigchi.org.

References

Abbasi, A. and Chen, H. (2008). Cybergate: A design framework and system for text analysis of computer mediated communication, *MIS Quarterly* **32**(4): 811–837.

Adams, L. and Courtney, J. (2004). Achieving Relevance in IS Research Via the DAGS Framework, in Proceedings of the 37th Hawaii International Conference on System Sciences (Honolulu, USA); Michigan: IEEE Computer Society Press 1–10.

Adomavicius, G., Bockstedt, J., Gupta, A. and Kauffman, R. (2008). Making Sense of Technology Trends in the Information Technology Landscape, *MIS Quarterly* **32**(4): 779–809.

Almquist, J. and Lupton, J. (2010). Design-oriented Research from the Humanities and Social Sciences, *Design Issues* **26**(1): 3–14.

Alter, S. (2006). Work Systems and IT Artifacts – Does the definition matter? *Communications of the Association of Information Systems* **17**(1): 299–313.

Andreasen, M.M., Wognum, N. and McAloone, T. (2002). Design Typology and Design Organization, in D. Marjanovic (ed.) *Design*, Vol. 1, Dubrovnik: The Design Society, pp. 1–6.

Archer, B. (1979). Whatever Became of Design Methodology? *Design Studies* **1**(1): 17–18.

Arnott, D. (2006). Cognitive Biases and Decision Support Systems Development: A design science approach, *Information Systems Journal* 16(1): 55–78.

Au, Y.A. (2001). Design Science I: The role of design science in electronic commerce research, *Communications of the Association for Information Systems* 7(1): Article 1.

Avital, M., Boland, R.J. and Lyytinen, K. (2009). Introduction to Designing Information and Organizations with a Positive Lens, *Information and Organization* 19(3): 153–161.

Bayazit, N. (2004). Investigating Design: A review of forty years of design research, *Design Issues* 20(1): 16–29.

Benbasat, I. and Zmud, R.W. (2003). The Identity Crisis within the IS Discipline: Defining and communicating the discipline's core properties, *MIS Quarterly* 27(2): 183–194.

Boland, R.J. (2004). Design in the Punctuation of Management Action, in R.J. Boland and F. Collopy (eds.) *Managing as Designing*, Stanford: Stanford Business Books, pp. 106–113.

Boland, R.J., Collopy, F., Lyytinen, K. and Yoo, Y. (2008). Managing as Designing: Lessons for organizational leaders from the design practice of Frank O. Gehry, *Design Issues* 24(1): 10–25.

Boztepe, S. (2007). User Value: Competing theories and models, *International Journal of Design* 1(2): 55–63.

Brown, A.L. (1992). Design Experiments: Theoretical and methodological challenges in creating complex interventions in classroom settings, *Journal of the Learning Sciences* 2(2): 141–178.

Buchanan, R. (1989). Declaration by Design: Rhetoric, argument and demonstration in design practice, in V. Margolin (ed.) *Design Discourse*, Chicago: University of Chicago Press, pp. 91–110.

Buchanan, R. (1992). Wicked Problems in Design Thinking, *Design Issues* 8(2): 5–21.

Buchanan, R. (1996). Myth and Maturity: Towards a new order in the decade of design, in V. Margolin and R. Buchanan (eds.) *The Idea of Design*, Cambridge: MIT Press, pp. 75–88.

Campbell, J.P. (1977). On the Nature of Organizational Effectiveness, in P.S. Goodman, J.M. Pennings *et al.* (eds.) *New Perspectives in Organizational Effectiveness*, San Francisco: Jossey-Bass, pp. 13–55.

Cao, J., Crews, J.M., Lin, M., Deokar, A., Burgoon, J.K. and Nunamaker, J.F. (2006). Interactions Between System Evaluation and Theory Testing: A demonstration of the power of a multifaceted approach to information systems research, *Journal of Management Information Systems* 22(4): 207–235.

Carlsson, S.A. (2006). Design Science in Information Systems: A critical realist perspective, in Seventeenth Australasian Conference on Information Systems, Adelaide, 6–8 December.

Carlsson, S.A. (2007). Developing Knowledge Through IS Design Science Research: For whom, what type of knowledge and how, *Scandinavian Journal of Information Systems* 19(2): 75–86.

Choi, J., Nazareth, D. and Jain, H. (2010). Implementing Service-Oriented Architecture in Organizations, *Journal of Management Information Systems* 26(4): 253–286.

Crilly, N. (2011). The Design Stance in User-System Interaction, *Design Issues* 27(4): 16–29.

Crilly, N. and Clarkson, P. (2007). What the Communicated-Based Models of Design Reveal and Conceal, in Design Semiotics in Use: 6th Nordcode Seminar & Workshop, 6–8 June, Helsinki, Finland.

Crilly, N., Good, D., Matravers, D. and Clarkson, P.J. (2008b). Design as Communication: Exploring the validity and utility of relation intention to interpretation, *Design Studies* 29(5): 425–457.

Crilly, N., Maier, A. and Clarkson, P.J. (2008a). Modelling the Relationship Between Designer Intent and Consumer Experience, *International Journal of Design* 2(3): 15–27.

Crilly, N., Moultrie, J. and Clarkson, P.J. (2009). Shaping Things: Intended consumer response and the other determinants of product form, *Design Studies* 30(3): 224–254.

Cross, N. (2001). Designerly Ways of Knowing: Design discipline versus design science, *Design Issues* 17(3): 49–55.

D'Aubeterre, F., Singh, R. and Iyer, L. (2008). A Semantic Approach to Secure Collaborative Inter-Organizational eBusiness Processes (SSCIOBP), *Journal of the Association for Information Systems* 9(3): 231–266.

Dilnot, C. (1984a). The State of Design History, Part I: Mapping the field, *Design Issues* 1(1): 4–23.

Dilnot, C. (1984b). The State of Design History, Part II: Problems and possibilities, *Design Issues* 1(2): 3–20.

Dilnot, C. (1982). Design as a Socially Significant Activity: An introduction, *Design Studies* 3(3): 139–146.

Dipert, R.R. (1995). Some Issues in the Theory of Artifacts: Defining 'artifact' and related notions, *The Monist* 78(2): 119–135.

Dorst, K. (2006). Design Problems and Design Paradoxes, *Design Issues* 22(3): 4–17.

Edelson, D.C. (2002). Design Research: What we learn when we engage in design, *Journal of the Learning Sciences* 11(1): 105–121.

El Sawy, O.A. (2003). The IS core – IX: The 3 faces of IS identity: Connection, immersion and fusion, *Communications of the Association of Information Systems* 12(1): 588–598.

Fallman, D. (2003). Design-Oriented Human – Computer interaction, *CHI Letters* 5(1): 225–232.

Friedman, B. (2008). Value Sensitive Design, in D. Schular (ed.) *Liberating Voices: A pattern language for communication revolution*, Cambridge, MA: MIT Press, pp. 366–368.

Friedman, K. (2003). Theory Construction in Design Research: Criteria, approaches and methods, *Design Studies* 24(6): 507–522.

Galle, P. (1999). Design as Intentional Action: A conceptual analysis, *Design Studies* 20(1): 57–81.

Germonprez, M., Hovorka, D. and Collopy, F. (2007). A Theory of Tailorable Technology Design, *Journal of the Association for Information Systems* 8(6): 351–367.

Gregor, S. and Jones, D. (2007). The Anatomy of a Design Theory, *Journal of the Association for Information Systems* 8(5): 312–335.

Hatchuel, A. (2001). Towards Design Theory and Expandable Rationality: The unfinished program of Herbert Simon, *Journal of Management and Governance* 5(3): 260–273.

Hevner, A.R., March, S.T. and Park, J. (2004). Design Science in Information Systems Research, *MIS Quarterly* 28(1): 75–105.

Hilpinen, R (1995). Belief Systems as Artifacts, *The Monist* 78(2): 136–155.

Hirschheim, R. and Klein, H. (2003). Crisis in the IS Field? A critical reflection on the state of the discipline, *Journal of the Association for Information Systems* 4(5): 237–293.

Hooker, J.N. (2004). Is Design Theory Possible? *Journal of Information Technology Theory and Application* 6(2): 63–72.

Hughes, T.P. (1987). The Evolution of Large Technological Systems, in W.E. Bijker, T.P. Hughes and T.F. Pinch (eds.) *The Social Constructions of Technological Systems: New directions in the sociology and history of technology*, Cambridge, MA: The MIT Press.

Iivari, J. (2007). A Paradigmatic Analysis of Information Systems as a Design Science, *Scandinavian Journal of Information Systems* 19(2): 39–64.

Jelinek, M., Romme, G.L. and Boland, R.J. (2008). Introduction to the Special Issue: Organization Studies as a Science for Design: Creating collaborative artifacts and research, *Organization Studies* 29(3): 317–329.

Jones, C. (2003). Theory After the Postmodern Condition, *Organization* 10(3): 503–525.

Jones, D., Gregor, S. and Lynch, T. (2003). An Information Systems Design Theory for Web-Based Education, IASTED Symposium on Web-Based Education, Rhodes, Greece, Anaheim: IASTED, pp. 603–608.

Kazmierczak, E. (2003). Design as Meaning Making: From making things to the design of thinking, *Design Issues* 19(2): 45–59.

Keys, P. (2007). Developing a Design Science for the Use of Problem Structuring Methods, *Systems Practice and Action Research* 20(4): 333–349.

Kimbell, L. (2011). Designing for Service as One Way of Designing Service, *International Journal of Design* 5(2): 41–52.

Kolfschoten, G. and De Vreede, G. (2009). A Design Approach for Collaboration Processes: A multimethod design science study in collaboration engineering, *Journal of Management Information Systems* 26(1): 225–256.

Krippendorff, K. (1996). On the Essential Contexts of Artifacts or on the Proposition That 'Design is Making Sense (of Things)', in V. Margolin and R. Buchanan (eds.) *The Idea of Design*, Cambridge: MIT Press.

Kroes, P. (2001). Technical Functions as Dispositions: A critical assessment, *TECHNE* 5(3): 1–16.

Kruger, C. and Cross, N. (2006). Solution Driven Versus Problem Driven Design: Strategies and outcomes, *Design Studies* 27(5): 527–548.

Kuechler, W. and Vaishnavi, V. (2008). The Emergence of Design Research in Information Systems in North America, *Journal of Design Research* 7(1): 1–16.

Lee, J., Wyner, G. and Pentland, B. (2008). Process Grammar as a Tool for Business Process Redesign, *MIS Quarterly* 32(4): 757–778.

Louridas, P. (1999). Design as Bricolage: Anthropology meets design thinking, *Design Studies* 20(6): 517–535.

Lundgren, N. (1978). Transportation and Personal Mobility, in B. Wilkins (ed.) *Leisure in the Twentieth Century*, London: Design Council, pp. 20–23.

Lunenfeld, P. (2003). The Design Cluster, in B. Laurel (ed.) *Design Research: Methods and Perspectives*, Cambridge, MA: MIT Press.

March, S.T. and Smith, G. (1995). Design and Natural Science Research on Information Technology, *Decision Support Systems* 15(4): 251–266.

Markus, M.L., Majchrzak, A. and Gasser, L. (2002). A Design Theory for Systems that Support Emergent Knowledge Processes, *MIS Quarterly* 26(3): 179–212.

Marxt, C. and Hacklin, F. (2005). Design, Product Development, Innovation: All the same in the end? A short discussion on terminology, *Journal of Engineering Design* 16(4): 413–421.

McKay, J. and Marshall, P. (2005). A Review of Design Science in Information Systems, in B. Campbell, J. Underwood and D. Bunker (eds.) *Socialising IT: Thinking about the people: Proceedings of the Australasian Conference on Information Systems (ACIS 2005)*, Sydney, Australia, pp. 1–11.

McKay, J. and Marshall, P. (2007). Science, Design, and Design Science: Seeking Clarity to Move Design Science Research Forward in Information Systems, *ACIS 2007 Proceedings* Paper 55, http://aisel.aisnet.org/acis2007/55.

Miller, W.R. (2004). Definition of design. [WWW document] http://www.google. com.au/search?q=...+static.userland.com%2Frack4%2Fgems%2Fwrmdesign% 2FDefinitionOfDesign1.doc&ie=utf-8&oe=utf-8&aq=t&rls=org.mozilla:en-US: official&client=firefox-a (accessed 9 June 2007).

Mittleman, D.D. (2009). Planning and Design Considerations for Computer Supported Collaboration Spaces, *Journal of the Association for Information Systems* 10: 278–305.

Mumford, E. (2000). A Socio-technical Approach to Systems Design, *Requirements Engineering* 5(2): 125–133.

Niehaves, B. (2007a). On Epistemological Pluralism in Design Science, *Scandinavian Journal of Information Systems* 19(2): 99–110.

Niehaves, B. (2007b). On Epistemological Diversity in Design Science – New vistas for a design-oriented IS research? In Twenty-Eighth International Conference on Information Systems, Montreal.

Niehaves, B. and Becker, J. (2006). Epistemological Perspectives on Design Science in IS Research, in Proceedings of the Twelfth Americas Conference on Information Systems (Acapulco, Mexico); 4–6 August.

Norman, D.A. (2009). Systems Thinking: A product is more than the product, *Interactions* 16(5): 52–54.

Parsons, J. and Wand, Y. (2008). Using Cognitive Principles to Guide Classification in Information Systems Modeling, *MIS Quarterly* 32(4): 839–868.

Peffers, K., Tuunanen, T., Rothenberger, M.A. and Chatterjee, S. (2008). A Design Science Research Methodology for Information Systems Research, *Journal of Management Information Systems* 24(3): 45–77.

Purao, S. (2002). Design Research in the Technology of Information Systems: Truth or dare, Atlanta: GSU Department of CIS Working Paper.

Redstrom, J. (2006). Towards User Design? On the shift from object to user as the subject of design, *Design Studies* 27(2): 123–139.

Redstrom, J. (2008). RE: Definitions of Use, *Design Studies* 29(4): 410–423.

Romme, A.G.L. (2003). Making a Difference: Organization as design, *Organization Science* 14(5): 558–573.

Roth, S. (1999). The State of Design Research, *Design Issues* 15(2): 18–26.

Ryan, D. (1997). Enzo Mari and the Process of Design, *Design Issues* 13(3): 9–36.

Schneider, B. (2007). Design as Practice, Science and Research, in M. Ralf (ed.) *Design Research Now: Essays and selected projects*, Basel: Birkhauser, pp. 207–218.

Secomandi, F. and Snelders, D. (2011). The Object of Service Design, *Design Issues* 27(3): 20–34.

Siponen, M., Baskerville, R. and Heikka, J. (2006). A Design Theory for Secure Information Systems Design Abstract Methods, *Journal of the Association for Information Systems* 7(11): 725–770.

Stewart, S. (2011). Interpreting Design Thinking, *Design Studies* 32(6): 515–520.

Stolterman, E. (2008). The Nature of Design Practice and Implications for Interaction Design Research, *International Journal of Design* 2(1): 55–64.

Storey, V., Burton-Jones, A., Sugumaran, V. and Purao, S. (2008). CONQUER: A methodology for context-aware query processing on the World Wide Web, *Information Systems Research* 19(1): 3–25.

Umapathy, K., Purao, S. and Barton, R. (2008). Designing Enterprise Integration Solutions Effectively, *European Journal of Information Systems* 17(5): 518–527.

van Aken, J., Berends, H. and van der Bij, H. (2007). *Problem Solving in Organizations: A methodological handbook for business students*, Cambridge: Cambridge University Press.

van Aken, J.E. (2004). Management Research Based on the Paradigm of the Design Sciences: The quest for field-tested and grounded technological rules, *Journal of Management Studies* 41(2): 219–246.

van Aken, J.E. (2005a). Valid Knowledge for the Professional Design of Large and Complex Processes, *Design Studies* 26(4): 379–404.

van Aken, J.E. (2005b). Management Research as Design Science: Articulating the research products of Mode 2 knowledge production in management, *British Journal of Management* 16(1): 19–36.

van Aken, J.E. (2007). Design Science and Organization Development Interventions: Aligning business and humanistic values, *Journal of Applied Behavioral Science* 43(1): 67–88.

van Aken, J.E. and Romme, G. (2009). Reinventing the Future: Adding design science to the repertoire of organization and management studies, *Organization Management Journal* 6(1): 5–12.

Walls, J.G., Widmeyer, G.R. and El Sawy, O.A. (1992). Building an Information System Design Theory for Vigilant EIS, *Information Systems Research* 3(1): 36–59.

Walls, J.G., Widmeyer, G.R. and El Sawy, O.A. (2004). Assessing Information System Design Theory in Perspective: How useful was our 1992 initial rendition? *Journal of Information Technology Theory and Application* 6(2): 43–58.

Wangelin, E. (2007). Matching Bricolage and Hermeneutics: A theoretical patchwork in progress, Design Semiotics in Use, SeFun International Seminar (Helsinki, Finland); 6–8 June.

Wastell, D. (2010). Managing as Designing: 'Opportunity knocks' for the IS field? *European Journal of Information Systems* 31: 1–10.

Wieringa, R. and Heerkens, H. (2007). Designing Requirements Engineering Research, Proceedings of the Comparative Evaluation in Requirements Engineering Conference (CERE 07), New Delhi, India.

Willem, R.A. (1990). Design and Science, *Design Studies* 11(1): 43–47.

Wolford-Ulrich, J. (2004). Seeing Servant Leadership Through the Lens of Design, Servant Leadership Research Roundtable, August 2004. [WWW document] http://www.regent.edu/acad/sis/publications/conference_proceedings/servant_leadershiup_roundtable/2004pdf/ulrich_seeing_servant.pdf (accessed 26 May 2007).

20
A Critical Analysis of Decision Support Systems Research Revisited: The Rise of Design Science

David Arnott[1,†] and Graham Pervan[2,†]
[1]Monash University, Australia;
[2]School of Information Systems, Curtin Business School,
Curtin University, Australia
[†]The contribution of the authors was equal

Introduction

Decision support systems (DSS) is the area of the information systems (IS) discipline that is focused on supporting and improving managerial decision making. In 2005 the *Journal of Information Technology* (*JIT*) published our paper that critically analyzed DSS research from 1990 to 2003 (Arnott and Pervan, 2005). That paper used bibliometric content analysis as its method and analyzed 1020 articles in 14 journals. The analysis illuminated a vibrant and important part of IS research. Personal DSS and group support systems (GSS) dominated DSS research and two-thirds of DSS research was empirical, a higher proportion than general IS research. Interpretive DSS research was growing from a low base while design-science research (DSR) and laboratory experiments were major research categories. Unfortunately, it was found that DSS research to 2003 was relatively poorly founded on judgment and decision-making theory and faced what was described as 'a crisis of relevance.'

It is now opportune to revisit published DSS research to examine the progress of the field. Since 2005 management support practice has seen the rise of business intelligence (BI) and business analytics (BA).

Reprinted from "A critical analysis of decision support systems research revisited: the rise of design science," by D. Arnott and G. Pervan in *Journal of Information Technology*, 29, 2014, pp. 269–293. With kind permission from the Association for Information Technology Trust. All rights reserved.

The much-hyped phenomena of big data will also affect large-scale DSS. The information technology (IT)-based support of managers is now a visible and significant part of enterprise-level IT and this fundamental 21st century change in DSS practice heightens the need to revisit the DSS literature analysis. In this paper, 7 years of publication have been added to the article sample, as have two new significant journals. The updated article sample in this paper now contains 1466 articles in 16 journals, representing 21 years of DSS research history.

The paper is structured as follows: first, the general trends that have occurred in DSS practice and research since the end of the previous article sample are outlined. This is followed by the codification of a number of expectations about the improvement of DSS research that focus the updated bibliometric analysis. These expectations arise from the recommendations of previous literature analyses. The research method and design is then outlined, followed by the results of the bibliometric content analysis. The discussion of the results is framed by the expectations identified in previous reviews. Speculations are then made about the likely future directions of the field in the form of forecasts for future analysis.

The evolution of the DSS field 2003–2010

This section discusses the major changes in DSS theory and practice that have occurred since the 2003 end of the original article sample. To help frame this discussion Figure 20.1 shows an update of Figure 20.1 in the 2005 *JIT* Critical Analysis paper. It now shows the genealogy of the DSS field over the last 50 years. The items in a genealogy are discrete individuals that share a common ancestry. Although they are unique entities they can exhibit a 'family resemblance.' Figure 20.1 does not address application areas (for example, corporate performance management) or technologies (for example, WWW and mobile devices). It focuses on DSS types and their theoretical foundations. The additions to the figure since 2005 are BI and BA. Hosack *et al.* (2012) extended the 2005 version of Figure 20.1 to include social and mobile computing. It is clear that social and mobile computing must be considered a core element of contemporary DSS but they are not DSS types.

BI and BA

Howard Dresner coined the BI term in 1989 and after joining Gartner Inc. popularized it through their industry publications (Power, 2012). However, the BI label did not gain widespread traction as a DSS movement until the early 2000s. The change in title of large-scale DSS from

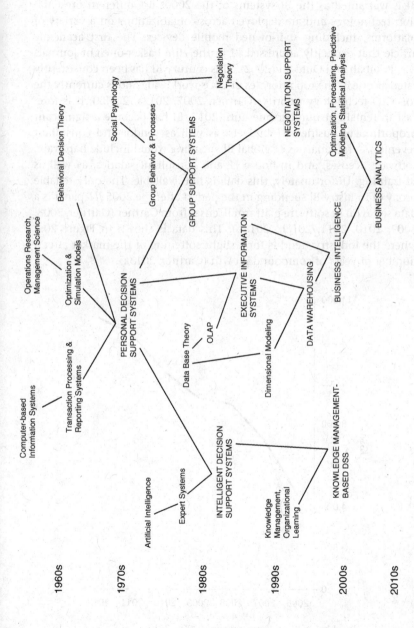

Figure 20.1 The genealogy of the DSS field, 1960–2010

executive information systems (EIS) and data warehousing (DW) to BI is warranted as the BI systems of the 2000s use different presentation technology and are deployed across organizations on a variety of platforms, including staff-owned mobile devices. The first academic article that explicitly addressed BI in the elite basket-of-eight journals was Rouibah and Ould-ali (2002). This century BI has been consistently rated as one of the top priorities of CIOs worldwide and is currently the top CIO technology priority (Gartner, 2007, 2012a, 2013a); it is forecast to remain at number one until 2017. BI has become a significant proportion of business IT budgets, as well as vendor and consultant revenues. A full analysis of global BI spending would include hardware, software licenses, and in-house IT and consultant salaries, as well as BI training. Unfortunately, this data is not available. The only reliable proxy of industry BI spending in the period after the 2005 *JIT* paper is a data series on BI software platform licenses from Gartner (Gartner, 2008, 2009, 2010, 2011, 2012b, 2013b). This data is shown in Figure 20.2 where the industry trend is for a slight softening of the market after a number of years of compound growth (Gartner, 2013a).

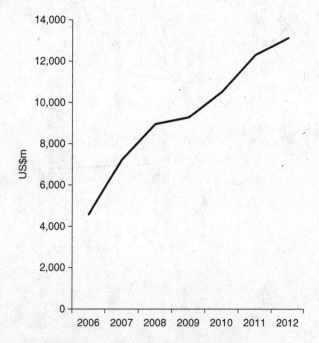

Figure 20.2   Worldwide BI platform revenue, 2006–2012

The term BA has also risen in prominence in the analysis period. A widely read professional article in the *Harvard Business Review*, Davenport (2006), was important in popularizing the term, as was the follow-on book (Davenport and Harris, 2007). Davenport and Harris's definition of BA is 'the extensive use of data, statistical and quantitative analysis, explanatory and predictive models, and fact-based management to drive decisions and actions.' This definition is similar, if not identical to BI. Most IT practitioners and managers do not see a significant difference between BA and BI although both terms are widely used by software vendors and consultants. Most contemporary large-scale DSS implementations are a complex combination of reporting and analysis-based applications.

Big data

Big data is currently an industry movement that is arguably the most hyped IT movement related to DSS in the field's history. There is no accepted definition of big data, but the essence of the concept is that data other than the traditional transactional data held in enterprise systems is now available for analysis in ever increasing volumes and velocities (McAfee and Brynjolfsson, 2012). The big data concept has largely been developed by consulting companies, especially McKinsey and Company (Brown *et al.*, 2013). How much value there is in the exabytes of big data available to organizations is yet to be determined but the importance for DSS is clear. The shared decision-making activity between a manager and a computer that is fundamental to DSS is highly compatible with the big data concept. As McAfee and Brynjolfsson (2012) relate, 'big data's power does not erase the need for vision or human insight.'

The actual implementation of big data applications by organizations does not mirror the marketing campaigns and its likely impact on large-scale DSS practice is unclear. Industry sources are beginning to question aspects of the big data hype. Gartner (2013a) found that only 8% of organizations have big data systems in production. Further, they note a negative influence of big data on the large-scale decision support area: 'Paradoxically, the confusion that surrounds the term "big data" and the uncertainty about the tangible benefits of big data are partly to blame for the soft BI and analytics market.' Ross *et al.* (2013) argue that 'you may not need big data after all' and that the priority for organizations should be to develop an evidence-based culture before investing heavily in big data applications. Industry bloggers such as Shander (2013) support this view and believe that big data and associated analytics are suitable for a certain type of company – those that are character-ized by extreme complexity. Shander asserts 'the rest should avoid the bandwagon altogether.'

While big data is certainly an important industry movement, it is yet to be reflected in the academic DSS publication sample that is the basis of this study. IS researchers are beginning to address big data: Chen *et al.* (2012) have developed a big data research agenda while Chiang *et al.* (2012) have analyzed the educational requirements for big data. Big data would be likely to feature strongly in any future update of this paper's analysis.

DSS industry changes

Another major development in the 2004–2010 period of the revisited DSS research sample was what has become known as 'the BI merger and acquisition year.' In 2007 three major enterprise systems and services companies acquired the major BI vendors. SAP AG acquired Business Objects SA for US$6.8 billion, IBM Corporation acquired Cognos Incorporated for $5 billion, and Oracle Corporation acquired Hyperion Solutions Corporation for $3.3 billion. These acquisitions fundamen-tally changed the structure of the DSS/BI industry, leaving SAS Institute Incorporated as the largest BI-only vendor. The acquisitions do empha-size the maturity of the large-scale DSS market and the place of BI in enterprise IT plans and budgets.

Advances in decision theory

Parallel to the rise of BI and BA in practice, there were also important developments in theory and research that concern all types of DSS. Two Nobel Prizes in Economics define the first of these developments. In 1978 Herbert Simon won the Nobel Prize for his theory of decision making. The seminal work for this theory is Simon (1960). Simon made the major advance of defining bounded rationality, a concept that recog-nized the limits of human information processing and the consequent inability of managers to make optimal decisions in an economically rational way. Further to bounded rationality, Simon's decision-making model is the most cited conceptualization of the phase theorem of deci-sion making. The iterative and recursive phases he identified were the famous intelligence, design, and choice phases. Simon's further concept of decision structuredness was one of the key constructs in DSS's semi-nal paper (Gorry and Scott Morton, 1971). The influence of the theory remains evident, as the 'intelligence' in BI is from Simon's first decision-making phase. Simon's theory of decision making is so embedded in management and IS research and practice that it has attained axiomatic status. Unfortunately, as Lipshitz and Bar-Ilan (1996) relate, 'this continuing popularity has not been based on empirical evidence.' In the significant time since the 1978 Prize there has been no experimental or field study that provides any support for the predictive validity of the phase theorem. Further, there is only modest support for the theory's descriptive validity. This means that although the phase theorem of Simon has widespread acceptance in research and practice it is actually based on little or no scientific evidence.

The decision-making theory of the second Nobel Prize for Economics in this discussion does not suffer like Simon's phase theory for lack of empirical evidence. It is based on the findings of hundreds of high quality laboratory and field experiments. It is also based on Simon's theory of bounded rationality. The 2002 Nobel Prize was awarded to Daniel Kahneman for the decision-making theory he developed with Amos Tversky (who unfortunately died before the Prize's award). Their theory is actually a set of theories that explains the cognitive processes of human decision making, and in particular its systematic failures. Knowing these systematic failures is the first step in designing corrective actions, that is, improving decision making. The Nobel Prize validated the Kahneman and Tversky approach and signaled a major shift in decision theory toward a post-Simon orthodoxy. Kahneman's 2011 best selling book, *Thinking Fast and Slow*, is aimed at the general public, including managers and IT professionals. It may be the vehicle for the Kahneman and Tversky approach to significantly affect practice.

The mainstreaming of DSR

In IS research and scholarship since the 2005 *JIT* paper the major methodological development has been the codification and acceptance of DSR as a research strategy. Although there were landmark DSR method articles in premier journals before 2004 (for example, Walls *et al.*, 1992; March and Smith, 1995) it was the publication of Hevner *et al.* (2004) in *MIS Quarterly* that legitimized and popularized the approach. This paper provided a set of guidelines for the execution of high quality DSR in IS. Following this, Hevner (2007) provided a three-cycle framework that can act as a context for detailed DSR methods. Kuechler and Vaishnavi (2012) is an important contribution to DSR methods, especially for theory development. Unlike the situation at the end of the original article sample in 2003, there now exists a critical mass of DSR method articles to direct and advise researchers on how to conduct quality DSR.

DSS theory and scholarship

During the new analysis period (2004–2010) there has been a number of reviews and analyses of DSS research. Jourdan *et al.* (2008) conducted a review of BI research from 1997–2006. It is difficult to compare their review with this paper (or previous analyses of DSS) as their definition of BI is more akin to competitive intelligence, and could also be interpreted to cover all of the DSS types in this paper. Only 22 of their 167 articles are in our sample (i.e. what is defined as DSS) and only 10 of them are in the BI category. This small sample size makes it difficult to use the Jourdan *et al.* results to inform BI and other DSS research agendas. Nevertheless, they called for a greater diversity of research methods in BI research.

A major contribution to scholarship in the analysis period is Hosack *et al.*'s (2012) conceptual article on the status and future of the DSS field. Their general theme is that 'decision support systems research is alive and well.' While their argumentation is strong, the empirical approach of bibliometric content analysis, while very time consuming, is needed to test the various expectations about the future of the field. Interestingly, Hosack *et al.* emphasize social media and mobility as the most important, even transformative, issues for DSS research in the near future.

Perhaps the most important general theoretical contribution to the DSS area in the analysis period is Clark *et al.*'s (2007) *MISQ* article that described a dynamic model of what they termed management support systems (MSS). Their MSS definition is essentially the same as our DSS definition. They subdivided MSS into DSS (our personal DSS), EIS, BI, and knowledge management systems. Their analysis was based on representative empirical and non-empirical papers in each grouping. They identified the key research constructs that cross all MSS groups and built a convincing causal model of the field. One of their most important findings is that the theory developed in one part of management support can be used in others, that is, MSS/DSS is a coherent academic field. This is particularly important for DSS researchers who want to shift their research agendas to the professionally important BI.

Summary of academic and industry change

In summary, the major professional development in DSS since the 2005 *JIT* paper is the rise of BI and, to a lesser extent, BA. Big data is a much-hyped area that may have a future impact on decision support. The vendor landscape was fundamentally reshaped by the acquisition of the major BI vendors by general IS vendors in 2007. In academic DSS, the major developments have been the Nobel Prize of Daniel Kahneman and the change in decision-making reference theory to a theory base that is scientifically validated. In research methodology, the codification and acceptance of DSR has been the significant development.

Expectations about the progress of the DSS field

This section identifies 15 major expectations and 4 corollary expectations that provide a structure for the analysis of the DSS field from 2004 to 2010. The expectations were developed from the conclusions of previous literature analyses of the 1990–2003 sample (Arnott and Pervan, 2005; Arnott et al., 2005), of the 1990–2004 sample (Arnott and Pervan, 2008), and of the 1990–2005 sample (Arnott and Pervan, 2012). While the expectations are grouped in logical sets, they are not independent and the processes that determine the outcome of one expectation can affect others. The expectations do not have equal importance to the field nor equal impact on practice.

The first set of seven expectations considers the overall nature of the DSS field. BI is now a major part of any organization's IT spending and BI vendor revenue is consistently growing. This should make BI an attractive area for IS researchers to study. It could also be expected that non-DSS IS researchers would change their research agendas to study BI (Arnott and Pervan, 2008). This leads to Expectation 1:

Expectation 1: In parallel with the rise of BI in IT practice, overall DSS publication will increase.

Arnott and Pervan (2005, 2008) argued strongly that DSS researchers should shift their agendas to BI. As discussed above, BI is the dominant decision support practice and its importance has grown significantly over the last decade. Also as argued by Clark et al. (2007), the theories, methods, and knowledge that have been used for PDSS and GSS are relevant to BI. It was expected that a phenomenon of researchers shifting topic to BI should have gained momentum in the 2004–2010 analysis period. This expectation is expressed as:

Expectation 2: BI will become an increasing share of DSS research.

Both Arnott and Pervan (2005, 2008) identified a significant conservatism in DSS research agendas. In the 2005 paper GSS occupied 29% of DSS publication. The 2008 paper criticized this situation, noting that DSS researchers seem to maintain research programs despite major shifts in industry practice. GSS is a DSS type that does not seem to warrant such a high presence in publishing and this allocation of research effort may be constraining research in more professionally relevant areas. This is not to say that GSS is not an important area of scholarship, quite the reverse; GSS research has much to offer research into the use of collaborative systems and social media for decision support. This situation leads to the expectation:

Expectation 3: GSS will decline in DSS publishing.

In both Arnott and Pervan (2005, 2008) concern was expressed about the low overall relevance evaluation of DSS research. It was found that case studies were the article type with the highest relevance scores. The previous literature analyses also showed that DSS researchers used case studies significantly less than general IS researchers. A strong recommendation from these earlier analyses was for DSS researchers to increase the use of the case study method in their projects. This leads to the next expectation:

Expectation 4: DSS research will have more case studies.

As a corollary to Expectation 4, Arnott and Pervan (2005) made further arguments for an increase in case studies using an interpretive approach. The high relevance scores of articles that used interpretive case studies was notable as was the obvious close ties that these researchers formed with their professional subjects. The corollary expectation is therefore:

Expectation 4a: DSS research will have more interpretive case studies.

Arnott and Pervan (2005, 2008) noted that DSR was a gradually increasing presence in DSS research. It was claimed in those reviews that experience with DSR could be the DSS field's most significant contribution to general IS research. The previous literature analyses argued for a further increase in DSS DSR. This was argued to be a factor in improving the relevance of DSS research as field-based DSR involves a close relationship with professionals and organizations. Expressed as an expectation this argument is:

Expectation 5: Design-science research will increase in DSS publication.

In addition to suggesting an increase in DSS DSR publishing, Arnott and Pervan (2005) also suggested that DSS DSR needed to improve in quality. This was also a central theme in Arnott and Pervan (2012) that analyzed DSS DSR from 1990 to 2005. Since 2005 it is possible that the quality of DSS DSR has significantly increased with the adoption of the Hevner *et al.* (2004) guidelines and the other methodological contributions that have been trigged by that paper. This leads to:

Expectation 6: DSS design-science research will increase in quality.

Arnott *et al.* (2005) provided a detailed analysis of how DSS research was funded between 1990 and 2003. A recommendation of that analysis was for DSS researchers to seek more external funding from both industry and competitive grant bodies (for example, the US National Science Foundation, Australian Research Council, Research Councils UK, and the Canadian National Research Council). This recommendation implies the following expectation:

Expectation 7: The external funding of DSS research will increase.

In addition to the 2005 recommendation on external funding, Arnott and Pervan (2008) argued that DSS researchers should seek more industry funding than they have in the past. Industry funding is important in ensuring the relevance of DSS research projects. This recommendation provides a corollary to Expectation 7:

Expectation 7a: The industry funding of DSS research will increase.

The next set of four major and two corollary expectations concern the quality of DSS research. Some of the previous expectations, especially Expectation 6, also address research quality. Arnott and Pervan (2008) identified the theoretical foundations of DSS research as one of the field's key issues. Unfortunately the 2005 and 2008 literature analyses did not code the quality of general theoretical foundations, only judgment and decision making. Arnott and Pervan (2012) did code general theoretical foundations as part of the assessment of research rigor. This coding was only for DSS DSR to 2005. The theoretical foundations of all DSS research needs assessment. This will be assessed using the following expectation:

Expectation 8: The theoretical foundations of DSS research will improve in quality.

A key finding of Arnott and Pervan (2005) was that DSS research was relatively poorly grounded in theories of judgment and decision making. The analysis argued for greater use of decision-making theory as well as a broader theoretical foundation. The first of these recommendations can be tested using the following expectation:

Expectation 9: DSS research will have better grounding in decision-making theory.

As mentioned in the previous section there are two important schools of behavioral decision-making; one associated with Simon and the other with Kahneman and Tversky. If DSS researchers are utilizing more recent and more scientifically valid decision-making theory, they will shift their foundation theory from Simon to Kahneman and Tversky. This leads to the two corollary expectations for Expectation 9:

Expectation 9a: DSS research will be more grounded in Kahneman and Tversky's theory of decision-making.

Expectation 9b: DSS research will be less grounded in Simon's theory of decision-making.

Arnott and Pervan (2008) argued that academic rigor in research articles is highly valued by IT professionals. This is what mainly separates academic articles from industry white papers, 'research reports,' and blogs. The 2008 literature analysis strongly recommended a much greater attention on the rigor of DSS research designs leading to the next expectation:

Expectation 10: DSS research designs will be more rigorous.

As part of increasing research rigor, Arnott and Pervan (2008) suggested that DSS researchers should aim to publish more in 'A' journals, especially the basket-of-six journals. In December 2011 the Association for Information Systems (AIS) Senior Scholars updated their journal ranking and expanded the basket-of-six to a basket-of-eight with the inclusion of *JIT* and *JSIS*. As a result, this literature analysis uses the AIS basket-of-eight rather than the basket-of-six. These journals are regarded as the pinnacle of IS publishing and any increase in the number of DSS articles in the basket-of-eight would indicate an increase in DSS research quality and impact. Accordingly, the next expectation is:

Expectation 11: DSS publication will increase in the basket-of-eight journals.

The final set of four expectations relate to what was identified as the most important issue in DSS research in the 2005 *JIT* paper, 'the crisis of relevance.' It was also identified as the first 'key issue' in Arnott and Pervan (2008). Both literature analyses viewed relevance as multifactorial and argued that a greater use of DSR and case studies, and greater attention to BI research would improve relevance. In the 2005 study the practical relevance of an article was judged in one question on a scale of very high to none. Hevner *et al.*'s (2004) discussion of relevance is useful for all DSS research, not just DSR. Unlike Arnott and Pervan (2005, 2008) Hevner *et al.* divided relevance into two types: relevance to IT professionals and relevance to managers. IT professionals are responsible for planning, developing, and maintaining the various types of DSS, whereas managers are the major sponsors and users of the systems, an important distinction for considering relevance. Hevner *et al.*'s approach leads to the following two expectations:

Expectation 12: DSS research will increase in relevance to IT professionals.

Expectation 13: DSS research will increase in relevance to managers.

Arnott and Pervan (2012), although only addressing DSS DSR to 2005, argued that in order to have increased organizational importance and impact, DSS projects should focus on more strategic problems than they have in the past. Refocused to the whole of DSS research this argument leads to the expectation:

Expectation 14: DSS will address more strategic decision tasks.

The final expectation about DSS research from 2003 to 2010 concerns the much discussed and debated tradeoff between research rigor and relevance for practice. Arnott and Pervan (2008) argued that there should be no tradeoff between rigor and relevance in DSS research. If the situation has improved since 2003 then the following expectation should be supported.

Expectation 15: DSS research will have less tradeoff between rigor and relevance.

Research method and design

General approach

There are two fundamental strategies for literature analysis. The first, thematic analysis, involves classifying and analyzing papers according to themes that are relevant to the theory and practice goals of a research project (Webster and Watson, 2002). Thematic analysis is the most common form of literature review in journal papers and doctoral theses. The second strategy is bibliometrics, which involves the measurement of publication patterns. The two most common bibliometric methods are citation analysis (Osareh, 1996) and content analysis (Weber, 1990). A third, and newer, bibliometric method is to use text-mining techniques to study a very large sample, even a population, of journal and conference papers in a field. Delen and Crossland (2008) performed this style of analysis on *MISQ, ISR*, and *JMIS* articles from 1994 to 2005.

Content analysis involves the coding and analysis of a representative sample of research articles. In this approach, data capture is driven by a protocol that can have both quantitative and qualitative aspects. This form of data capture is very labor intensive but it has the advantage that it can illuminate the deep structure of the field in a way that is impossible to achieve with other literature analysis approaches including text mining. To evaluate the expectations about the progress of the DSS field that were identified in the previous section, bibliometric content analysis of representative DSS research from 2004 to 2010 was undertaken. This was compared with existing bibliometric data on DSS research from 1990 to 2003.

The sample

The sample has a similar structure to that used in previous reviews of DSS research. A large set of quality journals was adopted as the basis of the sample because this best represents the invisible college of DSS research. Previous analyses of IS research have used a similar sampling approach (Benbasat and Nault, 1990; Alavi and Carlson, 1992; Chen and Hirschheim, 2004). Further, Webster and Watson (2002) have criticized the over emphasis on North American journals in review papers. In response we included five European IS journals (*ISJ*, *EJIS*, *I&O*, *JIT*, and *JSIS*) in the sample. Following Chen and Hirschheim (2004), the classification of a journal as US or European is largely based on the location of the publisher. Analyses of IS publishing have found significant differences between the nature of research published in North American and European journals (Cavaye, 1996; Galliers and Meadows, 2003). Two journals have been added to the 1990–2003 sample: *CAIS* from 1999, *JAIS* from 2000. These are the major journals of the premier academic association concerning IS. *JAIS* is particularly important for our study, as it is one of the basket-of-eight journals. At the time of the 2005 *JIT* paper *JAIS* was a relatively new journal and its status had not been established. The proposed journal sample was circulated to a number of editors-in-chief of major journals for comment and confirmation. Table 20.1 shows the article sample of DSS research from 1990 to 2010.

Table 20.1 shows that DSS is an important part of IS scholarship comprising 12% of articles published in the journals in the sample. When only general IS journals are analyzed, DSS comprises 18.7% of IS research. This significance is consistent with the citation-based analysis of Taylor *et al.* (2010) who identified 'group work and decision support' as one of the three core subfields of the IS discipline. They also identified DSS as persistently important to IS research since the 1980s.

Coding protocol and procedures

An amended coding protocol was used to collect data for the analysis in this paper; the new protocol appears in Appendix A. The two coding protocols that were used in previous work, the general DSS protocol of Arnott and Pervan (2005) and the DSS design-science protocol of Arnott and Pervan (2012) were amended and combined. Three significant changes have been made to the general section of the protocol. These changes relate to the article type classification, DSS types, and the relevance and rigor of the research. Details of the conversion and recoding of the original sample, in order to align it with the new protocol, are provided in Appendix B.

The first change to the protocol, and the subsequent analysis, is to abandon the Alavi and Carlson (1992) classification of article types. The Alavi and Carlson approach is a three-level taxonomy with 20 article types at the lowest level. We adopted a one-layer 10-item article typology that better characterizes contemporary DSS research, is easier to understand, and is more parsimonious for data coding decision making. Further, this classification allows better comparison with other IS review

Table 20.1 The DSS article sample by journal

Journal	Origin	2011 ISI 5-year impact factor	Journal orientation	Number of DSS articles published	Total Number of articles published	DSS articles as a percentage of published articles
Communications of the Association for Information Systems (CAIS) only since 1999	The United States	Not ranked	General IS	16	831	2
Decision Sciences (DS)	The United States	3.146	Multidiscipline	67	820	8
Decision Support Systems (DSS)	The United States	2.331	General IS	683	1652	41
European Journal of Information Systems (EJIS)	Europe	2.218	General IS	26	618	4
Group Decision and Negotiation (GDandN)	The United States	1.120	Specialist IS	193	499	39
Information and Management (I&M)	The United States	3.796	General IS	113	1171	10
Information and Organization (I&O)	Europe	0.667 (2-year)	General IS	16	241	7
Information Systems Journal (ISJ)	Europe	2.775	General IS	18	345	5
Information Systems Research (ISR)	The United States	4.131	General IS	37	463	8
Journal of Information Technology (JIT)	Europe	3.000	General IS	26	548	5
Journal of Management Information Systems (JMIS)	The United States	2.945	General IS	89	764	12

Journal	Region	Type				
Journal of Organizational Computing and Electronic Commerce (JOC and EC)	The United States	Specialist IS	0.628	76	319	24
Journal of Strategic Information Systems (JSIS)	Europe	General IS	2.000	11	348	3
Journal of the Association for Information Systems (JAIS) only since 2000	The United States	General IS	2.654	8	249	3
Management Science (MS)	The United States	Multidiscipline	3.304	46	2678	2
MIS Quarterly (MISQ)	The United States	General IS	7.497	41	593	7
Total				1466	12,139	12

studies (for example, Chen and Hirschheim, 2004; Guo and Sheffield, 2008). The new article types are:

- *Conceptual study:* 'Conceptual articles describe frameworks, models, and theories and offer explanations and reasons' (Alavi and Carlson, 1992);
- *Descriptive research:* 'Research in which one "paints a picture" with words or numbers, presents a profile, outlines stages, or classifies types' (Neuman, 2000: 508);
- *Experimental:* 'The experimenter manipulates one or more independent variables and holds constant all other possible independent variables while observing effects on dependent variables' (Zikmund *et al.*, 2010: 257);
- *Field study:* Has 'no manipulation of independent variables, involves experimental design but no experimental controls, (and) is carried out in the natural settings of the phenomenon of interest' (Alavi and Carlson, 1992);
- *Case study:* 'An empirical enquiry that investigates a contemporary phenomenon within its real-life context, especially when the boundaries between the phenomenon and context are not clearly evident' (Yin, 1994: 13);
- *Survey:* '"Snapshots" of practices, situations or views at a particular point in time, undertaken using questionnaires or (structured) interviews from which inferences may be made' (Galliers, 1991);
- *Literature review:* 'A directed search of published works ... that discusses theory and presents empirical results that are relevant to the topic at hand' (Zikmund *et al.*, 2010: 65);
- *Secondary data:* 'The reanalysis of previously collected survey or other data that were originally gathered by others' (Neuman, 2000: 305);
- *Action research:* 'Is focused on problem solving through social and organizational change' (Baskerville, 2008);
- *Design-science research:* The researcher 'creates and evaluates IT artifacts intended to solve identified organizational problems' (Hevner *et al.*, 2004: 77).

A major change to the categorization of types of DSS has also been made for this paper. The 2005 *JIT* paper included the DSS type 'executive information systems and business intelligence.' This category also included online analytical processing (OLAP) systems and reporting systems (e.g. corporate performance management systems) while DW was categorized as a separate DSS type. For this paper a DSS type 'BI' has been used. This new category includes the old BI, BA, OLAP, EIS, DW, and reporting systems. We believe that this categorization more clearly expresses the actual use of enterprise-scale DSS in practice and creates a large-scale DSS category that is clearly differentiated from the smaller scale and pervasive, personal DSS. The DSS types used in this paper are:

- *Personal Decision Support Systems (PDSS):* usually small-scale systems that are developed for one manager, or a small number of independent managers, to support a decision task;
- *Business intelligence (BI):* Large-scale systems that use data and analytics to support decision making at all levels of an organization. BI systems are often based on a data warehouse or data mart.
- *Group Support Systems (GSS):* The use of a combination of communication and DSS technologies to facilitate the effective working of groups;
- *Negotiation Support Systems (NSS):* DSS where the primary focus of the group work is negotiation between opposing parties;
- *Intelligent Decision Support Systems (IDSS):* The application of artificial intelligence techniques to decision support;
- *Knowledge Management-Based DSS (KMDSS):* Systems that support decision making by aiding knowledge storage, retrieval, transfer, and application by supporting individual and organizational memory and inter-group knowledge access.

The third major change to the coding protocol concerns a related set of questions: the importance of the business problem addressed by the article, the practice relevance of the article, and the rigor of theoretical foundations and the research methods used in the articles. These items were taken from the DSS design-science protocol used in Arnott and Pervan (2012). The importance of the business problem in an article was judged using Anthony's well-accepted typology of strategic, tactical, and operational problems (Anthony, 1965). By definition, a strategic task can have significantly more impact on an organization than tactical or operational tasks. Theoretical foundations and research methods were judged on a 3-point scale of strong, adequate, weak. Practical relevance to IT professionals and managers was judged on a 3-point scale of high, medium, low. These scales are ordinal and were analyzed accordingly.

The same coding procedures and practices that were used in previous DSS literature analyses were used for the coding of the updated sample and the recoding of the original sample. The coding was performed in intensive week-long retreats where the coders were able to challenge or confirm any question or issue as they arose. The ability to easily discuss interpretations improved the consistency of the coding. If after these discussions the coding could not be agreed on, a relevant expert in the specialist area was consulted by email. An important aspect of coding validity is that the two researchers have decades of experience in the DSS area, are experienced journal editors and reviewers, and have published DSS research in leading journals using DSR, experiments, case studies, and surveys. The coders have also worked in the IT industry mainly in the DSS area and are still involved at the highest levels of IT practice and formal IT professional bodies. The coders have also had significant senior management experience including divisional management and executive positions. This is important for judgments about the relevance of DSS research. The time taken to code each article varied considerably, ranging from over an hour for large, complex papers, to 15 min for the straightforward coding of a known paper.

In coding each paper the emphasis was on the dominant attribute of each factor for each paper. For identifying DSR articles we use the approach of Arnott and Pervan (2012) by considering whether the primary objective of the research was the development and evaluation of an important and novel IT artifact. Two passes through the 1466 articles were made to confirm the DSR article classification. Of the 529 articles coded as DSR only 17 (3.2%) explicitly defined their work as DSR, while 464 DSR articles (87.7%) did not define their research method in any way. Other popular terms for DSS DSR were 'description' (10 articles) and 'development' (10 articles). In coding relevance, consideration was given to the extent that a manager would be able to use the research in their work or the work of their organization, the extent that an IS professional could use the research in their work, and the extent that they would be likely to promote the research to a colleague. Each expectation was assessed on a 3-item scale of the expectation being strongly met, partly met, or not met all. These assessments were debated in a workshop/seminar of general IS academics who were provided with the data and the assessments of the coders. Two assessments were changed as a result of this structured critique.

The coded protocols were entered into an SPSS database for analysis by the second author, who also performed data-validity checks on the coding. Where possible the data was analyzed using cross-tabulation, Spearman's rank correlation, and ANOVA. When the word 'significant' is used in the text below it refers to test results that yielded a significance level of at least 0.05. The sample has been divided for analysis purposes into three 7-year eras: 1990–1996, 1997–2003, and 2004–2010. The third era is the addition to the article sample of the 2005 *JIT* paper.

Results and discussion

This section presents the quantitative results of the bibliometric content analysis of DSS research from 1990 to 2010. The discussion of the results is structured around the examination of the expectations for the progress of the field since 2003.

Expectations about the nature of the DSS field

Expectation 1: In parallel with the rise of BI in IT practice, overall DSS publication will increase.

Table 20.2 shows the share over time that DSS publishing occupies in the general IS journals that were identified in Table 20.1. The table shows that IS publication has grown 23.2% from the first to the second era, and 53.3% from the second to the third era. Overall, from 1990 to 2010 general IS publication has grown an impressive 89%. Unfortunately, in the same period DSS publication declined 21.6%. Table 20.2 shows that Expectation 1 has not been met.

To provide further detail to the results in Table 20.2, Figure 20.3 shows a year-by-year graph of DSS publishing from 1990 to 2010. The linear trend line shows a consistent reduction in publishing over the analysis period. There were fewer articles published in 2010 (36) than at the start of the sample in 1990 (42). Overall DSS publishing peaked in 1994 with 105 articles. Although the general trend is declining publication, there are periods of decline and growth: namely 1993–1997 and 1997–2006. It could be that this pattern will be repeated with significant growth in DSS publishing after 2010.

Figure 20.3 shows a significant decline in DSS publishing in the sample after 2007. This invites the question: What happened around and after 2007 for DSS researchers to change their research agendas to study other IS fields and phenomena? A particular concern for the field is that doctoral candidates and new faculty may have been part of this agenda shifting. One possible influence on researchers could be the rise in popularity of the technology acceptance model (TAM) (Davis, 1989). TAM became prominent in the late 1990s and early 2000s. Part of its appeal was that it offered a parsimonious model that was easy to use for surveys and field studies. Importantly, by 2007 TAM was a popular

64

Table 20.2 DSS publishing within general IS journals

| | 1990–1996 | | 1997–2003 | | 2004–2010 | | Total | |
	Number of articles	Percentage of IS	Number of articles	Percentage of IS	Number of articles	Percentage of IS	Number of articles	Percentage of IS
DSS papers	561	29.6	465	19.9	440	12.3	1,466	18.7
IS papers	1898		2339		3586		7823	

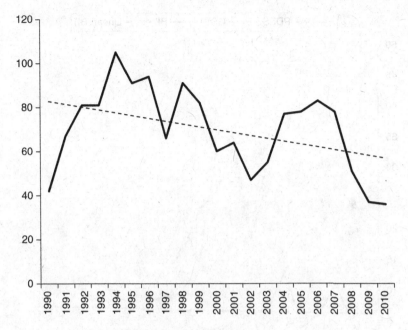

Figure 20.3   DSS articles published 1990–2010

theory for IS doctoral students. By the mid-2000s many IS academics had the feeling that TAM was swamping IS research. Hirschheim (2007: 205) lamented, 'TAM publications have been estimated to take up about 10% of our precious journal space.' It is likely that TAM was even more popular in the major IS conferences. TAM has not been as prominent in DSS research as it has in general IS. Benbasat and Barki (2007) argue that DSS research has produced important insights into IS usefulness that are more nuanced and detailed than that yielded by TAM research. As a result DSS researchers have been slow to embrace TAM.

Expectation 2: BI will become an increasing share of DSS research.

Figure 20.4 shows year-by-year publishing by three key DSS types: personal DSS, GSS, and BI. As shown in the figure, BI publishing increased steadily from 1999 but like the rest of DSS declined after 2007. The linear trend line for BI publishing shows absolute BI publishing is increasing over time. Table 20.3 provides data for the relative publishing increase or decrease of each DSS type. On a positive note, Table 20.3

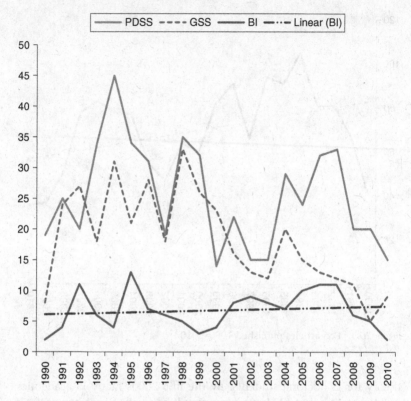

Figure 20.4   Publication by selected DSS types

shows that BI's share of DSS publishing has risen steadily from 8.4% of articles in 1990–1996 to 11.8% of 2004–2010. BI has been almost 10% of DSS publishing over time. Table 20.3 shows that Expectation 2 has been partly met. Importantly, there has been a significant increase in aggregate BI publishing from the second to the third analysis periods. An example of high quality BI research in the sample is Watson *et al.* (2002) who developed a framework for DW benefits and tested it with three case studies.

Expectation 3: GSS will decline in DSS publishing.

Table 20.3 shows that GSS publishing has significantly reduced in the last analysis era. GSS reduced from 30.3% of DSS research in 1997–2003 to 19.3% in 2004–2010, a drop of 11%. On the other hand, three DSS

Table 20.3 The sample by DSS type

DSS type	1990–1996		1997–2003		2004–2010		Total	
	Number of articles	Percentage of period	Number of articles	Percentage of period	Number of articles	Percentage of period	Number of articles	Percentage of sample
Personal DSS	208	37.1	152	32.7	173	39.3	533	36.4
Business intelligence	47	8.4	43	9.2	52	11.8	142	9.7
Group support systems	157	28.0	141	30.3	85	19.3	383	26.1
Intelligent DSS	86	15.3	63	13.5	50	11.4	199	13.6
Knowledge management-based DSS	4	0.7	18	3.9	16	3.6	38	2.6
Negotiation support systems	16	2.9	24	5.2	42	9.5	82	5.6
Many	43	7.7	24	5.2	22	5.0	89	6.1
Total	561		465		440		1466	

types have had significant increases; PDSS up 6.6%, BI up 2.6%, and NSS up 4.3%. This means that Expectation 3 has been strongly met.

Over time the primary focus of GSS research on face-to-face settings, using university-developed software on artificial problems with students as subjects, has had little impact on practice. However, there has been an explosion in commercial collaboration ITs for conferencing (for example, GoToMeetings, WebEx, MS Office Live Meeting, CU-SEEME, Skype), online communities (for example, Intranets, listservers, newsgroups, blogs), and proprietary groupware (IBM Lotus Notes, Novell GroupWise, Oracle Collaboration Suite). These products that support group work in a variety of time and place settings have the potential to redirect and rebuild GSS research, particularly in the field. A high quality example of this style of GSS research is Dennis *et al.* (2003) who studied the success and failure of groupware supported business process reengineering in two different armies, a food service company, and an IT company. Another very promising example is collaboration engineering, where GSS researchers have developed 'repeatable collaborative processes' (Briggs *et al.*, 2003: 32) that can be implemented by practitioners for the support of groups using modern project management platforms and social intranets.

Expectation 4: DSS research will have more case studies.

Table 20.4 shows an analysis of DSS publishing by article type. The table shows that case studies as a research type has reduced significantly in the period since 2003. This decline has been both absolute and relative; case studies now only occupy 6.6% of DSS articles. This means that Expectation 4 has not been met.

The expectation was developed because the 2005 *JIT* paper argued that more case studies would improve the relevance of DSS research without reducing research rigor. In fact, it is the rigor of academic case studies that professionals and managers value. The reduction of case study articles in the last analysis era would be a strong negative for the field except for the increase in DSR articles under Expectation 5 below. These changes combined may be beneficial for the relevance of DSS research.

Case studies can also be used as an evaluation method in DSR articles. They are the fourth most popular evaluation approach at 10.6% of DSS DSR articles. Their popularity in DSR has varied over the sample period with 10% of DSS DSR evaluation in the last analysis era being case studies. If these secondary case studies are added to the major case study article type they, unfortunately, do not affect the negative assessment

Table 20.4 Sample by article type

	1990–1996		1997–2003		2004–2010		Total	
	Number of articles	Percentage of period	Number of articles	Percentage of period	Number of articles	Percentage of period	Number of articles	Percentage of sample
Conceptual study	118	21.0	72	15.5	33	7.5	223	15.2
Descriptive study	37	6.6	36	7.7	17	3.9	90	6.1
Experimental	106	18.9	122	26.2	102	23.2	330	22.5
Field study	17	3.0	18	3.9	3	0.7	38	2.6
Case study	45	8.0	42	9.0	29	6.6	116	7.9
Survey	47	8.4	24	5.2	27	6.1	98	6.7
Literature review	9	1.6	7	1.5	9	2.0	25	1.7
Secondary data	3	0.5	3	0.6	5	1.1	11	0.8
Action research	0	0.0	2	0.4	4	0.9	6	0.4
Design science	179	31.9	139	29.9	211	48.0	529	36.1
Total	561		465		440		1466	

of Expectation 4. On a positive note, an exemplar of DSS DSR that uses case study as an evaluation method is Salo and Kakola (2005) who developed a design theory for a groupware-based requirements management system. They tested their theory by analyzing instantiations of product lines at Nokia.

Expectation 4a: DSS research will have more interpretive case studies.

Further examination of the epistemology underlying the case studies in Table 20.4 revealed that 35.6% of case studies were interpretivist in 1990–1996, 42.9% in 1997–2003, and 37.9% in 2004–2010. This means that Expectation 4a has not been met. It may be that the long-running positivism–interpretivism debate by IS scholars has matured and, in DSS research at least, the proportion of case studies in each epistemology is fairly stable. An example of a high quality DSS interpretive case study is Nandhakumar (1996) who investigated the critical success factors of EIS. He found important relationships between factors and important dynamic behaviors of factors. These insights would have been unlikely to emerge if quantitative methods had been used in his study.

Expectation 5: Design-science research will increase in DSS publication.

Table 20.4 shows that this expectation has been strongly met with DSR increasing from 29.2% of DSS research in 1997–2003 to 47.7% in 2004–2010; a rise of 18.5%. Figure 20.5 shows the data in different format, a histogram of DSS research by article type. This graph clearly shows the importance of design science as a research strategy for DSS researchers. If this trend continues DSR will be the majority of DSS research.

Expectation 6: DSS design-science research will increase in quality.

In assessing the quality of DSS DSR, two related constructs are available from the coding: the theoretical foundations of the research and the rigor of research methods. These two constructs can collectively indicate research quality. Table 20.5 shows the rigor of the theoretical foundations of DSS DSR from 1990–2010. These theoretical foundations are not restricted to judgment and decision making and include theories like TAM, task-technology fit (Goodhue and Thompson, 1995),

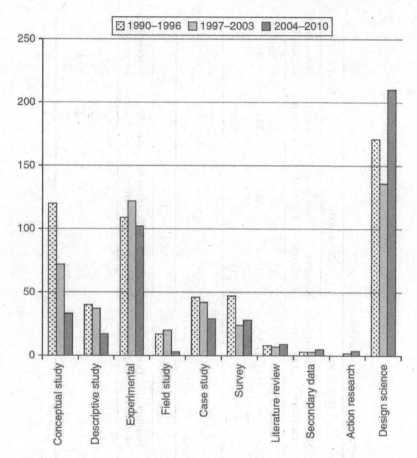

Figure 20.5 DSS articles by article type

and IS success (DeLone and McLean, 2003). Theory foundation rigor was judged on a 3-item scale of strong, adequate, and weak. Coding was performed with a generosity bias so when an article was near an item boundary (for example, weak/adequate) it was coded as the higher item (adequate in the example). Table 20.5 shows a virtually unchanging coding result for DSR quality over the 21 years of the sample. There has been a small shift of around 3% of articles from weak to adequate theoretical rigor, which is an improvement (although not significant).

Table 20.6 shows the analysis of the rigor of DSS DSR research methods. A similar coding scale and process to the rigor of theory

Table 20.5 The rigor of the theoretical foundations of DSS design-science research

	1990–1996		1997–2003		2004–2010		Total	
	Number of articles	Percentage of period	Number of articles	Percentage of period	Number of articles	Percentage of period	Number of articles	Percentage of sample
Strong	51	28.5	54	38.8	82	38.9	187	35.3
Adequate	84	46.9	66	47.5	107	50.7	257	48.6
Weak	44	24.6	19	13.7	22	10.4	85	16.1
Total	179		139		211		529	

Table 20.6 The rigor of the research methods of DSS design-science research

	1990–1996		1997–2003		2004–2010		Total	
	Number of articles	Percentage of period	Number of articles	Percentage of period	Number of articles	Percentage of period	Number of articles	Percentage of sample
Strong	6	3.4	4	2.9	18	8.5	28	5.3
Adequate	28	15.6	42	30.2	59	28.0	129	24.4
Weak	145	81.0	93	66.9	134	63.5	372	70.3
Total	179		139		211		529	

foundations was used. Table 20.6 shows a reasonable improvement in the strong category (up 5.6% in the last era) and a 3.4% reduction in the weak category. This small shift from weak to adequate and from adequate to strong is positive.

Taken together, Tables 20.5 and 20.6 show that Expectation 6 has been partly met, in that DSS DSR has had a modest improvement in quality. The most disappointing result was that only 8.5% of DSR articles in the final analysis era were judged as having strong rigor in their research methods. It could have been that the DSR guidelines of Hevner *et al.* (2004) would have had a greater positive impact in the 2004–2010 period. Perhaps the lag in quality improvement is longer than anticipated and could be because of the long publishing cycle of many journals in the sample. It is hoped that the DSR theory guidelines of Kuechler and Vaishnavi (2012) will also have a positive impact in time. As mentioned above, 87.7% of DSS DSR papers did not identify their research method in any way. It was clear during the coding process that many of the pre-2005 DSR papers were fitting their artifact development and evaluation work into the rubric of other methods (e.g. case studies). In the last analysis era there are examples of high quality DSS DSR in the sample like Shanks *et al.* (2009) where the artifact is a framework for the benefits of customer relationship management (CRM) systems. The framework is not only useful for DSS researchers but also for professionals who are building a business case for CRM, or who are conducting system evaluations.

Expectation 7: The external funding of DSS research will increase.

The Arnott *et al.* (2005) analysis of how DSS research was funded between 1990 and 2003 recommended that DSS researchers should seek more external funding from both grant funding bodies and industry. The 2005 analysis showed that DSS as a field relied excessively on internal university funding, mainly through faculty salaries. This was termed implicit funding, as it is part of the researcher's employment contract. Since the end of the 2003 sample the developed world has suffered the global financial crisis (GFC) and university budgets have been significantly constrained. Table 20.7 shows that in the 2004–2010 period the number of articles with competitive grant funding almost doubled over the previous era. As a result, Expectation 7 is strongly met. The increase suggests that DSS researchers have been able to secure funding from external grant sources to offset the internal effect of the GFC. Still, as Table 20.7 also shows, nearly two-thirds of DSS articles in 2004–2010

Table 20.7 DSS grant funding over time

Period	Some competitive grant funding		Some industry grant funding		Non-competitive grant funding only		No grant funding	
	Number of papers	Percentage of period	Number of papers	Percentage of period	Number of papers	Percentage of period	Number of papers	Percentage of period
1990–1996	80	14.5	39	7.0	38	6.8	421	75.0
1997–2003	70	15.1	14	3.0	25	5.4	363	78.1
2004–2010	119	27.0	17	3.9	29	6.6	284	64.5
Total	269	18.3	70	4.8	92	6.3	1068	72.9

did not report any grant or industry funding. This means that implicit funding remains the dominant source of support for DSS research. Further analysis of competitive grant funding by DSS types shows that PDSS accounts for the greatest share of articles with competitive grants; around 40% in the last analysis era.

Expectation 7a: The industry funding of DSS research will increase.

Table 20.7 also shows that the number of articles with some industry funding fell sharply in the first two analysis eras and then stabilized in the last era. This means that Expectation 7a has not been met. This is unfortunate as the industry funding of DSS research moves research agendas toward highly relevant topics. It can build lasting relationships between researchers and professionals. An explanation of why major competitive grants have grown while industry funding has stabilized could lie in the effects of the 2007/2008 GFC. Since the GFC organizations are likely to have significantly less scope to fund university research and are likely to have shifted their priorities toward organizational survival, especially in the United States and Europe. A post-GFC world may be more receptive to DSS industry-based research funding.

Expectations about the quality of DSS research

Expectation 8: The theoretical foundations of DSS research will improve in quality.

Expectation 6 has already examined the quality of the theoretical foundations of DSS DSR and found a modest improvement in the 2004–2010 analysis period. Expectation 8 expands this analysis to the whole of the DSS sample. Table 20.8 shows that the assessment of the quality of theoretical foundations of articles has had a moderate improvement in the last analysis era. The coding as weak has declined 4.4% and the coding as strong has increased by 4.9%. This means that Expectation 8 has been partly met; this is a positive sign for the field.

Expectation 9: DSS research will have better grounding in decision-making theory.

As DSS by definition involves supporting decision making, it follows that a significant proportion of DSS research should be grounded in appropriate theories of decision making. Table 20.9 shows the modest

Table 20.8 The quality of the theoretical foundations of DSS Research

	1990–1996		1997–2003		2004–2010		Total	
	Number of articles	Percentage of period	Number of articles	Percentage of period	Number of articles	Percentage of period	Number of articles	Percentage of sample
Strong	185	33.0	180	38.7	192	43.6	557	38.0
Adequate	214	38.1	195	41.9	182	41.4	591	40.3
Weak	162	28.9	90	19.4	66	15.0	318	21.7
Total	561		465		440		1,466	

Table 20.9 The use of judgment and decision-making reference theory

	1990–1996		1997–2003		2004–2010		Total	
	Number of articles	Percentage of period	Number of articles	Percentage of period	Number of articles	Percentage of period	Number of articles	Percentage of sample
JDM theory used	302	53.8	235	50.5	170	38.6	707	48.2
JDM theory not used	259	46.2	230	49.5	270	61.4	759	51.8
Total	561		465		440		1466	

decline in articles that use appropriate judgment and decision-making theory from 1990 to 2003 and the decline has accelerated in 2004–2010, dropping a serious 11.9% in the last era. Expectation 9 has not been met.

Table 20.10 builds on Table 20.17 from Arnott and Pervan (2005) and addresses Expectation 9 from another perspective. It shows the average number of judgment and decision-making citations per article from 1990 to 2010. Unfortunately, Table 20.10 confirms the analysis in Table 20.9. Mean citation was stable from 1990 to 2003 at 2.1 citations per article and then dropped to 1.2 in the last period. The decline is across most DSS types with only KMDSS showing an increased citation rate. This is a disappointing outcome for the field.

Expectation 9a: DSS research will be more grounded in Kahneman and Tversky's theory of decision-making.

Expectation 9b: DSS research will be less grounded in Simon's theory of decision-making.

Table 20.11 provides a citation analysis in the sample of works by Herbert Simon as one school of decision-making theory and by Daniel Kahneman and Amos Tversky as another school. The citations counted for Table 20.11 are those reference articles where Simon, Kahneman, or Tversky were authors or co-authors. This approach provides only a sample of the two schools' impact as it excludes the disciples of the founding researchers. It can also underestimate the impact of Simon's theory as, as discussed above, it has become axiomatic in business research and can be used in a research study without citation. Nevertheless, the

Table 20.10 Mean judgment and decision-making citation by DSS type

DSS type	1990–1996	1997–2003	2004–2010	Total
Personal DSS	2.3	2.1	1.3	2.0
Business intelligence	1.7	0.8	0.4	1.0
Group support systems	2.3	3.0	1.8	2.5
Intelligent DSS	0.8	0.7	0.4	0.7
Knowledge management-based DSS	1.3	1.3	2.1	1.7
Negotiation support Systems	2.8	2.1	1.4	1.9
Many	2.8	2.4	0.7	2.2
All articles in sample	2.1	2.1	1.2	1.8

Table 20.11 Citations to the major schools of decision-making reference theory

	1990–1996		1997–2003		2004–2010		Total	
	Number of cites	Percentage of period	Number of cites	Percentage of period	Number of cites	Percenatge of period	Number of cites	Percenatge of sample
Simon	160	72.7	81	66.4	37	59.7	278	68.8
Kahneman and Tversky	60	27.3	41	33.6	25	40.3	126	31.2
Total	220		122		62		404	

citation number of each school's founding fathers is an adequate proxy for the purpose of evaluating Expectations 9a and 9b.

The data in Table 20.11 shows that Expectations 9a and 9b have both been strongly met. Citations to Simon have declined from 72.7% of citations in the first era to 59.7% of citations in the final era. Conversely, citations to Kahneman and/or Tversky have increased from 27.3% of the first period to 40.3% of the final period. Figure 20.6 shows trend lines for the citations to each decision-making school. The data shows that DSS researchers are gradually and persistently moving from the Simon school to the Kahneman and Tversky school of decision making. If the literature analysis is updated in another 7 years, Kahneman and Tversky's theory may dominate DSS decision-making reference citation.

Expectation 10: DSS research designs will be more rigorous.

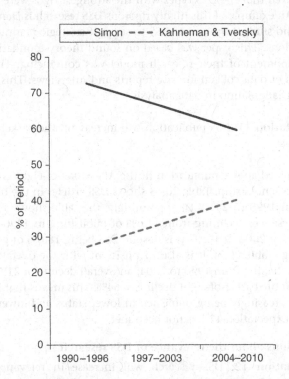

Figure 20.6 Citations to the major schools of decision-making reference theory

Table 20.12 shows the coding of the rigor of the research designs for DSS research from 1990 to 2010. As with other questions in the protocol the rigor of research designs was coded with a generosity bias at category boundaries. The table shows significant improvement in research rigor in the first two periods but shows virtually no change in the period from 2004 to 2010 that the expectation refers to. This means that Expectation 10 has not been met. Having 48.9% of articles coded as weak is a disappointing outcome for the field. Many articles did not even address research design at all. In 2005 it was noted that this was surprising given the journals in the sample, unfortunately the situation has not changed.

A cross-tab of research method rigor and journals showed that the most rigorous articles are published in *JAIS* and *MISQ*, while the least rigorous were found in *CAIS*, *DSS*, and *JOCEC*. Another cross-tab of the rigor of research methods and judgment and decision-making citation shows that papers that cite decision-making foundation theory are also significantly more rigorous. A final cross-tab using research methods rigor showed that the DSS types with the strongest rigor were GSS and KMDSS. An example of this highly rigorous DSS research is Dennis *et al.* (1997) who studied the use of GSS to support strategic planning in 30 organizations. This paper was based on sound theory foundations and the development of their research model was convincing. They used two types of data collection: case reports and interviews. This allowed effective triangulation in data analysis.

Expectation 11: DSS publication will increase in the basket-of-eight journals.

As discussed above, publication in the AIS basket-of-eight is the pinnacle of IS scholarship. Table 20.13 shows DSS articles in the basket-of-eight from 1990 to 2010. Disappointingly, the table shows a collapse of DSS presence, declining from 11.6% of publishing in 1990–1996 to only 2.7% of 2004–2010. This is despite DSS being 18.6% of general IS publishing (Table 20.2). It is also inconsistent with the overall decline of DSS publishing from 1990 to 2004; an overall decline of 21.6% compared with the basket-of-eight decline of 64%. This means that DSS articles are increasingly being published in lower status and lower impact journals. Expectation 11 has not been met.

Expectations about the relevance of DSS research

Expectation 12: DSS research will increase in relevance to IT professionals.

Table 20.12 The rigor of DSS research methods

Method rigor	1990–1996		1997–2003		2004–2010		Total	
	Number of articles	Percentage of period	Number of articles	Percentage of period	Number of articles	Percentage of period	Number of articles	Percentage of sample
Strong	89	15.9	110	23.7	105	23.9	304	20.7
Adequate	115	20.5	129	27.7	120	27.3	364	24.8
Weak	357	63.6	226	48.6	215	48.9	798	54.4
Total	561		465		440		1466	

Table 20.13 DSS publication in the basket-of-eight

Journal	1990–1996		1997–2003		2004–2010		Total	
	Number of articles	Percentage of journal	Number of articles	Percentage of journal	Number of articles	Percentage of journal	Number of articles	Percentage of journal
European Journal of Information Systems	14	11.2	7	8.1	5	11.1	26	10.2
Information Systems Journal	8	6.4	7	8.1	3	6.7	18	7.0
Information Systems Research	23	18.4	10	11.6	4	8.9	37	14.5
Journal of Information Technology	17	13.6	5	5.8	4	8.9	26	10.2
Journal of Management Information Systems	38	30.4	38	44.2	13	28.9	89	34.8
Journal of Strategic Information Systems	3	2.4	5	5.8	3	6.7	11	4.3
Journal of the Association for Information Systems	0	0.0	2	2.3	6	13.3	8	3.1
MIS Quarterly	22	17.6	12	14.0	7	15.6	41	16.0
Total	125	11.6	86	7.2	45	2.7	256	

Relevance to IT professionals and managers was judged on a 3-item scale (high medium, low) with the usual generosity bias. Table 20.14, which shows the article sample by relevance to IT professionals, is disappointing for the DSS field. What was a positive increase in high and medium relevance from the first to the second era has been more than reversed in the last analysis era. Unfortunately, in the last analysis period the decline in medium relevance has been added to the low category rather than to the strong. This means that Expectation 12 has not been met. One strategy to increase the relevance to IT professionals is to engage in more fieldwork. Arnott and Pervan (2010) found that in DSS DSR only 13.6% of design artifacts were actually used in the field. This indicates a significant scope for improvement.

A cross-tab of relevance to IS practitioners with DSS type shows that the DSS type that is performing far above the other types in terms of relevance is BI. Half of the BI articles in the sample scored high relevance. This is an impressive result as the next performing DSS type only had 10.5% of articles with high relevance. This supports the arguments in the 2005 *JIT* paper for researchers to shift DSS research agendas toward BI. An example of a DSS article with high relevance for IT professionals is Hwang *et al.* (2004) who studied the factors affecting the adoption of DW in the banking industry in Taiwan.

Expectation 13: DSS research will increase in relevance to managers.

Unlike the analysis of relevance to IT professionals under the last expectation, the analysis of the relevance of DSS research to managers is more positive. Table 20.15 shows that although there was a 2% decline of articles with high managerial relevance in the last era, the coding of medium relevance has been consistently growing over the sample period, with a growth of 7.7% in the last era mainly at the expense of low relevance articles. This means that Expectation 13 has been partly met and this is a healthy sign for the DSS field. An example of DSS research that is highly relevant to managers is Watson *et al.* (2004) who studied the governance of DW at a large health insurer. Their article provides guidance for a senior executive team that is designing IT governance structures and processes.

Expectation 14: DSS will address more strategic decision tasks.

To assess whether DSS research has increased in organizational importance and impact, articles were coded according to the nature

Table 20.14 The sample by practical relevance for IT professionals

Practical relevance	1990–1996		1997–2003		2004–2010		Total	
	Number of articles	Percentage of period	Number of articles	Percentage of period	Number of articles	Percentage of period	Number of articles	Percentage of sample
High	43	7.7	43	9.3	43	9.8	129	8.8
Medium	152	27.1	142	30.6	105	23.9	399	27.2
Low	366	65.2	279	60.2	292	66.4	937	64.0
Total	561		464		440		1466	

Table 20.15 The sample by practical relevance for managers

Practical relevance	1990–1996		1997–2003		2004–2010		Total	
	Number of articles	Percentage of period	Number of articles	Percentage of period	Number of articles	Percentage of period	Number of articles	Percentage of sample
High	76	13.5	65	14.0	53	12.0	194	13.2
Medium	140	25.0	135	29.1	162	36.8	437	29.8
Low	345	61.5	264	56.9	225	51.1	834	56.9
Total	561		464		440		1466	

of tasks that they support using the widely used strategic/tactical/operational classification (Anthony, 1965). It was hoped that DSS would address more strategic tasks. Table 20.16 shows the result of the coding. Unfortunately, Expectation 14 has not been met.

Although Expectation 14 has not been met, Table 20.16 gives some hope for the future. While strategic tasks have declined by 2.8%, tactical tasks have increased by 4%. Operational tasks remain at 67.3% overall, but the strong presence of tactical decision support is healthy for the field. A major constraint of research on strategic tasks, especially DSR, is access to participants and problems. There is no data on the strategic/tactical/operational breakdown of all IS publishing so it may be that DSS research at 8.2% strategic support in the last analysis period is an excellent result.

To further highlight the difficulties of strategic research in a field that is almost 50% DSR, Table 20.17 shows the coding for the primary user of the DSS in the article. Articles aimed at executive users have halved over the three analysis eras. Managers have been a steady proportion over time, while professionals have increased in attention.

A cross-tab of problem importance by DSS type showed that only BI, with 22.5% of articles coded as strategic, had a significant presence in strategic decision support. A further cross-tab of problem importance with article type showed that the types that had more strategic and less operational decision support were field study, case study, and action research. Significantly, all of these article types involve research in the field. An example of high quality DSS research that addresses strategic tasks is Leidner *et al.* (1999) who undertook survey research to investigate the role of culture in EIS use. They studied organizations in Mexico, Sweden, and the United States and found significant cultural differences in the use of EIS for strategic decision making.

Expectation 15: DSS research will have less tradeoff between rigor and relevance.

In Expectations 12 and 13, relevance was assessed in two dimensions, one that addressed relevance to IT professionals and one related to managers. Relevance was coded on the ordinal scale: high, medium, low. Under Expectation 6 rigor was assessed using two related constructs: the theoretical foundations of the research and the rigor of research methods. Both were coded on a 3-point ordinal scale: strong, adequate, weak. Spearman's rank correlations were performed on the two relevance and the two rigor constructs. The R^2 for the four correlations were all less

Table 20.16 The importance of business problems in DSS research

Problem Level	1990–1996		1997–2003		2004–2010		Total	
	Number of articles	Percentage of period	Number of articles	Percentage of period	Number of articles	Percentage of period	Number of articles	Percentage of sample
Strategic	56	10.0	51	11.0	36	8.2	143	9.8
Tactical	118	21.0	95	20.5	108	24.5	321	21.9
Operational	387	69.0	318	68.5	296	67.3	1,001	68.3
Total	561		465		440		1466	

Table 20.17 The primary user of DSS

User	1990–1996		1997–2003		2004–2010		Total	
	Number of articles	Percentage of period	Number of articles	Percentage of period	Number of articles	Percentage of period	Number of articles	Percentage of sample
Executive	45	8.0	27	5.8	18	4.1	90	6.1
Manager	53	9.4	42	9.0	40	9.1	135	9.2
Professional	55	9.8	69	14.8	78	17.7	202	13.8
Other knowledge worker	18	3.2	17	3.7	20	4.5	55	3.8
Many	51	9.1	48	10.3	54	12.3	153	10.4
Unclear	339	60.4	262	56.3	230	52.3	831	56.7
Total	561		465		440		1466	

than or equal to 0.01. This means that there is no relationship between rigor and relevance in the article sample and that Expectation 15 has not been met.

This is not to say that DSS research cannot be both rigorous and relevant. Inspecting the four measures of rigor and relevance for individual articles identified seven articles (of the total 1466) with perfect scores, that is, they are strongly rigorous and highly relevant to both IT professionals and managers. Examples of this research excellence are Marginson *et al.* (2000) who compared the executive use of email and accounting IS to investigate why executives use IT, and Gottschalk (2000) who investigated the use of knowledge management to support senior professionals in Norwegian law firms.

Overall assessment of the expectations about DSS research

Table 20.18 summarizes the assessment of the expectations about the development of the DSS field since the 2003 end of the sample in the 2005 *JIT* Critical Analysis article. Five of the 19 expectations were judged as having being strongly met, 4 partly met, and 10 were not met at all. That 9 of the 19 expectations about the development of DSS research in the 7 years to 2010 were in some way realized is positive for the field, the 10 other unmet expectations are a cause for concern.

The assessment of the expectations shows a field that is undergoing a major transition. Some of the activities of the field are pushing DSS research in a positive direction, others in a negative direction. This situation is visualized in Figure 20.7 where, as an alternative to Table 20.18, the forces determining the health of the DSS field are shown as strong, medium, or weak effects according to the discussion around the assessment of the expectations. Figure 20.7 is inspired by force-field analysis (Lewin, 1943). Force-field analysis is used by clinical psychologists and psychiatrists to develop an overall impression of the mental health of a patient. The interpretation of Figure 20.7 is by definition subjective but it can provide an overall impression of the health of the DSS field. Importantly, it is based on empirical data obtained through bibliometric analysis, as detailed above, rather than being based on non-empirical argumentation and opinion.

In terms of negative effects, or Lewin's hindering forces, the analysis shows that DSS research addressed fewer strategic problems after 2003 than it had before. It also shows that DSS has had a significant reduction in aggregate publishing from 2004 to 2010, and that its presence in the elite basket-of-eight journals has declined at an even faster rate than the overall DSS publishing decline. The relevance of DSS

Table 20.18 Expectations about the progress of DSS research since 2003

Number	Expectation	Level of meeting expectation
The nature of the DSS field		
1	In parallel with the rise of BI in IT practice, overall DSS publication will increase	None
2	BI will become an increasing share of DSS research	Partly
3	GSS will decline in DSS publishing	Strong
4	DSS research will have more case studies	None
4a	DSS research will have more interpretive case studies	None
5	Design-science research will increase in DSS publication	Strong
6	DSS design-science research will increase in quality	Part
7	The external funding of DSS research will increase	Strong
7a	The industry funding of DSS research will increase	None
The quality of DSS research		
8	The theoretical foundations of DSS research will improve in quality	Part
9	DSS research will have better grounding in decision-making theory	None
9a	DSS research will be more grounded in Kahneman and Tversky's theory of decision-making	Strong
9b	DSS research will be less grounded in Simon's theory of decision-making	Strong
10	DSS research designs will be more rigorous	None
11	DSS publication will increase in the basket-of-eight journals	None
The relevance of DSS research		
12	DSS research will increase in relevance to IT professionals	None
13	DSS research will increase in relevance to managers	Part
14	DSS will address more strategic decision tasks	None
15	DSS research will have less tradeoff between rigor and relevance	None

research to IT professionals has declined and DSS research design rigor has not improved from its low previous assessment. Industry funding of DSS research has reduced significantly. The use of judgment and decision-making foundation theory in DSS research has declined, but

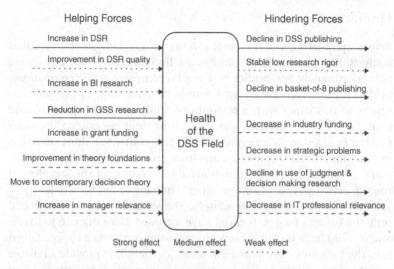

Figure 20.7 Forces acting on the DSS field

on a positive note what theory that is used is trending toward the more recent decision-making theory of Kahneman and Tversky.

In terms of positive forces, or Lewin's helping forces, on DSS research, an important finding is that design science has significantly increased as a DSS research strategy. Unlike the situation for IT professionals, the relevance of DSS research to managers is improving. There has also been some improvement in the rigor of DSS DSR. In addition, there has been a major increase in DSS grant funding, an increase that is particularly important after the GFC. GSS publication has declined significantly and now occupies a more balanced fraction of DSS research. Unfortunately, this GSS reduction has mainly shifted toward personal DSS, the oldest part of the field, rather than to BI. There has, however, been a significant increase in BI publishing in the last 7 years. The shift of research designs toward design science should be positive for the DSS field. Importantly, DSS DSR is significantly better than the remainder of DSS research in terms of relevance to managers and quality of research methods (one-way ANOVA, $P<0.01$). The theory foundations of DSR have improved significantly over the analysis period. Further, DSR naturally involves greater engagement with the IT industry and organizations.

The assessment of a number of the expectations has identified exemplary DSS research articles. These articles show that DSS researchers are capable of the highest quality IS research.

Limitations

Before speculating on the implications of the bibliometric content analysis, it is important to consider the limitations of the study. There are unfortunately few studies that can be compared with the quantum of data analyzed in this study. It would be interesting to compare the results of this paper with a text-mining study of all DSS journals and conferences in the style of the analysis of multiple criteria decision-making research by Bragge *et al.* (2012). This content analysis study has similar limitations to previous literature analyses (Arnott and Pervan, 2005, 2008, 2012). These limitations are the nature of the sample and the subjective aspects of some coding. The sample of DSS articles in 16 journals is only one possible sample. The sample could have included only the basket-of-eight, it could have included more than 16 journals, and it could have included book chapters and conference papers. Given this, the basket-of-eight plus eight other journals does provide a reliable sample of DSS research. The large size of the sample (1466 articles) and the 21-year time period also adds to the strength of the sample. In terms of coding limitations, four of the protocol items (R7, R8, R10, R11 in Appendix A) involve a subjective judgment by the coder on a 3-point ordinal scale. The procedures used in coding aimed at ensuring the reliability of this coding. The judgment of how well each expectation was met also used a subjective 3-item scale and judgment of the strength of each force in the force-field diagram was also subjective. Both these sets of judgments were tested in a seminar environment. It is highly likely that other experienced DSS researchers and professionals using the same protocol and procedures would yield similar results. Importantly, and as described above, a generosity bias was used in coding to mitigate any negative framing effect (Tversky and Kahneman, 1981). Keeping in mind the limitations of the study, the analysis of the expectations does provide a foundation for speculating about the future directions of the DSS field and its importance to IS in general.

Speculations about the future of the DSS field

The depiction of positive and negative forces on DSS research in Figure 20.7 invites the questions: What is the net effect of the various forces? Has DSS as a field improved over the 7 years of the updated sample? Unfortunately, there is no quantitative score that can summarize these effects, because as mentioned, force-field analysis is subjective in nature and the various forces are of varying strength. What is clear from the data analysis is that the DSS field has a very different feel to the field that was analyzed in the 2005 *JIT* Critical Analysis paper. This section speculates on trends from the analysis and identifies a number of forecasts about the likely development of the DSS field in the next 7 years (the interval of analysis in this paper). These forecasts are similar in nature to the expectations that guided the research in this paper; they are based on bibliometric content analysis as seen through the lens of the researchers' experiences. There are 10 forecasts provided below, a smaller set than the 15 expectations that guided the analysis in this paper. The forecasts for DSS's future do cover the most important trends and issues that arose from the analysis and discussion of the context of the field.

Forecast 1: Design science will dominate DSS research

In the first analysis era statistical hypothesis testing and conceptual studies comprised 48.3% of articles, in the last era their proportion reduced to 36.8%. DSR grew to 48% of DSS research in the last era. The linear trend analysis shows that DSR will be the majority of DSS research during the forecast period. The transition from a field dominated by what can be termed orthodox IS research methods, to one dominated by DSR, is a major finding of this paper.

Forecast 2: DSS DSR will increase in quality

Since the 2005 *JIT* paper there has been a number of significant publications that DSS DSR researchers can use to inform their work. These include Hevner *et al.* (2004), Hevner (2007), Iivari (2007), Gregor and Jones (2007), Vaishnavi and Kuechler (2008), Kuechler and Vaishnavi (2012), Germonprez *et al.* (2011), and Venable *et al.* (2012). The lack of consensus about what constitutes quality DSR before the 2003 end of the previous article sample has hampered DSS DSR quality and acceptance. High quality DSR may provide DSS researchers with the opportunity to progress the DSS field to a situation where it is respected and influential with DSS users and developers.

Forecast 3: DSS DSR will increase in relevance

DSS DSR has a higher relevance to managers than other parts of DSS research. It does lag with relevance to IT professionals. DSS DSR has been slow to embrace a *techne* conceptualization of relevance (Lee, 2010). In this form of relevance a DSS DSR project can argue a significant contribution to relevance when it effectively shows professionals and managers how to accomplish a decision support task in a new or novel way. With greater academic acceptance of this form of contribution we expect that DSS researchers will naturally increase their attention on relevance to IT professionals while maintaining their managerial relevance.

Forecast 4: The rise in DSS DSR will lead to greater research on tactical and strategic decision support

Although around two-thirds of DSS papers currently address operational tasks, DSS researchers have the opportunity to lift their attention to more tactical and strategic tasks. DSS through its support of managerial work is the part of the IS discipline that arguably is the most exposed to tactical and strategic decision making. By definition these tasks have the greatest impact on an organization and by supporting strategic decisions in a DSR context, DSS will increase its importance to practitioners and organizations.

Forecast 5: Information Systems DSR will learn from, and be guided by, DSS DSR

As predicted in Arnott and Pervan (2005) and confirmed in Arnott and Pervan (2012), experience with design science could be one the most important contributions that DSS research can make to the IS discipline. The only guidance through literature analysis regarding the size of DSR in IS research is the study by Indulska and Recker (2008). They analyzed DSR articles in the five main AIS-sponsored conferences (ICIS, ECIS, PACIS, AMCIS, ACIS) from 2005 to 2007 and found that DSR only comprised 3% of IS research. If their 3-year sample was extended to 2010, the percentage of IS DSR may have increased. Indulska and Recker noticed that an overproportional share of DSR was published by European authors, which is understandable as European IS has had a long design-science tradition (Winter, 2008). It could be that these European researchers were not restricted by the statistical hypothesis-testing research that is the orthodoxy in North American business schools. The current study has found that DSS research was 12.3% of IS research in the 2004–2010 period. It also found that DSR was 48% of DSS research in that period. This means that 5.9% of IS research from 2004 to 2010 was DSS DSR, a very significant fraction of total IS research. Unlike the situation with TAM where IS researchers ignored the progress that DSS research had made on understanding usability and usefulness (Benbasat and Barki, 2007), IS design-science researchers may improve their work by familiarizing themselves with quality DSS DSR. It is no accident that when Hevner *et al.* (2004) analyzed three exemplars of DSR they chose two DSS articles or when Kuechler and Vaishnavi (2012) analyzed DSR articles for theorizing they only chose DSS studies.

Forecast 6: DSS research will be largely based on the decision theory of Kahneman and Tversky

DSS should make better use of the current orthodoxy of behavioral decision theory, the theories typified by the work of Kahneman and Tversky. As the testing of Expectation 9a found, the move in foundation theory away from Simon's phase model is well underway. Simon's theory of bounded rationality is still valid and useful. However, given the lack of empirical validation of the phase model, and the availability of alternative scientifically tested theory, there is simply no reason to use Simon's phase model in DSS research. Kahneman and Tversky's theories have the potential to transform DSS research and practice.

Forecast 7: BI publishing will increase in the sample's journals

There is also a concerning trend in BI research, the most strategic and most relevant type of DSS research. Despite some improvement from 2004 to 2010, there is still inadequate attention being given to BI, the major DSS movement in industry. It could be that a significant amount of BI research is being published in journals outside the sample especially as there has been a number of DSS- and BI-titled journals created in this century (for example, *International Journal of Business Intelligence Research, International Journal of Business Intelligence and Data Mining,* and the *International Journal of Decision Support System Technology*). If BI publishing has shifted to these new outlets, the impact of DSS research will reduce because new journals, by their nature, have limited readership and library availability. Articles in newer journals are therefore less likely to be cited and less likely to influence other researchers' agendas.

Forecast 8: Big data, social media, and mobile computing will figure significantly in DSS research

These three areas did not figure significantly in the sample used for the analysis in this paper. Hosack *et al.* (2012) have argued strongly for social media and mobile computing as potentially transformative tech-nologies for DSS. In a similar way Chen *et al.* (2012) have argued for big data as a major new area for DSS research. These conceptual articles may be followed by empirical research papers in the near future.

Forecast 9: The level of DSS publishing will stabilize

One of the most marked trends in the analysis is the overall decline in DSS publication, a decline that indicates that IS scholars are shifting their research agendas away from DSS. On the other hand, at 12.3% of IS research it could be that DSS has reached a more balanced proportion of the discipline. With increased publishing on BI, emergence of social media, big data, mobile computing, and increased interest in DSR, it could be that the long term declining trend for publishing will stabilize in the next analysis era.

Forecast 10: DSS publishing will increase in the Basket-of-Eight journals

The analysis of Expectation 11 showed a significant shift of DSS publi-cation away from the basket-of-eight journals – the pinnacle of IS schol-arship. This is a disappointing situation, as there is nothing intrinsic to DSS or BI research that precludes publication in the basket-of-eight. The direction that DSS research will likely take in the immediate future is toward even more BI research and toward more articles being published in higher impact journals (particularly the basket-of-eight). The 2011 move by the AIS from a basket-of-six to a basket-of-eight set of elite journals could help the DSR push of DSS as half of the basket-of-eight are European in origin, half are North American in origin, only one-third of the basket-of-six was European. As Indulska and Recker (2008) have found, non-North American researchers have tended to dominate DSR publishing. The greater acceptance of DSR in North America that has followed the publication of Hevner *et al.* (2004) should also assist DSS DSR authors publishing in the best journals.

Conclusion

In conclusion, using IT-based systems to support the decision-making activities of managers and other senior personnel has been a key aspect of IS research and practice since the IS discipline emerged in the 1960s and 1970s. There is no reason to suggest that this situation will change in the future, especially as BI is currently rated as the most important IT issue for CIOs worldwide and DSS research is currently over 10% of the IS discipline. Despite some disappointing outcomes with the assessment in this paper of expectations about the development of the field, there is considerable scope for improvement and greater impact in the future of the DSS field. We believe that that future will be based on high quality, highly relevant DSS DSR. Through the rise of design science the future of DSS research is taking a very interesting path.

Acknowledgements

We thank Sindy Madrid Torres for her work as a research assistant on the project, especially with support for the recoding of the original sample.

References

Alavi, M. and Carlson, P. (1992). A Review of MIS Research and Disciplinary Development, *Journal of Management Information Systems* 8(4): 45–62.

Anthony, R.N. (1965). *Planning and Control Systems: A framework for analysis*, Cambridge, MA: Harvard University Press.

Arnott, D. and Pervan, G. (2005). A Critical Analysis of Decision Support Systems Research, *Journal of Information Technology* 20(2): 67–87.

Arnott, D. and Pervan, G. (2008). Eight Key Issues for the Decision Support Systems Discipline, *Decision Support Systems* 44(3): 657–672.

Arnott, D. and Pervan, G. (2010). How Relevant is Fieldwork to DSS Design-Science Research? in A. Respicio, F. Adam, G. Phillips-Wren, C Teixeira and J. Telhada (eds.) *Bridging the Socio-Technical Gap in Decision Support Systems: Challenges for the next decade*, Amsterdam: IOS Press, pp. 199–210.

Arnott, D. and Pervan, G. (2012). Design Science in Decision Support Systems Research: An assessment using the Hevner, March, Park, and Ram guidelines, *Journal of the Association for Information Systems* 13(11): 923–949.

Arnott, D., Pervan, G. and Dodson, G. (2005). Who Pays for Decision Support Systems Research? Review, Directions and Issues, *Communications of the Association for Information Systems* 16: 356–380.

Baskerville, R. (2008). What Design Science is Not, *European Journal of Information Systems* 17(5): 441–443.

Benbasat, I. and Barki, H. (2007). Quo Vadis, TAM? *Journal of the Association for Information Systems* 8(4): 211–218.

Benbasat, I. and Nault, B. (1990). An Evaluation of Empirical Research in Managerial Support Systems, *Decision Support Systems* 6(3): 203–226.

Bragge, J., Korhonen, P., Wallenius, H. and Wallenius, J. (2012). Scholarly Communities of Research in Multiple Criteria Decision Making: A bibliometric research profiling study, *International Journal of Information Technology and Decision Making* 11(2): 401–426.

Briggs, R.O., de Vreede, G.-J. and Nunamaker, Jr. J.F. (2003). Collaboration engineering with ThinkLets to Pursue Sustained Success with Group Support Systems, *Journal of Management Information Systems* 19(4): 31–64.

Brown, B., Court, D. and Willmott, P. (2013). Mobilizing your C-suite for Big Data Analytics, *McKinsey Quarterly*, November.

Cavaye, A.L.M. (1996). Case Study Research: A multi-faceted research approach for IS, *Information Systems Journal* 6(3): 227–242.

Chen, H., Chiang, R. and Storey, V. (2012). Business Intelligence and Analytics: From big data to big impact, *MIS Quarterly* 36(4): 1165–1188.

Chen, W.S. and Hirschheim, R. (2004). A Paradigmatic and Methodological Examination of Information Systems Research from 1991 to 2001, *Information Systems Journal* 14(3): 197–235.

Chiang, R.H.L., Goes, P. and Stohr, E.A. (2012). Business Intelligence and Analytics Education, and Program Development: A unique opportunity for the information systems discipline, *ACM Transactions on Management Information Systems* 3(3): 1–13.

Clark, Jr T.D., Jones, M.C. and Armstrong, C.P. (2007). The Dynamic Structure of Management Support Systems: Theory development, research focus, and direction, *MIS Quarterly* 31(3): 579–615.

Davenport, T.H. (2006). Competing on Analytics, *Harvard Business Review* 84(1): 98–107.

Davenport, T.H. and Harris, J.G. (2007). *Competing on Analytics: The new science of winning*, Boston, MA: Harvard Business School Press.

Davis, F.D. (1989). Perceived Usefulness, Perceived Ease of Use, and User Acceptance of Information Technology, *MIS Quarterly* 13(3): 319–339.

Delen, D. and Crossland, M.D. (2008). Seeding the Survey and Analysis of Research Literature with Text Mining, *Expert Systems with Applications* 34(3): 1707–1720.

DeLone, W.H. and McLean, E.R. (2003). The DeLone and McLean Model of Information Systems Success: A ten-year update, *Journal of Management Information Systems* 19(4): 9–30.

Dennis, A.R., Carte, T.A. and Kelly, G.G. (2003). Breaking the Rules: Success and failure in groupware-supported business process reengineering, *Decision Support Systems* 36(1): 31–47.

Dennis, A.R., Tyran, C.K., Vogel, D.R. and Nunamaker, Jr J.F. (1997). Group Support Systems for Strategic Planning, *Journal of Management Information Systems* 14(1): 155–184.

Galliers, R.D. (1991). Choosing Appropriate Information Systems Research Approaches: A revised taxonomy, in H.-E. Nissen, H.K. Klein and R. Hirschheim (eds.) *Information Systems Research: Contemporary approaches and emergent traditions*, Amsterdam: North-Holland, pp. 327–345.

Galliers, R.D. and Meadows, M. (2003). A Discipline Divided: Globalization and parochialism in information systems research, *Communications of the Association for Information Systems* 11: 108–117.

Gartner (2007). *Creating Enterprise Leverage: The 2007 CIO agenda (Gartner EXP CIO Report)*, Stamford, CT: Gartner Inc.

Gartner (2008). Gartner says worldwide business intelligence platform market grew 13 percent in 2007, *Gartner Newsroom*, [WWW document] http://www.gartner.com/it/page.jsp?id=700410 (accessed 7 November 2012).

Gartner (2009). Gartner says worldwide business intelligence, analytics and performance management grew 22 percent in 2008, *Gartner Newsroom*, [WWW document] http://www.gartner.com/it/page.jsp?id=1017812 (accessed 7 November 2012).

Gartner (2010). Gartner says worldwide business intelligence, analytics and performance management software market grew 4 percent in 2009, *Gartner*

Newsroom, [WWW document] http://www.gartner.com/it/page.jsp?id=1357514 (accessed 7 November 2012).

Gartner (2011). Gartner says worldwide business intelligence, analytics and performance management software market surpassed the $10 billion mark in 2010, *Gartner Newsroom*, [WWW document] http://www.gartner.com/it/page.jsp?id=1642714 (accessed 7 November 2012).

Gartner (2012a). *Amplifying the Enterprise: The 2012 Gartner CIO agenda report*, Stamford, CT: Gartner Inc.

Gartner (2012b). Gartner says worldwide business intelligence, analytics and performance management software market surpassed the $12 billion mark in 2011, *Gartner Newsroom*, [WWW document] http://www.gartner.com/it/page.jsp?id=1971516 (accessed 7 November 2012).

Gartner (2013a). Gartner predicts business intelligence and analytics will remain top focus for CIOs through 2017, *Gartner Newsroom*, [WWW document] http://www.gartner.com/newsroom/id/2637615 (accessed 18 February 2014).

Gartner (2013b). Gartner says worldwide business intelligence software revenue to grow 7 percent in 2013, *Gartner Newsroom*, [WWW document] http://www.gartner.com/newsroom/id/2340216 (accessed 18 February 2014).

Germonprez, M., Hovorka, D. and Gal, U. (2011). Secondary Design: A case of behavioral design science research, *Journal of the Association for Information Systems* 12(10): 662–683.

Goodhue, D.L. and Thompson, R.L. (1995). Task-Technology Fit and Individual Performance, *MIS Quarterly* 19(2): 213–236.

Gorry, G.A. and Scott Morton, M.S. (1971). A Framework for Management Information Systems, *Sloan Management Review* 13(1): 1–22.

Gottschalk, P. (2000). Predictors of IT Support For Knowledge Management in the Professions: An empirical study of law firms in Norway, *Journal of Information Technology* 15(1): 69–78.

Gregor, S. and Jones, D. (2007). The Anatomy of a Design Theory, *Journal of the Association for Information Systems* 8(5): 312–335.

Guo, Z. and Sheffield, J. (2008). A Paradigmatic and Methodological Examination of Knowledge Management Research: 2000 to 2004, *Decision Support Systems* 44(3): 673–688.

Hevner, A.R. (2007). The Three Cycle View of Design Science Research, *Scandinavian Journal of Information Systems* 19(2): 87–92.

Hevner, A.R., March, S.T., Park, J. and Ram, S. (2004). Design Science in Information Systems Research, *MIS Quarterly* 28(1): 75–106.

Hirschheim, R. (2007). Introduction to the Special Issue on 'Quo Vadis TAM – Issues and reflections on technology acceptance research', *Journal of the Association for Information Systems* 8(4): 203–205.

Hosack, B., Hall, D., Paradice, D. and Courtney, J.F. (2012). A Look Toward the Future: Decision support is alive and well, *Journal of the Association for Information Systems* 13(5): 315–340.

Hwang, H.-G., Ku, C.-Y., Yen, D. and Cheng, C.C. (2004). Critical Factors Influencing the Adoption of Data Warehouse Technology: A study of the banking industry in Taiwan, *Decision Support Systems* 37(1): 1–21.

Indulska, M. and Recker, J.C. (2008). Design Science in IS Research: A literature analysis, in S. Gregor and S. Ho (eds.) *Proceedings of the 4th Biennial ANU Workshop on Information Systems Foundations*, Canberra, Australia: ANU.

Iivari, J. (2007). A Paradigmatic Analysis of Information Systems as a Design Science, *Scandinavian Journal of Information Systems* 19(2): 39–64.

Jourdan, Z., Rainer, R.K. and Marshall, T.E. (2008). Business Intelligence: An analysis of the literature, *Information Systems Management* 25(2): 121–131.

Kahneman, D. (2011). *Thinking Fast and Slow*, New York: Farrar, Straus and Giroux.

Kuechler, W. and Vaishnavi, V. (2012). A Framework for Theory Development in Design Science Research: Multiple perspectives, *Journal of the Association for Information Systems* 13(6): 395–423.

Lee, A.S. (2010). Retrospect and Prospect: Information systems research in the last and next 25 years, *Journal of Information Technology* 25(4): 336–348.

Leidner, D.E., Carlsson, S., Elam, J. and Corrales, M. (1999). Mexican and Swedish Managers' Perceptions of the Impact of EIS on Organizational Intelligence, Decision Making, and Structure, *Decision Sciences* 30(3): 633–658.

Lewin, K. (1943). Defining the 'Field at a Given Time', *Psychological Review* 50(3): 292–310.

Lipshitz, R. and Bar-Ilan, O. (1996). How Problems are Solved: Reconsidering the phase theorem, *Organizational Behavior and Human Decision Processes* 65(1): 48–60.

March, S. and Smith, G.F. (1995). Design and Natural Science Research on Information Technology, *Decision Support Systems* 15(4): 251–266.

Marginson, D., King, M. and McAulay, L. (2000). Executives' Use of Information Technology: Comparison of electronic mail and an accounting information system, *Journal of Information Technology* 15(2): 149–164.

McAfee, A. and Brynjolfsson, E. (2012). Big Data: The management revolution, *Harvard Business Review* (October): 61–68.

Nandhakumar, J. (1996). Design for Success?: Critical success factors in executive information systems development, *European Journal of Information Systems* 5(1): 62–72.

Neuman, W.L. (2000). *Social Research Methods: Qualitative and quantitative approaches*, 4th edn, Needham Heights, MA: Allyn and Bacon.

Osareh, F. (1996). Bibliometrics, Citation Analysis and Co-Citation Analysis: A review of literature I, *Libri* 46(3): 149–158.

Power, D.J. (2012). A brief history of decision support systems (version 4.1). [www document] http://dssresources.com/history/dsshistory.html, accessed 3 July 2012.

Ross, J.W., Beath, C.M. and Quaadgras, A. (2013). You May Not Need Big Data After All, *Harvard Business Review* (December): 90–98.

Rouibah, K. and Ould-ali, S. (2002). PUZZLE: A concept and prototype for linking business intelligence to business strategy, *Journal of Strategic Information Systems* 11(2): 133–152.

Salo, A. and Kakola, T.K. (2005). Groupware Support for Requirements Management in New Product Development, *Journal of Organizational Computing and Electronic Commerce* 15(4): 253–284.

Shander, B. (2013). Does your company actually need data visualization? HBR blog network [www document] http://blogs.hbr.org (accessed 14 November 2013).

Shanks, G., Jagielska, I. and Jayaganesh, M. (2009). A Framework for Understanding Customer Relationship Management Systems Benefits, *Communications of the Association for Information Systems* 25: 263–288.

Simon, H.A. (1960). *The New Science of Management Decision*, New York: Harper.

Taylor, H., Dillon, S. and Van Wingen, M. (2010). Focus and Diversity in Information Systems Research: Meeting the dual demands of a healthy applied discipline, *MIS Quarterly* 34(4): 647–667.

Tversky, A. and Kahneman, D. (1981). The Framing of Decisions and the Psychology of Choice, *Science* 211(4487): 453–458.

Vaishnavi, V.K. and Kuechler, Jnr W. (2008). *Design Science Research Methods and Patterns: Innovating information and communication technology*, Boca Raton, FL: Auerbach Publications.

Venable, J., Pries-Heje, J. and Baskerville, R. (2012). A Comprehensive Framework for Evaluation in Design Science Research, in K. Peffers, M. Rothenberger and B Kuechler (eds.) Proceedings of the 7th Conference on Design Science in Information Systems (DESRIST'12) Berlin: Springer-Verlag, pp. 423–438.

Watson, H.J., Fuller, C. and Ariyachandra, T. (2004). *Data Warehouse* Governance: Best practices at blue cross and blue shield of North Carolina, *Decision Support Systems* 38(3): 435–450.

Watson, H.J., Goodhue, D.L. and Wixom, B.H. (2002). The Benefits of Data Warehousing: Why some organizations realize exceptional payoffs, *Information & Management* 39(6): 491–502.

Walls, J.G., Widmeyer, G.R. and El Sawy, O.A. (1992). Building an Information Systems Design Theory for Vigilant EIS, *Information Systems Research* 3(1): 36–59.

Weber, R.P. (1990). *Basic Content Analysis*, 2nd edn, Newbury Park, CA: Sage Publications.

Webster, J. and Watson, R.T. (2002). Analyzing the Past to Prepare for the Future: Writing a literature review, *MIS Quarterly* 26(2): xiii–xxiii.

Winter, R. (2008). Design Science Research in Europe, *European Journal of Information Systems* 17(5): 470–475.

Yin, R.K. (1994). *Case Study Research: Design and methods*, 2nd edn, Newbury Park, CA: Sage Publications.

Zikmund, W.G., Babin, B.J., Carr, J.C. and Griffin, M. (2010). *Business Research Methods*, 8th edn, Mason, OH: South-Western, Cengage Learning.

Appendix A

Coding protocol

RESEARCH FACTORS

R1. Dominant Research Stage: 1 Theory Building   2 Theory Testing   3 Theory Refinement   4 Unclear

R2. Epistemology: 1 Positivist   2 Interpretivist   3 Critical   5 N/A

R3. Article Type

1 Conceptual study	2 Descriptive research	3 Experimental
4 Field study	5 Case study	6 Survey
7 Literature review	8 Secondary data	9 Action research
10 Design science		

R5. Did the paper acknowledge the support of a formal grant?   1 Yes   2 No
R6. If yes: 1 Major Competitive 2 University 3 Industry 4 MCandU 5 MCandI
   6 UandI 7 All 3

Research Rigor

R7. Theoretical Foundations   1 Strong   2 Adequate   3 Weak
R8. Research Methodologies   1 Strong   2 Adequate   3 Weak

Problem Relevance

R9. Importance of business problem 1 Strategic 2 Tactical   3 Operational
R10. Relevance to IS practitioners   1 High   2 Medium   3 Low
R11. Relevance to managerial users   1 High   2 Medium   3 Low

DSS FACTORS

D1. What type of DSS is the paper addressing?
   1 Personal DSS   2 Group support system   3 Business Intelligence
   5 Intelligent DSS   6 KM-based DSS   8 Negotiation-based DSS
   7 Many

D2. What organizational level is addressed?
   1 Individual   2 Small no. of ind.managers   3 Group
   4 Department   5 Division   6 Organization   7 Unclear

D3. What is the decision support focus of the paper?
   1 Development   2 Technology   3 Decision outcome/organization impact
   4 Decision process   5 Many   6 Unclear

JUDGMENT and DECISION MAKING FACTORS

J1. Who is the primary client?
           1 Executive   2 Manger   3 Professional   4 Other   5 Unclear

J2. What is the primary user's functional area?   Unclear

J3. Who is the primary user?
   1 Executive   2 Manager   3 Professional   4 Other   5 Unclear   6 Many

J4. Is judgment and decision-making reference research cited? Yes No
J5. If cited what reference theories? (author/date citations)

What general approach to decision-making is used?
J6.   1 Descriptive   2 Prescriptive   3 Unclear
J7.   1 Economic   2 Behavioral   3 Both   4 Unclear

J8. Is a phase model of decision-making used?   Yes   No
J9.   If yes, then which?

Design Science Section (completed if R3=10)

Guideline 1 – The Design Artifact
1.1 Type of Artifact   1 Construct   2 Model   3 Method   4 Instantiation

1.2 What was the artifact?
1.3 Was the artifact actually used in a field environment?   Yes   No

(Guideline 2 is covered by R7 through R11)

Guideline 3 – Design Evaluation
3.1 Type of evaluation
    Observational 1 Case study 2 Field study
    Analytical   3 Static   4 Architecture 5 Optimization 6 Dynamic
    Experimental 7 Controlled experiment   8 Simulation
    Testing   9 Functional (black box) 10 Structural (white box)
    Descriptive   11 Informed argument   12 Scenarios
              13 None

3.2 Choice of evaluation method   1 Highly Appropriate 2 Adequate
                                  3 Poor Choice
3.3 Quality of execution of evaluation   1 High   2 Medium 3 Low

Guideline 4 – Research Contributions
4.1 Contribution Area   1 The design artifact   2 Foundations
                            3 Evaluation Methodologies

Guideline 6 – Design as a Search Process
6.1 Decomposition into sub-problems   Yes No
6.2 Iteration from sub-problem solution to overall problem solution Yes No
6.3 Satisficing used to decide on solution convergence point   Yes No

Guideline 7 – Communication of Research
7.1 Effectiveness of tech-oriented presentation   1 High 2 Medium 3 Low
7.2 Effectiveness of mgt-oriented presentation   1 High 2 Medium 3 Low

8.1 Did the paper mention "design science"?   Yes No
8.2 If "No" what did it call it?   or "Nothing"

9. Design Science Reference Citations

Appendix B

Appendix B Converting and recoding the 1990–2003 sample

The original protocol appears as an appendix in Arnott and Pervan (2005). The original sample's article types were based on Alavi and Carlson (1992). The process of converting article types from the original to the new protocol appears in Table 20.B1.

Articles were assigned to the new article type 10 DSR using the process adopted by Arnott and Pervan (2012). In that paper, articles coded as the original article types 7, 8, 10, and 16 were inspected to see if they satisfied the Hevner *et al.* (2004) DSR definition. This sampling approach was identified as a potential limitation in Arnott and Pervan (2012). To overcome this in this study the remaining 957 articles were inspected for recoding as type 10 DSR; 8 were recoded as type 10.

Table 20.B1 Conversion of original article types

Original article type	New article type	Recoding required
1. DSS frameworks	1. Conceptual study	By SPSS script
2. Conceptual models	1. Conceptual study	By SPSS script
3. Conceptual overview	1. Conceptual study	By SPSS script
4. Theory	1. Conceptual study	By SPSS script
5. Opinion and example	1. Conceptual study	By SPSS script
6. Opinion and personal experience	1. Conceptual study	By SPSS script
7. Tools, techniques, methods, model applications	2. Descriptive research	By SPSS script
8. Conceptual frameworks and their application	1. Conceptual study	By SPSS script
9. Description of type or class of product, technology, systems, and so on	2. Descriptive research	By SPSS script
10. Description of specific application, system, and so on	2. Descriptive research	By SPSS script
11. Lab experiment	3. Experimental	By SPSS script
12. Field experiment	3. Experimental	By SPSS script
13. Field study	4. Field study	By SPSS script
14. Positivist case study	5. Case study	By SPSS script
15. Interpretivist case study	5. Case study	By SPSS script
16. Action research	9. Action research	By SPSS script
17. Survey	6. Survey	By SPSS script
18. Development of DSS instrument	None	5 articles were recoded to other types
19. Secondary data	7. Literature review 8. Secondary data	39 articles were recoded into new types 7 and 8
20. Simulation	3. Experimental	By SPSS script

For DSS Type conversion, the old '3. EIS (includes BI, OLAP, and enterprise wide reporting)' and '4. DW' were combined into a new type '3. BI'. This new category also includes BA.

For the rigor and relevance items (R7 through R11) in the new protocol, the coding of the 521 DSR articles was transferred to the new fields. For the remaining 957 articles a special recoding protocol was developed. This recoding took 98 person-hours.

21

Design Theory for Dynamic Complexity in Information Infrastructures: The Case of Building Internet

Ole Hanseth
Department of Informatics, University of Oslo, Norway

Kalle Lyytinen
Department of Information Systems, Weatherhead School of Management, Case Western Reserve University, USA

Introduction

Increased processing power and higher transmission and storage capacity have made it possible to build increasingly integrated and versatile Information Technology (IT) solutions whose complexity has grown dramatically (BCS/RAE, 2004; Hanseth and Ciborra, 2007; Kallinikos, 2007). Complexity can be defined here as the dramatic increase in the number and heterogeneity of included components, relations, and their dynamic and unexpected interactions in IT solutions. Unfortunately, software engineering principles and design methodologies have not scaled up creating a demand for new approaches to better cope with this increased complexity (BCS/RAE, 2004). The growth in complexity has brought to researchers' attention novel mechanisms to cope with it like architectures, modularity or standards (Parnas, 1972; Schmidt and Werle, 1998; Baldwin and Clark, 2000). Another, more recent stream of research has adopted a more holistic, socio-technical and evolutionary approach putting the growth in the combined social and technical complexity at the center of an empirical scrutiny (see, e.g., Edwards *et al.*, 2007). These scholars view these complex systems as new types

Reprinted from "Design theory for dynamic complexity in information infrastructures: the case of building internet," by O. Hanseth and K. Lyytinen in *Journal of Information Technology*, 25, 2010, pp. 1–19. With kind permission from the Association for Information Technology Trust. All rights reserved.

of IT artifacts and denote them with a generic label of *Information Infrastructures* (IIs). So far, empirical studies have garnered significant insights into the evolution of IIs of varying scale, functionality and scope including Internet (Abbate, 1999; Tuomi, 2002), electronic market places and EDI networks (Damsgaard and Lyytinen, 2001; Wigand *et al.*, 2006), wireless service infrastructures (Funk, 2002; Yoo *et al.*, 2005) or ERP systems (Ciborra *et al.*, 2000). At the same time effective design of IIs holds considerable benefits for individuals, businesses and society at large as testified, for example, by the success of Internet. Yet, failures to design IIs are more common incurring huge losses in foregone investments, opportunity costs, and political and social problems. A case in point is current the difficulty to implement a nation wide e-health system in the UK (Sauer and Willcocks, 2007; Greenhalgh *et al.*, 2008).

One challenge in the II research has been in the difficulty of translating vivid empirical descriptions of IIs evolution into effective *sociotechnical* design principles that promote their evolution, growth and complexity coordination. In this paper we make some steps in addressing this challenge by formulating a new design approach to address the *dynamic complexity of IIs*. From a technical view point designing an II involves discovery, implementation, integration, control and coordination of increasingly heterogeneous IT capabilities. Socially, it requires organizing and connecting heterogeneous actors with diverging interests in ways that allow for II growth and evolution. In the proposed approach we posit that the growing complexity of IIs originates from local, persistent and limitless shaping of II's IT capabilities due to the enrollment of diverse communities with new learning and technical opportunities. We argue that one common reason for the experienced II design culprits is that designers cannot design IIs effectively by following traditional top-down design. In particular, the dynamic complexity poses a chicken-egg problem for the would-be II designer that has been largely ignored in the traditional approaches. On one hand, IT capabilities embedded in II gain their value by being used by a large number of users demanding rapid growth in the user base (Shapiro and Varian, 1999). Therefore, II designers have to come up early on with solutions that persuade users to adopt while the user community is non-existent or small. This requires II designers to address head on the needs of the very first users before addressing completeness of their design, or scalability. This can be difficult, however, because II designers must also anticipate the completeness of their designs. This defines the *bootstrap problem of II design*. On the other hand, when the II starts to expand by benefitting from the network effects, it will switch to a period of rapid growth. During this growth, designers need to heed for unforeseen and diverse demands and produce designs that cope technically and socially with these increasingly varying needs. This demands infrastructural flexibility in that the II adapts technically and socially. This defines the *adaptability problem of II design* (Edwards *et al.*, 2007). Clearly, these two demands contradict and generate tensions at any point of time in II design (Edwards *et al.*, 2007).

In this paper we will address this tension by examining emergent properties of IIs as *adaptive complex systems*. As IIs exhibit high levels of dynamic complexity, they cannot be designed in the traditional way starting with a 'complete' set of requirements. II designers cannot design IIs just based on the 'local' knowledge, but they can increase the likelihood for successful emergence and growth of IIs by involving elements in their designs that take into account socio-technical *features* of IIs generated by their dynamic complexity. We call this engagement *design for IIs*.[1] While designing *for* IIs, the designers need to ask how they can generate designs that promote continued growth and adaptation of IIs. To this end we outline a socio-technical II design theory (Walls *et al.*, 1992, 2004) consisting of design principles and rules (Walls *et al.*, 1992, 2004; Baldwin and Clark, 2000; Markus *et al.*, 2002). This theory can guide design behaviors in ways that allow IIs grow and adapt *as self-organizing systems*. It is a socio-technical theory, because its design domain involves both technical and social elements and their relationships. It is a design theory, because it consists of 'how to' design principles and rules (Walls *et al.*, 1992, 2004; Markus *et al.*, 2002) backed by 'because of' justifications derived from a kernel theory – Complex Adaptive Systems (CAS) theory (Holland, 1995). We illustrate the validity of these design principles and rules by following the exegesis of Internet.

The remainder of this essay is organized as follows. In the next section we define IIs and characterize their dynamic complexity. The following section formulates the design theory based on CAS to address dynamic complexity by deriving design principles. In the subsequent section we detail the design rules to address dynamic complexity and illustrate their use during the design of the Internet. In the final section we offer concluding remarks and note some avenues for future research.

Information infrastructures

IT capabilities, applications and platforms

As noted, IIs form a different 'unit'[2] of design when compared with traditional classes of IT solutions. These design classes can be defined in their order of increasing complexity as: (1) IT capabilities, (2) applications, (3) platforms, and (4) IIs. The main differences between these classes lie in their overall complexity, how they relate to their design and use environments, and how they behave over time in relation to those environments. They pose different challenges during the design, are organized differently, controlled differently and obtain distinct emergent properties. The main features of each class are depicted in Table 21.1.

We denote an *IT capability* as the possibility and/or right of the user or a user community to perform a set of actions on a computational object or process. An example of such capability would be a text editor. An IT capability is defined and managed locally by single or a small group of designers. They typically control its evolution locally. IT capabilities are viewed here solely as engineered artifacts.

Applications consist of suites of IT capabilities. They are developed to meet a set of specified user needs within a select set of communities. They can grow amazingly complex in terms of effort and scope, but despite this, they still can be viewed as applications, if governed by a set of specifications[3] through which their design scope remains bounded. An application is *a priori* determined by choice of design context, user groups and functional goals. Consequently, the application can be developed, and preferably should be done so, by a hierarchy assuming centralized control.[4] Therefore, most proposed design theories address the design of applications by promoting ways of generating effectively a closure in the included IT capabilities as to meet user's needs (Boehm, 1976; Ross and Schoman, 1977; DeMarco, 1978; Olle *et al.*, 1983; Agresti, 1986; Walls *et al.*, 1992; Freeman, 2007).

Platforms differ from applications due to their heterogeneous and growing user base, that is their design context is not fixed due to the constant generification of included IT capabilities (Williams and Pollock, 2008). Platforms include, for example, office software platforms (MS Office, Officestar), operating system platforms (Windows, Unix), application frameworks like ERP or CRM packages (SAP, Oracle, SalesForge) or application development platforms (e.g. Service Oriented Architecture). Platform designs draw upon architectural principles that organize IT capabilities into frameworks allowing the software to address a family of generic functional specifications that meet the needs of multiple, heterogeneous and growing user communities (Evans *et al.*, 2006; Williams and Pollock, 2008). Platforms are composed by formulating a design framework (architecture) that allows organizing a growing set of IT capabilities into a relatively well-bounded and controlled

Table 21.1 Applications, platforms and information infrastructures

Property/Type of IT system	Application	Platform	Information infrastructure
Emergent properties			
Shared	Yes, locally and through specified functions	Yes, across involved user communities and across a set of IT capabilities	Yes, universally and across multiple IT capabilities (Star and Ruhleder, 1996; Porra, 1999)
Open	No, closed by user group and functionality	Partially, depends on design choices and managerial policies	Yes, universally allowing unlimited connections to user communities and new IT capabilities (Weill and Broadbent, 1998; Kayworth and Sambamurthy, 2000; Freeman, 2007)
Heterogeneous	Yes, partially and mainly by involved social groups	Partially, mainly by social groups but also by technical connections	Yes, increasingly heterogeneous both technically and socially (Kling and Scacchi, 1982; Hughes, 1987; Kling, 1992; Edwards et al., 2007)
Evolving	Yes, but limited by time horizon and user community. Linear growth	Yes, and limited by architectural choices and functional closure. Mostly linear growth	Yes, unlimited by time or user community (Star and Ruhleder, 1996; Freeman, 2007; Zimmerman, 2007) Both linear and nonlinear growth (Hughes, 1987)
	Evolution bounded and context free	Evolution path dependent	Evolution path dependent (Star and Ruhleder, 1996; Porra, 1999; Edwards et al., 2007)
Structural properties			
Organizing principle	Direct composition of IT capabilities within a homogeneous platform	Direct composition of a set of horizontal IT capabilities within a set of homogeneous platforms	Recursive composition of IT capabilities, platforms and infrastructures over time (Star and Ruhleder, 1996; Edwards et al., 2007)
Control	Centralized	Centralized	Distributed and dynamically negotiated (Weill and Broadbent, 1998) Can involve only basisorganizing principles (standards) and rely on installed base inertia (Star and Ruhleder, 1996; Edwards et al., 2007).

system. The platforms provide thus a (semi)-closed, and highly complex suite of IT capabilities, which, thanks to the original architecting, can be extended. A platform's initial design starts with a set of closed specifications determining included IT capabilities and anticipated requirements for their extensions and combinations. Their evolution is also governed and constrained by these initial specifications. Therefore, the design context remains controlled and the relationships between the user and design communities do not change significantly during the platform's lifetime. Platforms typically grow in complexity as designers take into account heterogeneous user needs while maintaining backward compatibility and horizontal compatibility across different combinations of capabilities. Therefore, many platforms, originally conceived as limited sets of IT capabilities, obtain later emergent features; they start growing in seemingly unlimited fashion and serve unexpected user communities generating exponentially growing technical and social complexity. Consider, for example, the growth of the MS Office platform, or Linux operating system due to the increasingly distributed and open character of their design and user communities (Scacchi, 2009).

Defining II

Based on an extensive literature review we will define next *II*. Hughes (1987) recognized early on heterogeneity, socio-technical nature and unbounded growth as essential features of infrastructures. Kling (1992) and Kling and Scacchi (1982) drew attention to additional material requirements of infrastructures like connectivity. Porra (1999) and Star and Ruhleder (1996) have recently emphasized the criticality of sharing and learning within and across communities, while Kayworth and Sambamurthy (2000), Weill and Broadbent (1998) and Chung *et al.* (2003) have pinpointed the possibility to shape infrastructures by local choice. Finally, recent definitions of IIs recognize tensions between the local and the global, their recursive nature, their unique coordination challenges due to the lack of global control (Star and Ruhleder, 1996; Edwards *et al.*, 2007; Freeman, 2007; Zimmerman, 2007) (Table 21.1).

Accordingly, we will define an *II* as a *shared*, *open* (and unbounded), *heterogeneous* and *evolving* socio-technical system (which we call *installed base*) consisting of a set of IT capabilities and their user, operations and design communities. This definition highlights both the structural properties and the emergent properties of IIs that *distinguish* IIs from their constituent elements (Table 21.1).

Structurally an II is recursively composed of other infrastructures, platforms, application and IT capabilities. Recursion forms the organizing principle implying that IIs return 'onto' themselves by being composed of similar elements (Lee *et al.*, 2006). Socially, IIs are also recursively organized in that they are both outcomes and conditions of design action and involve rule-following and rule-shaping activity (Giddens, 1984). The control of II is distributed and episodic and an outcome of negotiation and shared agreements. Distributed forms of control form often the only way to coordinate II evolution and thus IIs are never changed from above (Star and Ruhleder, 1996). Therefore, they cannot be truly 'designed' in a traditional sense as in traditional approaches a designer assumes control over the design space (Edwards *et al.*, 2007; Freeman, 2007). Episodic forms of control determine which groups of designers control which parts or elements of the II; what IT capabilities become integrated and how; who has access to the capabilities and so on (Tuomi, 2002; Edwards *et al.*, 2007).

IIs become *shared* across multiple communities in a myriad and unexpected ways. In principle, they exhibit unbounded *openness*: new components can be added and integrated with them in unexpected ways and contexts. In addition, there are no clear boundaries between those that can use an II and those that cannot; and there are no clear boundaries between those that can design the II and those that may not. As a result, II designs need to be approached *as if* no closure, in principle, is assumed in their form or content, capability, form or scope of access.

The openness of IIs implies that during their lifetime the social and technical diversity and *heterogeneity of IIs* will increase (Edwards *et al.*, 2007). IIs become increasingly heterogeneous as the number of different kinds of technological components are included, but first of all because IIs include (an increasing number of) components of very different nature: user communities, operators, standardization and governance bodies, design communities, etc.

Finally, because IIs are open, they *evolve*, seemingly, *ad infinitum*. IIs are never built in a green field, nor do they die – though they may wither to rise in new forms (Edwards *et al.*, 2007). IIs are often bootstrapped by experimenting and thereby enrolling new communities. For example, Berners-Lee designed the first web service to meet information sharing needs among high energy physicists (Berners-Lee and Fischetti, 1999). As this design unfolded, designers and users discovered additional IT capabilities, or transformed the existing ones to new uses, or to other design contexts thereby expanding the web (Ciborra *et al.*, 2000) generating its fractal evolution. Hence, the evolution of 'Infrastructure is fixed in modular increments, not all at once or globally' (Star and Ruhleder, 1996).

Overall, the evolution of infrastructures is both enabled and constrained by the *installed base*,[5] that is the existing configuration of II components (Hughes, 1987; Star and Ruhleder, 1996; Porra, 1999). Whatever is added needs to be integrated and made *compatible* with this base. This sets up demands for horizontal and/or backwards compatibility and imposes constraints on what can be designed at any time. Accordingly, II evolution is path dependent and shaped by neighboring infrastructures, existing IT capabilities, user and designer learning, cognitive inertia, etc. (Hughes, 1987; Kling, 1992; Star and Ruhleder, 1996; Hanseth and Monteiro, 1997; Porra, 1999).

Related research

Most II research has aimed at identifying the main features and characteristics of IIs – their 'nature' as they evolve and developers and users are struggling to make them work (Star and Ruhleder, 1996; Ciborra *et al.*, 2000; Kallinikos, 2004, 2006, 2007; Edwards *et al.*, 2007; Contini and Lanzara, 2009).

Standards are core elements of IIs; hence standards research constitutes a major part of II research (Star and Ruhleder, 1996; Edwards *et al.*, 2007). A large part of this research has focused on and disclosed a very dense and complex web of relations between technical and social (or non-technical) issues and elements of the standards (Hanseth and Monteiro, 1997; Bowker and Star, 1999; Lyytinen and Fomin, 2002) Another key part of the research has focused on the creation and role of network effects, that is self-reinforcing processes leading to lock-ins (Shapiro and Varian, 1999; Hanseth, 2000).

A minor part of II research has focused explicitly on strategies for developing standards and infrastructures. Cordella (2004), Hanseth and Lundberg (2001), Grisot (2008) and Pipek and Wulf (2009) describe how infrastructures emerge in use while users appropriate a variety of IT capabilities and bring them together in novel ways by making them components of IIs. Even without technically integrating the capabilities, they are *de facto* becoming integrated and interdependent in work practices (Pipek and Wulf, 2009).

A few researchers have addressed design strategies for infrastructure development. Hanseth *et al.* (1996) recognize the need to manage the tension between standardization and flexibility (see also Egyedi, 2002). Hanseth and Aanestad (2003) argue, using telemedicine as an illustration, that II design needs to be seen as a bootstrapping process, which utilizes network effects and spillovers within a growing user base by using simple solutions as a sort of 'stunts,' which offer 'detours' on the road toward infrastructures (Aanestad and Hanseth, 2002). Hanseth (2001) also demonstrates the importance of gateways in flexible II design by reviewing the history of the Internet design in Scandinavia. Lessig (2001) and David (2001) note the criticality of Internet's architectural features – especially its end-to-end architecture – in supporting adaptability at the 'edge of chaos' (Saltzer *et al.*, 1984). Benkler (2006) emphasizes the importance of the local 'programmability' of terminals, and its mutual dependency on the end-to-end architecture. Finally, Zittrain (2006) recently combined these features into an encompassing concept of a generative technology – a notion close to our idea of dynamic complexity. We add next to Zittrain's concept a more coherent design framework formulated as a design theory.

Design theory for addressing adaptive complexity in II evolution

IT design theories

Since the publication of Walls *et al.*'s (1992) article, the term 'IS design theory' has denoted a set of concepts, beliefs and 'laws' – either natural or social – which help designers map a class of design problems to effective solutions that meet design goals. Design theories are about 'how to' principles and rules of form and function, and justificatory 'because of' explanatory knowledge that can be mobilized during the design (Gregor, 2006). They encapsulate three elements: (1) a set of design goals shared by a family of design problems; (2) a set of system features that meet those goals; and (3) a set of design principles and rules to guide the design so that a set of system features is selected to meet chosen design goals. Design principles state broad guidelines how the design can be carried out and where the designer can focus his or her attention during function and form shaping. They can be further detailed into design rules that formulate in concrete terms how to generate and select desired system features as to achieve stated system goals.

The crux of a design theory is its 'kernel theory' (Walls *et al.*, 1992). It postulates falsifiable predictions for a class of design solutions (i.e. product theories), or design processes (i.e. process theories) in relation to system goals. They vary significantly in their generality, structure and predictive power (Gregor, 2006). Each design theory applies *in a certain design context* in which *a specific set of system goals* have been selected, and *apply to a specific class of systems* and *associated design processes*. The design context is determined by the nature of the system, its size, the design phase, the type of technology, the type of users or designers

(Walls *et al.*, 1992, 2004). Next we will focus on II design theory for dynamic complexity. Our main interest is in generating technical and social components of the IIs in ways that address the tensions between the bootstrap and the adaptability problems.

CAS as a design theory about dynamic complexity in II

We draw upon CAS theory as our kernel theory (Holland, 1995; Benbya and McKelvey, 2006). CAS addresses nonlinear phenomena within physics and biology, but also in social domains including financial markets (Arthur, 1994). CAS investigates systems that *adapt* and *evolve* while they *self-organize*. The systems are made up of autonomous agents with the ability to adapt according to a set of rules in response to other agent's behaviors and changes in the environment (Holland, 1995). Key characteristics of CAS are: (1) nonlinearity, that is small changes in the input or the initial state can lead to order of magnitude differences in the output or the final state; (2) order emerges from complex interactions; (3) irreversibility of system states, that is, that change is path dependent; and (4) unpredictability of system outcomes (Dooley, 1996).

We chose CAS as our kernel theory as it recognizes factors that generate the dynamics associated with the II bootstrap and adaptability problems and helps describe II evolution as an example of path-dependent and nonlinear change. CAS brings theoretical rigor to generate insights to these two design challenges. In addition, these challenges are not highlighted in two pet theories among II scholars: the social shaping of technology (Edwards *et al.*, 2007), and Bateson's ecological theory (Star and Ruhleder, 1996). Next, the design principles are deductively derived from CAS. In the section 'Design rules to manage dynamic complexity – the Internet case' we instantiate these principles with a set of 19 design rules whose application is illustrated with concrete episodes from the design history of Internet.[6]

CAS categories and design principles for dynamic complexity in IIs

CAS helps characterize how the IIs can be initiated and how they grow and evolve while they self-organize. This is addressed by following the two principles: (1) create an attractor that feeds system growth to address the bootstrap problem; and: (2) assure that the emerging system will remain adaptable at 'the edge of chaos' while it grows to address the adaptability problem. We surmise that these principles can promote design for IIs in ways that lead them to self-organize and to grow. We will next describe key categories of CAS theory and the logic that underpins these design principles and their 'because of reasons' as suggested in Table 21.2.

Addressing growth in II

A central claim in CAS is that order *emerges* – it is not designed by an omnipotent 'designer.' Typical example is the dynamic arrangements among cells and the establishment of standards without anyone ever intending to design them as such (e.g. QWERTY, TCP/IP). According

Table 21.2 CAS-based design theory for dynamic complexity in Information Infrastructures (IIs)

Design goals	Bootstrap the IT capability into an installed base so that it gains momentum Manage and allow for maximum II adaptability.
A set of system features	II as an unbounded, evolving, shared, heterogeneous and open recursively organized system of IT capabilities whose evolution is enabled and constrained by its installed base and the nature and content of its components and connections.
Kernel theory of flexible IIs	CAS informs how to address *bootstrap problem* in II designs by suggesting that • Designer can gain momentum in the growth of II through attracting a critical mass of users • Designer can enable nonlinear growth by new combinations of the installed base CAS informs how to address the *adaptability problem* in II designs by suggesting that • Designer needs to recognize path dependencies within the installed base • Designer needs to create lock-in through network externalities that exclude alternative pathways • Designer need to achieve modularity to accommodate the growing need for openness and heterogeneity in future
Design principles	For the II bootstrap problem: 1. Design initially for usefulness 2. Draw upon existing installed base 3. Expand installed base by persuasive tactics For the II adaptability problem: 4. Make each IT capability simple 5. Modularize the II by building separately its principal functions and sub-infrastructures using layering and gateways

to CAS, such orders emerge around *attractors*, that is a limited range of states within which the system growth can stabilize, and which allow the system to bootstrap (Holland, 1995). The simplest attractor is a single point in the system state space. Attractors can also come in other forms, which are called 'strange attractors' (Carpa, 1996) that stabilizes the system into a specific region (David, 1986). De-facto standards (e.g. MS Windows, QWERTY, Internet standards) are examples of such attractors. Attractors stabilize a system through *feed-back* loops (also called network effects or 'increasing returns'). In case of standards this happens because the value of a standard defining an IT capability depends on the number of users having adopted it. So when a user adopts a standard its value increases. This again makes it more likely that another user will adopt it, which further increases its value and so on (Arthur, 1994; Shapiro and Varian, 1999). A large installed base will also attract complementary IT capabilities thereby making the original capability increasingly attractive (Shapiro and Varian, 1999). A larger installed base increases also the credibility associated with the capability and reduces user risks of foregone investments. Together these features make an IT capability more attractive leading to increased adoption that further increases its installed base (Grindley, 1995). Some describe this process of getting 'the bandwagon moving.'

Positive network effects lead to self-reinforcing *path-dependent* processes. Overall, the involved path dependency suggests that past events – for example a serendipitous adoption, or correctly timed designs – can change history by generating irreversible effects – called butterfly effects. Such path-dependent growth will eventually lead to a *lock-in* when the adoption rates cross a certain threshold (David, 1986). Such a lock-in happens when a system's growth reaches what Hughes (1987) calls a momentum. This creates a new lasting order with irreversible effects (Arthur, 1994).

We distinguish two facets of path dependence in IIs: *cumulative adoption* and *technology traps*. Cumulative adoption takes place when an II designer builds up an installed base ahead of its alternatives and accordingly becomes cumulatively attractive, and starts growing in an unbounded manner. Bootstrapping for cumulative growth is possible when the timing is right and users can still be persuaded (Edwards *et al.*, 2007; Zimmerman, 2007). Design choices for II thereby become path dependent, as conditions for cumulative adoption are created during the early stages of growth (Grindley, 1995; Shapiro and Varian, 1999). *Technology traps* suggest that many times blind early design decisions later constrain the further expansion of II and become reverse salients (Hughes, 1987). Design for expansion is typically carried out technically and socially in ways that is compatible with the early installed base and its predicted trajectory. Thereby, early design decisions can later block the expansion as new communities join, or technological trajectories change, and create adverse constraints for growth. Such adverse constraints we call *technology traps*. Examples of technology traps are, for example, the need to support archaic computer architectures (e.g. IBM 9010, IBM360 or Intel 8086), operating systems (DOS, Windows95) (Mashey, 2009) or the effects of architecture choices for the growth of the French Minitel system (Cats-Baril and Jelassi, 1994).

Addressing adaptability in II

All systems evolve, but all systems do not adapt equally well. Systems that reach early on lock-in, or exhibit a large number of 'reverse salients' (Hughes, 1987) will fail to do so. According to CAS, highly adaptable systems are characterized by the increased variety achieved through high modularity: 'variation is the raw material for adaptation' (Axelrod and Cohen, 1999: 32). In other words, the larger the variety of agents and pathways for evolution, the more design alternatives can be tried out, and the more agents learn (Holland, 1995; Benbya and McKelvey, 2006). Accordingly, the larger the variety of IT capabilities and the larger the number of II designers the larger is II adaptability. At the same time a certain level of order is necessary in order to maintain stability in the design context. This stability is achieved through modularity. According to CAS, modularity creates a balance between variety and order by localizing the change and permitting fast and deep change in parts of the system. Engineered as well as living systems must thus be modular to remain robust and at the same time to generate variety (Simon, 1969; Baldwin and Clark, 2000; Wagner, 2007). Adaptation becomes optimal at 'the edge of chaos' (Stacey, 1996), where variety generation and modularity are balanced.[7] To wit, traditional application design theory assumes the complete order of stasis as designers are assumed to control all the system states during the design. In contrast, random order excludes the possibility for any design as no order can be detected in the context. Hence, in designing *for* II, designers need to establish a self-organization, where the II will remain 'at the edge of chaos.'

Design rules to manage dynamic complexity – the Internet case

The design principles listed in Table 21.2 guide II designers to conceive their designs in ways where they can generate 'natural' order at the edge of chaos. To carry out effectively designs that conform to these principles we need to break down the five design principles into *design rules* that govern designer's behaviors influencing specific II components or their environments. In this section we will articulate such design rules. The next section introduces some modularity concepts necessary in stating design rules. The following section offers a summary of their content and reports how we used Internet design to illustrate them. The section after that introduces each design rule with illustrative examples from Internet design.

Modularization of II

In formulating the design rules we need to distinguish properties of IIs that help modularize them. We therefore next define analytical types of (sub) IIs that allow – when composed *together* – the generation of *modular* IIs. We apply recursively de-composition, that is identify separate subsets of IT capabilities within any II, which also are IIs, but which share either a set of common functions and/ or internal or external connections without having strong dependencies with the remaining IIs (Baldwin and Clark, 2000; Kozlowski and Klein, 2000).

We will first split IIs into *vertical application* IIs and of *horizontal support* IIs. The former will deliver functional capabilities, which are deployable directly by one or more user communities. An example of application capability would be e-mail. The latter – support infrastructures – offer generic services often defined in terms of protocols or interfaces necessary in delivering most, if not all application services. They are primarily deployed by designer communities while building application capabilities[8] and include capabilities for data access and identification (addressing), transportation (moving) and presentation (formatting). They also constitute part of the installed base, which II designers need to take into account when bootstrapping an application infrastructure or making changes in support IIs.

We can further recursively decompose both application and support IIs. Thus, any II can be split into its application and support infrastructures until a set of 'atomic' IT capabilities are reached (per recursive definition of II). In addition, any support infrastructure can be split into *transport* and *service* IIs. This split is justified as transport infrastructure is necessary to make any service infrastructure work. The transport IIs offer data or message transportation services like the UDP/TCP/IP protocol stack (Leiner *et al.*, 1997). On the other hand service infrastructures support, for example, direct addressing, service identification, service property discovery, access and invocation, or security capabilities.

They become useful when IIs start to grow in complexity and scale, and designers need more powerful capabilities to configure application capabilities. A classic example of a service II is the Domain Name Service (DNS) in the Internet, which maps mnemonic identifiers like amazon. com to varying length bit representations, that is IP addresses. Both application and service IIs can be finally linked together horizontally through *gateways*. These offer flexible pathways for II expansion and navigation (Hanseth, 2001; Edwards *et al.*, 2007). An example of a gateway would be an IT capability, which supports multiple e-mail services running on different e-mail protocols.

Design rules for dynamic complexity in II's

Derivation and summary of the design rules

In total, we propose 19 design rules for II dynamic complexity shown in Table 21.3. Overall, the design rules characterize: (1) appropriate ways to organize and relate II components technically and socially (modular design, organize recursively) that address dynamic complexity similar to Baldwin and Clark's (2000) design rules; (2) desirable properties of specifications of II components (e.g. simplicity), (3) desirable sequences for design (e.g. design one-to-many IT capabilities before many-to-many IT capabilities) (4) desirable ways to relate II specifications and associated components to one another (modularity, recursive application).

Illustrating II design rules- the case of Internet

Below we illustrate the deployment of each design rule by referring to episodes of Internet design. We chose Internet design as an illustration as its design history offers rich insights into the situated application of the proposed design theory 'in use.' We chose to illustrate the theory with the design of Internet, because it qualifies as a grand 'success' story about II design *par excellence* (Table 21.4). By any criterion its design involved cultivating an II, which is shared, open and heterogeneous, organized recursively and operates without centralized control. We also content that the success of Internet testifies to the plausibility of the design rules discussed below.

We gleaned the design rules by content analyzing design episodes, that is, moments when new IT capabilities were added, modified, expanded or purged in the Internet regime. A review of these design situations permit us generalize identified design rules by triangulating data with the emerging theory (Eisenhardt, 1989). Documents like the Internet Engineering Task Force (IETF) rules for Requests For Change, but also the *credo* coined in Clark's famous speech in 1992: 'We reject:

Table 21.3 Design rules for dynamic complexity in the design for IIs

Design problem	Element of CAS	Design principles	Design rules	
Bootstrap problem Design goal: Generate attractors that bootstrap the installed base	Create an IT capability that can become an attractor for the system growth.	1. Design initially for direct usefulness.	DR1.	Target IT capability to a small group
			DR2.	Make IT capability directly useful without the installed base
			DR3.	Make the IT capability simple to use and implement
			DR4.	Design for one-to-many IT capabilities in contrast to all-to-all capabilities.
	Avoid dependency on other II components that deflect away from the existing attractors	2. Build upon existing installed bases	DR5.	Design first IT capabilities in ways that do not require designing and implementing new support infrastructures
	Use installed base as to build additional attractors by increasing positive network externalities		DR6.	Deploy existing transport infrastructures
			DR7.	Build gateways to existing service and application infrastructures
			DR8.	Use bandwagons associated with other IIs
	Exclude alternative attractors by persuasive tactics Offer additional positive network externalities by expanding learning in the user community	3. Expand installed base by persuasive tactics to gain momentum	DR9.	'Users before functionality' – grow the user base always before adding new functionality
			DR10.	Enhance any IT capability within the II only when needed

(continued)

Table 21.3 Continued

Design problem	Element of CAS	Design principles	Design rules
			DR11. Build and align incentives so that users have real motivation to use the IT capabilities within the II in new ways
			DR12. Develop support communities and flexible governance strategies for feedback and learning
	Build capabilities that enable growth based on experience and learning	4. Make the IT capability as simple as possible	DR13. Make the II as simple as possible in terms of its technical and social complexity by reducing connections and governance cost
	Use abstraction and gateways to separate II components by making them loosely coupled		DR14. Promote partly overlapping IT capabilities instead of all-inclusive ones.
Adaptability problem Design Goal: Make the system maximally adaptive and variety generating as to avoid technology traps	Design IT capabilities and their combinations in ways that allow II growth	5. Modularize the II	DR15. Divide II recursively always into transportation, support and application infrastructures while designing the II
	Use evolutionary strategies in the evolution of II that allow independent incremental change in separate components		DR16. Use gateways between standard versions
	Draw upon II designs that enable maximal variations at different components of the II		DR17. Use gateways between layers
			DR18. Build gateways between infrastructures
			DR19. Develop transition strategies in parallel with gateways

Table 21.4 Internet as an II

	Internet as an II
Structural properties	
Organizing principles	Internet is composed of multiple layers of distinct IT capabilities that carry out similar functions at different layers (e.g. transport and application layer). It consists of or draws upon multiple platforms, IT capabilities and social groups that design, implement and maintain its functionality.
Control	The control of Internet design is distributed among a large set of designers, user communities and forms of governance. The control of different capabilities is separated and distributed and the control forms are loosely coupled through architectural principles. Control forms vary among different communities (IETF, W3C or OASIS) as well as governance structures (Nickerson and Zur Muehlen, 2006; Russell, 2006).
Emergent properties	
Shared	Shared by an increasingly growing number of heterogeneous user communities, designers, regulators and other social actors.
Open	Any new IT capability, designer or user group can be added as long as it conforms to the architectural principles of Internet and thus abstracts data transfer into a transfer of data streams to a specified set of IP addresses.
Heterogeneous	Internet has grown immensely in heterogeneity both socially and technically since its inception and during its exponential growth.
Evolving	Evolving set communication and distributed computing capabilities C'For any set of users at any time Internet is seen as a distinct set of capabilities (telnet, ftp, smtp, http, etc.) that are available. Internet evolves because this set has grown significantly during its evolution integrating new users and design communities.

kings, presidents, and voting. We believe in rough consensus and running code' (Russell, 2006), and personal biographies all exemplify the behaviors of the Internet designers and consequently their design theories-in-use. To this end we probed Internet standardization archives and primary secondary sources on Internet history – especially Abbate's (1999) excellent narrative. We also examined personal accounts of Internet design (Leiner *et al.*, 1997; Berners-Lee and Fischetti, 1999), and recent scholarly analyses of the Internet growth (Tuomi, 2002). Finally, we interviewed Robert Kahn, one of the original developers and sponsors of Internet protocols. As a result we were able to solicit 19 design rules as summarized in Table 21.5 founded on CAS that had 'worked' during Internet design.

For sure, not all designers at all times and consciously followed these rules. But many of them acted consistent with these rules. For example, they underpin many common 'interaction rules' in the Internet design ecology. Many key figures have also openly embraced proposed design principles. For instance, throughout Internet's history, from Kahn's and Cerf's initial design to the creation of BitTorrent, the Internet designers have favored bottom-up, experimental design and utilization of network effects. At the core was also the recognition of high uncertainty related to desired IT capabilities. Bob Kahn noted vividly this:

> They (DoD) didn't have a problem. And that's why it's so hard for those kinds of things to actually get in motion. If you're saying, 'Can I imagine a problem that somebody might have at some unspecified point in the future?' Absolutely, that was what was driving it. And, so you had to really trust what was in your mind's eye. And that was the basis on which the internal justifications were eventually made. But it took a while to get there. (Kahn, 2006)

Therefore, he argued that the only way to design was experimental:

> But when you're dealing with something as really state of the art, it's hard to know what to build upfront because a lot of what makes it what it is a function of, you know, iterating with users and feedback and allowing the system to evolve and grow and to see how it would work. This is not something that most people, who are, you know, in management chain, are very uncomfortable with because they don't exactly know what to expect. So it's very hard for those people, you know, to deal with those kinds of creative processes. (Kahn, 2006)

Design rules for dynamic complexity in the design for II

We next discuss in detail how the 19 design rules in Table 21.3 were inferred from the CAS theory offering a 'because of' justification for the design principles. To wit, each design rules offers a falsifiable statement of design outcomes to validate the theory. By analyzing whether the designer followed the rule and related design outcomes, we can

Table 21.5 Design principles and rules for Internet

Challenge: Bootstrap problem

Design principle	Design rules		Followed	Evidence from Internet design history
1. Design initially for usefulness	DR1.	Target IT capability to a small group	✓	Designed originally as a support capability for Defense Advanced Research Projects Agency (DARPA) researchers to share expensive and centralized computing resources
	DR2.	Make IT capability directly useful without an installed base	✓	Designed as application for log in and file downloads The developed IT capability was well suited for experimenting with distributed Unix and LAN technologies, in which originally reaching large installed base was not an issue
	DR3.	Make the IT capability simple to use and implement	✓	Obtain experience based on the use of simple prototypes and capabilities. This has been an important design principle in the Internet community, in particular during the early adoption (Leiner *et al.*, 1997; Abbate, 1999)
	DR4.	Design for one-to-many IT capabilities in contrast to all-to-all	✓	Remote login as a first capability
2. Build upon existing installed bases	DR5.	Design IT capability that does not depend on new support infrastructure	✓	A principal design rule in implementing the TCP/IP protocol stack was to make it run on top of multiple underlying physical access layers: telephone, radio, satellite, LAN technologies, etc. (Abbate, 1999)
	DR6.	Deploy existing transport infrastructures	✓	All early capabilities were introduced without any new related transport infrastructures

(continued)

Table 21.5 Continued

Challenge: Bootstrap problem

Design principle	Design rules	Followed	Evidence from Internet design history
	DR7. Build gateways to existing service and application infrastructures	✓	Gateways were developed for example to other e-mail protocols and other IT capabilities. Recently gateways (e.g. CGI) to databases and application capabilities have been important in making Web-services useful
	DR8. Use bandwagons associated with other IIs	✓	During the 1980s, Internet increased its acceptance with the diffusion of workstation/Unix/LAN technologies
3. Expand installed base by persuasive tactics to gain momentum	DR9. Users before functionality	✓	Many Internet capabilities have been added when their needs have been recognized. The development of TCP/IP and its new versions IPv6, the introduction of DNS, enhancement of the web by XML and CCS are examples of this
	DR10. Enhance the IT capability within the II only when needed	✓	Internet offered low cost and innovative ways for many scientific and engineering communities to communicate and share information and build associated services. Important allies were research funding agencies and research communities
	DR11. Build and align incentives as needed	✓	Development and use intertwined to build communities. A large community (critical mass) was, e.g., built originally to learn from distributed computing. The same applies to Web, Instant messaging or multicasting
	DR12. Develop support communities	✓	Developers and users are both innovators for IT capabilities and organized support communities to do so

4. Make the design of IT capability as simple as possible	DR13. Make the II in terms of its technical and social complexity as simple as possible	✓	This rule was explicitly stated early on (RFC, 1994) and has been important throughout the design history of the Internet
	DR14. Promote partly overlapping IT capabilities instead of all-inclusive ones	✓	This rule is enabled by the principle that standards are open and any one can design at the edge new functionality resulting in multiple overlapping capabilities
5. Modularize the II	DR15. Divide infrastructure recursively into transportation, support and application infrastructures	✓	The architectural principle of 'end-to-end' architecture that promotes independence and modularization (David, 2001) Internet is composed of a large number of separate capabilities, sub-infrastructures that are established and operated by independent actors including ISPs, etc.
	DR16. Use gateways between specification versions	✓	The paradigmatic example of this is the use of tunneling in the transition from version 4 to 6 of the IP protocol
	DR17. Use gateways between layers	✓	This is key architectural principle of Internet that separates applications, transport, addressing and physical connections. All these layers are connected through open gateways
	DR18. Build gateways between infrastructures	✓	This was originally used to connect different networks (BITNET, Decnet) with Internet e-mail protocols. The same took place with AOL and Progidy
	DR19. Develop transition strategies in parallel with gateways	✓	Consideration of transition strategies is carefully introduced into the new versions of the protocol specifications

determine whether the rule following did not lead to the predicted outcome thus falsifying (partly) the proposed design theory.

Design rules for the bootstrap problem

Often new IT capabilities are not adopted despite their novelty, because users wait others to adopt first: early adopters face high risks and costs, but few benefits. In light of CAS, an II designer must generate attractors to propel users to adopt the IT capability so that its growth will reach a momentum (Hanseth and Aanestad, 2003). We observe three design principles decomposed into 12 design rules that help generate and manage such attractors (see Tables 21.3 and 21.5).

Design rules for principle #1: Design initially for direct usefulness: Early users cannot be attracted to IT capabilities reasons like the size of their installed base. Therefore, we need design rules that foster relationships between the proposed IT capability and user adoption. Therefore, a small user population needs to be identified and targeted (Design Rule 1 (DR1[9])). The proposed IT capability has to offer the group *immediate* and *direct* benefits (DR2). Because first adopters accrue high adoption costs and confront high risks, the IT capability to-be-adopted must be simple, cheap and easy to learn (DR3). Here cheap is defined in relation to both design and learning costs. Simple means that the design covers only the essential functionality expected and the capability is designed so that it is easy to integrate the IT capability with the installed base. Significant user investments cannot be expected because a small user base does not contribute either to the demand or the supply side economies of scale.

IT capabilities have varying impacts on the scale of increasing returns and the amount of positive feedback. They vary significantly between capabilities where every user interacts symmetrically with every user (like e-mail) and capabilities where one user interacts uni-directionally with the rest. Capabilities can also have multiple possible implementation sequences. In general, IT capabilities supporting asymmetrical interactions (one-to-many) and thus less dependent on network effects should be implemented first as the growth can be promoted locally (DR4). These capabilities have lower adoption barriers as they do not need to reach a critical mass to generate fast adoption.

The Internet's success has been widely attributed to its successful bottom-up bootstrapping (Leiner *et al.*, 1997; Abbate, 1999; Tuomi, 2002; Kahn, 2006). Though early on Internet designers built bold scenarios of how the future of telecommunications would unfold (Tuomi, 2002), the early uses of packet switching were targeted to small groups of researchers, who were interested in accessing powerful and expensive computers (DR1). The aim was to provide a limited range of directly useful IT capabilities: remote login and file transfer (DR1). Among these capabilities, remote login was a perfect choice, because each user could adopt it independently from others and users had the skills and motivation to do so (DR3, DR4). While the number of users grew, they could start share data through file transfer. Later on, new capabilities have been introduced in the same way (DR2). E-mail, for instance, was originally developed to support communications between persons responsible for maintaining the network when only four computers were connected to it (Abbate, 1999) (DR1 and DR2). The design of transportation services (TCP) followed also an evolutionary approach as multiple versions of increasingly complete protocols for TCP and IP were implemented in the early 1980s (DR3).

Design rules for principle #2: build on installed bases: The second principle promotes connections with the existing installed base during design time. The II designer should thus design toward existing support infrastructures that the targeted user groups use (DR5). If an IT capability is designed so that it requires a new support infrastructure, this will erect heightened adoption barriers as, per our definition, the support infrastructure will be *sui generis* an II, which then needs to be bootstrapped with high learning barriers (Attewell, 1992). As noted, transport infrastructures form the base for implementing II while the need for service infrastructures depends on the size and sophistication of application capabilities, or the size of installed base. While the installed base remains small, the II does not need advanced service infrastructures. The II designer should therefore design toward the simplest possible service infrastructure (DR6). Next, capabilities associated with separate service and application infrastructures should be connected, when possible, through gateways increasing connections between isolated user communities and benefitting adopters with larger positive network effects (DR7). As the designers link the new IT capabilities to the existing IIs, they need to take into account the speed and direction of the adoption of IT capabilities in neighboring infrastructures, and capitalize on their bandwagon effects (DR8).

The Internet's early success resulted from exploiting established infrastructures as transport infrastructures (DR5) when TCP/IP was first implemented using modems over the telephone lines (Abbate, 1999). In addition, each adopted capability has served to develop more advanced capabilities (Abbate, 1999) (DR6). Currently, the Internet provides, for example, capabilities for electronic commerce including transaction support (e.g. EbXML[10]), identification support (e.g. digital certificates) or security (e.g. SET) built as separate capabilities on top of TCP/IP and http (Faraj *et al.*, 2004; Nickerson and Zur Muehlen, 2006). Another example is the initial growth of Internet's service infrastructures (DR6). In the beginning there was none and their need was discovered later when new service capabilities started to grow. Yet, the scale of Internet was still relatively small so that it was easy to design DNS capabilities and link it to a (now) stable transportation infrastructure. Later on DNS became critical as it increased flexibility of use through the management of dynamic IP addresses (DHCP). The Internet designers have also increased the installed base through gateways (DR7). The expansion of the Web functionality is a case in point. The Web was originally thought to be useful for static information provisioning so that HTML tagged files could be downloaded using the http protocol (Tuomi, 2002). A significant added value for Web was created by building gateways that leveraged upon data residing in organizational databases. This added dynamic or 'deep' web features: a call to data base could be now embedded in HTML as defined by Common Gateway Interface (CGI) specifications,[11] and later expanded with Java standards (RMI[12]).

Design rules for principle #3: expand installed base with persuasive enrollment tactics: After establishing the first attractor (usefulness), the II designers have to sustain growth. Therefore, when a simple version of the IT capability is available, the II designer needs to seek as many users as possible (DR9). This principle is captured well in a slogan: 'users before functionality' emphasizing the criticality of generating positive network effects: the IT capability derives its value from the size of its user base – *not* from its superior functionality. New functionality should be added only when it is truly needed, and the original capability obtains new adoption levels so that the proposed capability will have enough users willing to cover the extra cost of design and learning (DR10). Many times useful new functionality emerges when users start deploy the IT capability in unexpected ways through learning by doing and trying, or re-organizing the connections between the user communities and the IT capability (DR11). A growing installed base urges II designers to find means to align heterogeneous user interests and persuade them to continue to participate in the II. One approach is to use the installed base as a source of useful learning by creating user communities that offer feedback. This helps introduce new capabilities based on feedback and unexpected actor interactions (DR12) (Tuomi, 2002; Zimmerman, 2007).

Many capabilities during Internet design were established at times when the capabilities could be expected to work satisfactorily and serve a useful purpose (DR9). As a result increasingly sophisticated application capabilities emerged including Gopher (Minnesota), WAIS (Cambridge, Mass) and irc (University of Oulu) (Rheingold, 1993). As a result Internet has grown over the years enormously in terms of new services and protocols. Typically these capabilities emerged as local community responses to an identified local need (DR10), and only a tiny fraction of the Internet's current protocol stack was part of the initial specifications (DR10). Main reason for this was that most innovations took place at the 'edge' as design capability and application functionality were early on moved to the network boundary. New capabilities could be conceived and tried out whenever a user with a 'problem' and enough transportation capability could leverage upon the new functionality (Tuomi, 2002). Internet was also widely adopted by computer science and associated engineering communities as their research-computing infrastructure (DR11 and DR12). The open packet switching standards turned out to be perfectly suited for the research vision shared by this movement (Kahn, 2006).

Design rules for the adaptation problem

When the bandwagon starts rolling, the II designers need to guarantee that the II will grow *adaptively* and re-organize constantly with new connections between II components. *Ad hoc* designs, which were originally created for early users will now threaten to create technology traps. If designers continue to generate highly interdependent and local IT capabilities, the whole system will become inflexible and reach a stasis. In contrast, if IT capabilities are organized modularly through loosely coupled 'layers,' which can change independently, this will generate higher component variation for successful adaptation. The following two design principles decomposed into seven rules offer guidance to promote modularity.

Design rules for principle #4: make the organization of IT capabilities simple: The first principle asks for the use of simple architectural principles during the initial design of the IT capabilities (DR13). It is easier to change something that is simple than something that is complex. What makes a collection of IT capabilities simple or complex is a function of its technical complexity as defined by the number of its technical elements, their connections and rate of change (Edwards *et al.*, 2007). Therefore following information hiding, simple interface protocols and functional abstraction can help make the design simple. But, just as important is it to recognize the socio-technical complexity of the design space: the number and type of connections between technical and the social elements. In the lingo of Actor Network Theory (Latour, 1999) the actor network constituted by the II, that is its data elements, use practices, specifications and their discovery and enforcement practices, the relationships to other infrastructures, the multiplicity of developers, the role of organizations, the variety of users, the regulatory bodies etc. – and a myriad of links between all affect what can be changed and how (Star and Ruhleder, 1996; Latour, 1999). Simpler actor networks can be created by making them initially as small as possible, and keeping them loosely connected, and avoiding confrontations with competing networks. This is achieved by pursuing separate specifications for distinct domains and separating the concerns of different social and technical actors through functional abstraction (Tilson, 2008). Limiting the functional scope of application infrastructures to a minimum keeps the related infrastructures separate. Decomposing service IIs into a set of layers and separating their governance achieves the same goal. These principles decrease the technical complexity of specifications but, more importantly, reduce their social complexity. Finally, designs should promote partly overlapping IT capabilities instead of all-inclusive ones. This increases variance and stimulates innovation at different pockets by making it operate at 'the edge of chaos' (DR14).

The principles of early Internet design promoted simplicity (DR13). Its protocols were lean and simple, and therefore had less ambiguity and errors. As a result the implementations were simpler, and easier to test and change. Origins of this approach date back to early designs, which confronted early on the challenge of how to promote change, but at the same time to avoid technology traps. This was expressed early in the Internet's specification approach:

> From its conception, the Internet has been, and is expected to remain, an evolving system whose participants regularly factor new requirements and technology into its design and implementation. (RFC, 1994: 6)

This vision was opposite to traditional design strategies in the telecommunication industry followed in the design of the ISO/OSI protocol stack where designers assumed one homogeneous, complete and controllable network, which had to be completely specified (Abbate, 1999; Russell, 2006). This difference was later at the center of the controversy between the Internet community and the ISO/OSI committee (Schmidt and Werle, 1998; Russell, 2006). The OSI standardizers argued that Internet lacked critical functions; in contrast, the Internet community advocated technical simplicity and pragmatic value. As Kahn observed:

> So the only way that you could ever get anything to be a standard was: you had to have built it first; it had to be deployed; and basically, people would speak by adoption. So the things that became standard ... were the things that were starting to become in widespread use and they would eventually become standards when they were already used. This is the equivalent of ratification after the fact, the standard is simply a means of ratifying what has become in widespread use ... a very different approach than specifying upfront and hoping people will build it. (Kahn, 2006)

Many scholars have attributed the demise of the OSI to its disregard to this pragmatic approach (Rose, 1992; Stefferud, 1994). Finally, Internet always promoted designs that were partly overlapping increasing variety. For example it has generated several transportation protocols, e-mail protocols, information distribution protocols and so on (DR14).

Design rules for principle #5: modularize the II: As noted, II designers need to organize modularly capabilities into loosely coupled sub-infrastructures (Parnas, 1972; Baldwin and Clark, 2000). Therefore, IIs should be decomposed recursively into separate application, transport and service sub-infrastructures (DR15). Each II interface must hide mechanisms that implement these capabilities as to maintain loose couplings between the connected IIs. IIs need to be also decomposed vertically into independent neighboring application infrastructures, and II designers need to build gateways to connect them. Consequently, gateways must connect regions of II that run different versions of the same IT capabilities (DR16), or between different IT capability layers, for example, transport or service (DR17), or between several dedicated application infrastructures (DR18) (Edwards *et al.*, 2007). Finally, transitions between incompatible IT capabilities need to be supported by navigation strategies that allow local changes in different versions of the IT capability that run on the current installed base (DR19).

One reason for the speed of innovation in Internet was its initial modular design (DR15) (Tuomi, 2002). The Internet's simple end-to-end architecture, which puts the 'intelligence' into the end nodes, has proven to be a critical for its adaptive growth (DR15, DR16, DR17) (Abbate, 1999; David, 2001). The design stimulated continued local application or service infrastructure innovation laid on top of separate transportation infrastructure of TCP/IP or UDP (DR15) (Rheingold, 1993; Tuomi, 2002). Each of these capabilities was designed independently and its design decisions were insulated from potential changes in the underlying transport infrastructures. They were also governed separately.[13] The erection of the W3C and governance of the web service community forms a case in point (Berners-Lee and Fischetti, 1999). Gateways continue to play a critical role in the evolution of Internet and extensive use of gateways has prevented designers to act like 'blind giants,' and made early decisions easier to reverse (Hanseth, 2001). Multiple gateways prevail, for instance, between the Internet's e-mail service and proprietary e-mail protocols (DR17). Another important family of gateways has been built between the Internet's access services and organization's applications and databases through web servers (DR18). Over the years Internet protocols have been revised and extended (DR16, DR19). One example is the revision of the transportation protocol from IPv4 to IPv6. The need to add new capabilities while attempting to overcome installed base inertia has been a major design challenge (RFC, 1994; Monteiro, 1998; Hovav and Schuff, 2005). Between 1974 and 1978, four versions of the IP protocol were developed in fast experimental cycles until IPv4 was released (Kahn, 1994). For the next 15 years IPv4 remained stable. In the early 1990s Internet's address space was expected to run out due to the Internet's exponential growth. Moreover, the addressing scheme in IPv4 did not support multicasting and mobility. This triggered a new round of designs to deliver a new IP version called IP version 6.[14] The final version, however, fulfilled only few of the original requirements – the most important one being the extension of the reverse salient – address space – to awesome 2^{128} addresses.[15] The most important criterion in accepting the final specifications was in determining mechanisms that would introduce the new version in a stepwise manner (DR19), though initially this was not at all in the requirements (RFC, 1995; Steinberg, 1995; Hovav and Schuff, 2005).[16]

Concluding remarks

Today's IT systems involve complexity that extends beyond what can be addressed by traditional design approaches. Accordingly, we need to theorize in fresh ways how to design complex IT systems. To this end we have formulated a design theory based on CAS theory that tackles IIs' dynamic complexity. The theory was derived by scrutinizing design histories of large infrastructures, a review of CAS theory principles and illustrated by the analysis of Internet exegesis. The theory formulation follows an approach similar to Lindgren *et al.* (2004), and Markus *et al.* (2002). By formulating this design theory we make a contribution to IS Design and Software Engineering research on how to develop large and complex ICT solutions viewed as IIs. We do so by drawing extensively on prior research on II evolution and soliciting the empirical insights into a coherent design theory.

The proposed theory defines its unit of analysis, its essential properties and related kernel theory – CAS – as to derive five design principles, and19 design rules. It recognizes and draws upon earlier research on IIs (Kling, 1992; Star and Ruhleder, 1996) by observing pivotal relationships between technical and social elements, and their dynamic interactions. In contrast to earlier II research (Freeman, 2007; Zimmerman, 2007), the proposed theory adopts the viewpoint òf designers: how to 'cultivate' an installed base and promote its dynamic growth by proposing *design rules* for II bootstrapping and adaptive growth. Opposed to other design theories and methodologies, which are all 'design from scratch' approaches, our design theory puts the installed base at the center: II development is about how to create a self-reinforcing installed base by drawing upon existing ones, and how to avoid being trapped by the force of the installed base.

All theories are incomplete (Weick, 1989) and so is our proposed theory. Hence, the key question is not to ask whether the proposed theory is incomplete (as it will be), but rather: what are the implications of its limits? We will address this in two ways: (1) how to address incompleteness in the scope of our theoretical formulation, (2) and how to improve consequently its external validity. We drew upon CAS as to account for the feedback-based growth within complex socio-technical systems. The principles that underlie CAS are widely accepted as illustrating how complex systems evolve. Our contribution has been to revise CAS into a form that can be utilized in design thinking in the context of IIs. In doing so we drew upon extant II and other literatures to propose a set of falsifiable design rules (Baldwin and Clark, 2000). Unfortunately, our theory refinement still does not offer detailed recommendations of how to decide in specific contingencies about II designs. We are confident that in some situations the theory has limited applicability. For example, the design of IIs that necessitate single 'point' coordination through significant early investments like the design of wireless systems may follow a more centralized specification driven approach. Likewise, the theory does not help estimate the economic consequences of choosing between infrastructural alternatives (Fichman, 2004). The theory is also limited in its scope. It says nothing about the politics during II design and how a designer can cope with the power. To do so, we would have to integrate the theory with theories that recognize power like actor network theory (Latour, 1999), or institutional theory (Scott, 2001). Finally, it cannot account for all critical features of II design like security.

The proposed theory was kept simple as we preferred generality over accuracy (Weick, 1989). Consequently, it is composed of a small set of concepts offering design abstractions across a set of IT capabilities and their growth patterns. These concepts hide differences by applying abstraction and composition (Kozlowski and Klein, 2000). Therefore, the simplicity of the theory comes at a cost: its design rules offer no silver bullet for prediction, and it has at most a pragmatic legitimacy (Robey, 2003). Its knowledge claims can thus improve II designs instead of suggesting the 'optimal' design. One use of the theory is in explaining *post hoc* to what extent design processes with observed outcomes followed or did not follow principles derived from the CAS theory. Another use is to guide designs through enacting rules that promote increased II adaptability by stating what 'thou shall not,' that is: (1) what *not* to *assume* (e.g. complete control), or (2) what *not* to *do* (keep it simple stupid!).

We illustrated the theory through an investigation of successful design episodes around Internet. In this application we viewed the theory through its use *utility* – that is did the enactment of the design rules lead to stated design goals? These principles and rules have also been applied during the successful design of national IIs for health care in developing countries including South Africa, Ethiopia, Tanzania, Nigeria, India and Vietnam (Braa *et al.*, 2007). These programs emphasized bottom-up and iterative development and relied on simple solutions using flexible standards. Our question for all these experiences is: did the theory make a difference and how would we evaluate it under counter-factual conditions? Had it made a difference in the Internet case had the designers *not* pursued the design rules?[17] Naturally, we can never be completely certain about this as we cannot carry out a new 'experiment' under the same conditions. We content, however, that, had designers followed alternative design rules, the Internet would not have been bootstrapped as effectively. Many other II designs with similar goals followed different rules, but failed despite huge institutional backing and deep resource commitments (like ISO/OSI). We have neither examined situation where *not following* the design rules led to successful outcomes, or where following the design rules led to failures.[18]

In future, we will expand the proposed theory by analyzing other II design episodes. Some candidates are: the digital transformation in industries including architecture and construction (Boland *et al.*, 2006), health care (Hanseth and Monteiro, 1997) or financial services (Markus *et al.*, 2006). Another route is the creation of service infrastructures for web services (Nickerson and zur Muehlen, 2006), and broadband mobile services (Yoo *et al.*, 2005; Tilson and Lyytinen, 2006).

Our theory has significant practical implications. If its design rules were widely adopted, the II designers would have to prefer continuous, local innovation, to increase chaos, and to apply simple designs and crude abstractions. This change is not likely, as design communities are often locked into institutional patterns that reinforce design styles assuming vertical control and complete specifications. The best example of this is perhaps Tim Berners-Lee's legacy. He successfully introduced the Web by following design rules that address dynamic complexity, but later changed into a specification-driven approach during the development of the semantic web. This process, however, has been more onerous. The lesson learned is: designers learn often superstitiously (March, 1991). We hope, however, that this essay highlights why changing such superstitions makes a lot of sense in today's design.

Acknowledgements

The paper has benefited from the helpful comments of Nick Berente, Sean Hansen, David Tilson, Youngjin Yoo, Vallabh Sambamurthy, Bo Dahlbom, Eric Monteiro, Margunn Aanestad, Petter Nielsen, Lynne Markus and Omar El-Sawy, the senior editor Jannis Kallinikos and two reviewers for their constructive comments. We also thank faculties at the Helsinki School of Economics, Umea University, University of Oslo and Case Western Reserve University for constructive feedback. Finally, we want to thank all the people who participated in the study for sharing their experience and thoughts.

Notes

1. In one sense infrastructures just evolve, if we rely on biological metaphor and the idea of 'blind' mutation. But, because infrastructures are artifacts created by intentional action, we prefer to use the term 'design for' instead of 'design of' as designer's behaviors matter how, and to what extent the infrastructure can evolve. We have elsewhere proposed the term 'cultivate' for this type of design activity.
2. We use the term information infrastructure as a symmetrical concept to that of an application, that is an information system. Both are

socio-technical artifacts, and thus 'designed.' Both consist of elements of hardware, software and data that are integrated into a suite of IT capabilities and designed, used and regulated by social groups. But their behavior, design parameters and characteristics that define good 'designs' are different as argued below.

3. Consider, for example, the design of the aviation application embedded in a modern airplane like Airbus A380. Its specifications are derived from a host of avionics engineers, regulators, airline managers and so on, and developed and controlled by a group of developers who are organized into a hierarchy. The Airbus 380 software is therefore also useful immediately. It will, however, gradually obtain new features that differentiate it from its initial specification. For example, the navigation systems of A380 may have to communicate with new air-traffic control systems and be integrated with new media and communication software, or airplane maintenance and control systems. During its use Airbus380 avionics software will thus evolve in unanticipated ways based on user learning, regulatory demands and innovation around IT that support new avionic tasks. Accordingly, the Airbus A380 applications, when used over time, become connected with multiple external IT capabilities that expand in unanticipated ways. As a result the applications become a critical component in a complex web of interlocked set of IT capabilities in the modern avionics acquiring infrastructural features.

4. This is an idealized view as many times user needs are unknowable, poorly expressed or change too fast to truly address them.

5. II specifications are often called standards and regarded essential in building IIs (Star and Ruhleder, 1996; Edwards *et al.*, 2007). Standards are shared and agreed upon specifications among a set of communities. We deem them not analytically necessary for II design. They are, however, one of the most effective means to coordinate the distributed design of IIs, and they play a prominent role to expand, coordinate and deploy IT capabilities in a distributed manner.

6. The theory has also been influenced by our experiences in designing other types of IIs. These include mobile infrastructures, ERP implementations in large organizations and electronic patient record infrastructures.

7. For example, Google follows 70-20-10 rule to maintain a balance between order and chaos. They use 70% of their resources and attention to improve the current order of the core businesses, 20% to work on related and incremental adaptations and 10% in other, non-related new 'permutations.'

8. This principle is similar to decomposition of dedicated IT applications if we distinguish between user defined computational functions (e.g. computing a salary), and generic horizontal system functions (e.g. retrieving or storing an employee record).

9. This refers to the rule label in Table 21.3.

10. See http://www.ebxml.org/.

11. See http://hoohoo.ncsa.uiuc.edu/cgi/overview.html.

12. See http://java.sun.com/products/jdk/rmi/.

13. This was not always done without friction (see, e.g., Nickerson and Zur Muehlen, 2006).

14. For a definition see http://playground.sun.com/pub/ipng/html/ipng-main.html.

15. It has been later observed that other 'workarounds' like DHCP and NAT actually could circumvent the address space problem and the value of IPv6 in this solving the original requirement has been questionable.
16. See, e.g., http://www.ipv6.org/.
17. Falsification principle followed is contingent in the sense that we can never be sure that the strategy would work successfully in all future cases, that is, the theory remains always falsifiable.
18. We have no such evidence after analyzing multiple cases.

References

Aanestad, M. and Hanseth, O. (2002). Growing Networks: Detours, stunts and spillovers, Proceedings of COOP 2002, Fifth International Conference on the Design of Cooperative Systems, St. Raphael, France, 4–6th June 2002.

Abbate, J. (1999). *Inventing the Internet*, Cambridge, MA: MIT Press.

Agresti, W.W. (1986). The Conventional Software Life-Cycle Model: Its evolution and assumptions, in W.W. Agresti (ed.) *New Paradigms for Software Development*, Washington, D.C: IEEE Computer Society.

Arthur, W.B. (1994). *Increasing Returns and Path Dependence in the Economy*, Ann Arbor: The University of Michigan Press.

Attewell, P. (1992). Technology Diffusion and Organizational Learning: The case of business computing, *Organization Science* 3(1): 1–19.

Axelrod, R.M. and Cohen, M.D. (1999). *Harnessing Complexity: Organizational implications of a scientific frontier*, New York: Free Press.

Baldwin, C. and Clark, K. (2000). *Design Rules*, Cambridge, MA: MIT Press.

BCS/RAE (2004). The challenges of complex IT projects, British Computer Society and Royal Academy Engineering Project [www document], http://www.bcs.org/upload/pdf/complexity.pdf (accessed August 2009).

Benbya, H. and McKelvey, B. (2006). Toward Complexity Theory of Information System Development, *Information, Technology and People* 19(1): 12–34.

Benkler, Y. (2006). *The Wealth of Networks. How Social Production Transforms Markets and Freedom*, New Haven, CT; London: Yale University Press.

Berners-Lee, T. and Fischetti, M. (1999). *Weaving the Web-The Original Design and Ultimate Destiny of World Wide Web by Its Inventor*, San Francisco: Harper-Collins.

Boehm, B.W. (1976). Software Engineering, *IEEE Transactions on Computers* C-25(12): 1226–1241.

Boland, R., Lyytinen, K. and Yoo, Y. (2006). Path Creation with Digital 3D Representations: Networks of innovation in architecture, engineering and construction, *Organization Science* 18: 631–647.

Bowker, G. and Star, S.L. (1999). *Sorting Things Out. Classification and Its Consequences*, Cambridge, MA: MIT Press.

Braa, J., Hanseth, O., Mohammed, W., Heywood, A. and Shaw, V. (2007). Developing Health Information Systems in Developing Countries – The flexible standards strategy, *MIS Quarterly* 31(2): 381–402.

Carpa, F. (1996). *The Web of Life. A new scientific understanding of living systems*, London: Harper Collins.

Cats-Baril, W. and Jelassi, T. (1994). The French Videotext System Minitel: A successful implementation of national information technology infrastructure, *MIS Quarterly* 18(1): 1–20.

Chung, S., Kelly Rainer, R. and Lewis, B. (2003). The Impact of Information Technology Infrastructure Flexibility on Strategic Alignment and Applications Implementation, *Communications of the Association of Information Systems* 11: 191–206.

Ciborra, C., Braa, K., Cordella, A., Dahlbom, B., Failla, A., Hanseth, O., Hepsø, V., Ljungberg, J., Monteiro, E. and Simon, K. (2000). *From Control to Drift. The Dynamics of Corporate Information Infrastructures*, Oxford: Oxford University Press.

Contini, F. and Lanzara, G.F. (eds.) (2009). *ICT and Innovation in the Public Sector*, Basingstoke, England: Palgrave Macmillan.

Cordella, A. (2004). Standardization in Action, Paper presented at European Conference on Information Systems, Turku, Finland, 14–16th June 2004.

Damsgaard, J. and Lyytinen, K. (2001). Building Electronic Trading Infrastructure: A private or public responsibility, *Journal of Organizational Computing and Electronic Commerce* 11(2): 131–151.

David, P.A. (1986). Understanding the Economics of QWERTY, in W.N. Parker (ed.) *Economic History and the Modern Economist*, Oxford and New York: Basil Blackwell.

David, P.A. (2001). The Beginnings and Prospective Ending of 'End-to-End' – An evolutionary perspective on internet architecture, Working Papers 01012, Stanford University, Department of Economics [www document] http://ideas. repec.org/p/wop/stanec/01012.html.

DeMarco, T. (1978). *Structured Analysis and System Specification*, New York, NY: Yourdon Press.

Dooley, K. (1996). Complex Adaptive Systems: A nominal definition, [www document] http://www.public.asu.edu/~kdooley/papers/casdef.PDF (accessed 13th August 2009).

Edwards, P., Jackson, S., Bowker, G. and Knobel, C. (2007). Report of a Workshop on 'History and Theory of Infrastructures: Lessons for new scientific infrastructures', University of Michigan, School of Information [www document] http://www.si.umich.edu/InfrastructureWorkshop/documents/ UnderstandingInfrastructure2007.pdf (accessed 15th March 2007).

Egyedi, T.M. (2002). Standards Enhance System Flexibility? Mapping Compatibility Strategies Onto Flexibility Objectives [www document] http://www.tudelft.nl/ live/binaries/0b330c26-def4-45e3-a367-43b61bf0ae45/doc/mapping.pdf.

Eisenhardt, K. (1989). Building Theories from Case Study Research, *Academy Management Review* 14(4): 532–550.

Evans, D.S., Hagiu, A. and Schmalensee, R. (2006). *Invisible Engines: How software platforms drive innovation and transform industries*, Cambridge, MA: MIT Press.

Faraj, S., Kwon, D. and Watts, S. (2004). Contested Artifact: Technology sensemaking, actor networks, and the shaping of the web browser, *Information Technology & People* 17(2): 186–209.

Fichman, R. (2004). Real Options and IT Platform Adoption: Implications for theory and practice, *Information Systems Research* 15(2): 132–154.

Freeman, P.A. (2007). Is 'Designing' Cyberinfrastructure – or, even, defining it – possible? *First Monday* 12(6), June [www document] http://firstmonday.org/ issues/issue12_6/freeman/index.html (accessed 8th August 2007).

Funk, J.L. (2002). *Global Competition Between and within Standards: The case of mobile phones*, New York: Palgrave.

Giddens, A. (1984). *The Constitution of Society*, London: Polity Press.

Greenhalgh, T., Stramer, K., Bratan, T., Byrne, E., Mohammad, Y. and Russell, J. (2008). Introduction of Shared Electronic Records: Multi-site case study using diffusion of innovation theory, *British Medical Journal*, (Clinical research edn) 337: a1786.

Gregor, S. (2006). The Nature of Theory in Information Systems, *MIS Quarterly* 30(3): 611–642.

Grindley, P. (1995). *Standards, Strategy, and Politics. Cases and Stories*, New York: Oxford University Press.

Grisot, M. (2008). Foregrounding Differences: A performative approach to the coordination of distributed work and information infrastructures in use, Ph. D. Thesis, Departments of Informatics, University of Oslo, Norway.

Hanseth, O. (2000). The Economics of Standards, in Ciborra *et al.* (eds.), *From Control to Drift. The Dynamics of Corporate Information Infrastructures*, Oxford: Oxford University Press, pp. 56–70.

Hanseth, O. (2001). Gateways – Just as important as standards. How the internet won the 'religious war' about standards in Scandinavia, *Knowledge, Technology and Policy* 14(3): 71–89.

Hanseth, O. and Aanestad, M. (2003). Bootstrapping Networks, Infrastructures and Communities, *Methods of Information in Medicine* 42: 384–391.

Hanseth, O. and Ciborra, C. (2007). *Risk, Complexity and ICT*, Cheltenham, UK; Northampton, MA, USA: Edward Elgar Publishing.

Hanseth, O. and Lundberg, N. (2001). Information Infrastructure in Use – An empirical study at a radiology department, *Computer Supported Cooperative Work (CSCW). The Journal of Collaborative Computing* 10(3–4): 347–372.

Hanseth, O. and Monteiro, E. (1997). Inscribing Behaviour in Information Infrastructure Standards, *Accounting Management and Information Technology* 7(4): 183–211.

Hanseth, O., Monteiro, E. and Hatling, M. (1996). Developing Information Infrastructure: The tension between standardization and flexibility, *Science, Technology and Human Values* 21(4): 407–426.

Holland, J. (1995). *Hidden Order*, Massachusetts: Addison-Wesley Reading.

Hovav, A. and Schuff, D. (2005). 'The Changing Dynamic of the Internet' Early and Late Adopters of Ipv6 Standard, *Communications of the Association of the Information Systems* 15: 242–262.

Hughes, T.P. (1987). The Evolution of Large Technical Systems, in W.E. Bijker, T.P. Hughes and T. Pinch (eds.) *The Social Construction of Technological Systems*, Cambridge, MA: MIT Press.

Kahn, R.E. (1994). The Role of Government in the Evolution of the Internet, *Communications of the ACM* 37(8): 415–419, Special issue on Internet technology.

Kahn, R.E. (2006). Personal interview on phone 6th December 2006.

Kallinikos, J. (2004). Deconstructing Information Packages: Organizational and behavioural implications of large scale information systems, *Information Technology and People* 17(1): 8–30.

Kallinikos, J. (2006). Information out of Information: On the self-referential dynamics of information growth, *Information Technology and People* 19(1): 98–115.

Kallinikos, J. (2007). Technology, Contingency and Risk: The vagaries of large-scale information systems, in O. Hanseth and C. Ciborra (eds.) *Risk, Complexity and ICT*. Cheltenham, UK; Northampton, MA: Edward Elgar Publishing, pp. 46–74.

Kayworth, T. and Sambamurthy, S. (2000). Facilitating Localized Exploitation of Enterprise Wide Integration in the use of IT Infrastructures: The role of PC/LAN infrastructure standards, *The Data Base for Advances in Information Systems* 31(4): 54–80.

Kling, R. (1992). Behind the Terminal: The critical role of computing infrastructure in effective information systems' development and use, in W. Cotterman and J. Senn (eds.) *Challenges and Strategies for Research in Systems Development*, London: John Wiley, pp. 153–201.

Kling, R. and Scacchi, W. (1982). The Web of Computing: Computing technology as social organization, *Advances in Computers*, New York: Academic Press, Vol. 21, pp. 3–87.

Kozlowski, S. and Klein, K. (2000). A Multi-Level Approach to Theory and Research in Organizations: Contextual, temporal and emergent processes, in K. Klein and S. Kozlowski (eds.) *Multilevel Theory, Research and Methods in Organizations*, San Francisco: Jossey-Bass, pp. 3–90.

Latour, B. (1999). *Pandora's Hope. Essays on the Reality of Science Studies*, Cambridge, MA; London, UK: Harvard University Press.

Lee, C., Dourish, P. and Mark, G. (2006). The Human Infrastructure of the Cyberinfrastructure, Proceedings of CSCW'06 (Banf, Canada); New York: ACM Press, 483–492.

Leiner, B.M., Cerf, V.C., Clark, D.D., Kahn, R.E., Kleinrock, L., Lynch, D.C., Postel, J., Roberts, L.G. and Wolff, S.S. (1997). The Past and Future History of the Internet, *Communications of the ACM* 40(2): 102–108.

Lessig, L. (2001). *The Future of Ideas: The fate of the commons in a connected world*, New York: Random House.

Lindgren, R., Hendfridsson, O. and Schultze, U. (2004). Design Principles for Competence Management Systems: A synthesis of an action research study, *MIS Quarterly* 28(3): 435–472.

Lyytinen, K. and Fomin, W. (2002). Achieving High Momentum in the Evolution of Wireless Infrastructures: The battle over the 1G solutions, *Telecommunications Policy* 26: 149–190.

March, J.G. (1991). Exploration and Exploitation in Organizational Learning, *Organization Science* 2(1): 71–78.

Markus, M.L., Majchrzak, A. and Gasser, L. (2002). A Design Theory for Systems That Support Emergent Knowledge Processes, *MIS Quarterly* 26(3): 179–212.

Markus, M.L., Steinfield, C.W., Wigand, R.T. and Minton, G. (2006). Industry-Wide Information Systems Standardization as Collective Action: The case of the US residential mortgage industry, *MIS Quarterly* 30(Special Issue on Standardization August 2006): 439–465.

Mashey, J. (2009). The Long Road to 64 Bits, *Communications of the ACM* 52(1): 45–53.

Monteiro, E. (1998). Scaling Information Infrastructure: The case of the next generation IP in internet, *The Information Society* 14(3): 229–245.

Nickerson, J.V. and zur Muehlen, M. (2006). The Ecology of Standards Processes: Insights from internet standard making, *MIS Quarterly* 30(5): 467–488.

Olle, T.W., Soland, H.G. and Tully., C.J. (eds.) (1983). *Information Systems Design Methodologies: A feature analysis*, Amsterdam, The Netherlands: Elsevier Science Publishers B.V.

Parnas, D.L. (1972). A Technique for Software Module Specification with Examples, *Communications of the ACM* 15(5): 330–336.

Pipek, V. and Wulf, V. (2009). Infrastructuring: Toward an integrated perspective on the design and use of information technology, *Journal of the Association for Information Systems* 10(5): 447–473.

Porra, J. (1999). Colonial Systems, *Information Systems Research* 10(1): 38–69.

RFC (1994). The Internet Standards Process – Revision 2, RFC 1602, IAB and IESG [www document] http://www.ietf.org/rfc/rfc1602.txt.

RFC (1995). The Recommendation for the IP Next Generation Protocol, RFC 1752, IAB and IESG [www document] http://www.ietf.org/rfc/rfc1752.txt.

Rheingold, H. (1993). *The Virtual Community: Homesteading the electronic frontier*, Reading, MA: Addison Wesley.

Robey, D. (2003). Identity, Legitimacy, and the Dominant Research Paradigm: An alternative prescription for the IS discipline, *Journal of the Association of for Information Systems* 4(6): 352–359.

Rose, M.T. (1992). The Future of OSI: A modest prediction, in G. Neufeld and B. Plattner (eds.) Proceedings of the Usenix Conference 1992; Berkley USA: USENIX Association.

Ross, D.T. and Schoman Jr., K.E. (1977). Structured Analysis for Requirements Definition, *IEEE Transactions of Software Engineering* SE 3(1): 69–84.

Russell, A. (2006). Rough Consensus and Running Code' and the Internet – OSI standards war, *IEEE Annals of the History of Computing* 28(July–September): 48–61.

Saltzer, J.H., Reed, D.P. and Clark, D.D. (1984). End-to-End Arguments in Systems Design, *ACM Transactions on Computer Systems* 2: 277–288.

Sauer, C. and Willcocks, L. (2007). Unreasonable Expectations – NHS IT, Greek choruses and the games institutions play around mega-programmes, *Journal of Information Technology* 22: 195–201.

Scacchi, W. (2009). Understanding Requirements for Open Source Software, in K. Lyytinen, P. Loucopoulos, J. Mylopoulos and W. Robinson (eds.) *Design Requirements Engineering: A ten-year perspective*, LNBIP 14, Berling and Heidelberg: Springer-Verlag, pp. 467–494.

Schmidt, S.K. and Werle, R. (1998). *Coordinating Technology. Studies in the International Standardization of Telecommunications*, Cambridge MA: MIT Press.

Scott, R.W. (2001). *Institutions and Organizations*, London: Sage.

Shapiro, C. and Varian, H.R. (1999). *Information Rules: A strategic guide to the network economy*, Boston, MA: Harvard Business School Press.

Simon, H. (1969). *The Sciences of the Artificial*, Cambridge, MA: MIT Press.

Stacey, R.D. (1996). *Complexity and Creativity in Organisations*, San Francisco: Berrett-Koehler.

Star, L.S. and Ruhleder, K. (1996). Steps Toward an Ecology of Infrastructure: Design and access of large information spaces, *Information Systems Research* 7(1): 111–134.

Stefferud, E. (1994). Paradigms Lost, *Connexions. The Interoperability Report* 8(1).

Steinberg, S.G. (1995). Addressing the Future of the Net, *WIRED* 3(May): 141–144.

Tilson, D. (2008). Reconfiguring to Innovate: Innovation networks during the evolution of wireless services in the United States and the United Kingdom, Ph.D. Thesis, Department of Information Systems, Case Western Reserve University.

Tilson, D. and Lyytinen, K. (2006). The 3G Transition: Changes in the US wireless industry, *Telecommunication Policy* 30: 569–586.

Tuomi, I. (2002). *Networks of Innovation. Change and Meaning in the Age of the Internet*, Oxford, UK: Oxford University Press.

Wagner, A. (2007). *Robustness and Evolvability in Living Systems*, Princeton, NJ: Princeton University Press.

Walls, J.G., Widmeyer, G.R. and El Sawy, O.A. (1992). Building an Information System Design Theory for Vigilant EIS, *Information Systems Research* 3(1): 36–59.

Walls, J.G., Widmeyer, G.R. and El Sawy, O.A. (2004). Assessing Information System Design Theory in Perspective: How useful was our 1992 rendition? *Journal of Information Technology Theory and application* 6(2): 43–58.

Weick, K.E. (1989). Theory Construction as Disciplined Imagination, *Academy of Management Review* 14(4): 516–531.

Weill, P. and Broadbent, M. (1998). *Leveraging the New Infrastructure*, Cambridge, MA: Harvard Business School Press.

Wigand, R.T., Lynne Markus, M., Steinfield, C.W. and Minton, G. (2006). Standards, Collective Action and IS Development – Vertical information systems standards in the US home mortgage industry, *MIS Quarterly*, Special Issue on Standards and Standardization 30: 439–465.

Williams, R. and Pollock, N. (2008). *Software and Organisations – The biography of the enterprise-wide system or how SAP conquered the world*, London: Routledge.

Yoo, Y., Lyytinen, K. and Yang, E. (2005). The Role of Standards in Innovation and Diffusion of Broadband Mobile Services: The case of South Korea, *Journal of Strategic Information Systems* 14(2): 323–353.

Zimmerman, A. (2007). A Socio-Technical Framework for Cyberinfrastructure Design, in Proceedings of e-Social Science Conference (Ann Arbor, Michigan, October).

Zittrain, J. (2006). The Generative Internet, *Harward Law Review* 119: 1974–2040.

22
Understanding the Dominance and Advocacy of the Design-Oriented Research Approach in the Business Informatics Community: A History-Based Examination

Lutz J. Heinrich and René Riedl
Department of Business Informatics – Information Engineering, Johannes Kepler
University Linz, Austria

Introduction

Information Systems (IS) is a scientific discipline with global reach that investigates the development, use, and impact of information and communication technologies (IT). In this article, we focus on historical investigation of one major scientific community within the larger IS discipline, namely that of *Wirtschaftsinformatik* (Business Informatics or BI). Business Informatics, which had its genesis in the 1960s, is now the dominant IS community in the German-speaking countries (Austria, Germany, Switzerland). This community is best characterized by its strong connections to industry and its concentration on engineering (e.g., Heinrich, 2005; Frank *et al.*, 2008; Buhl *et al.*, 2012). Thus, even though most BI scholars acknowledge that both research *and* development are equally important objectives of scientific enquiry, the focus of BI has been on the development of IT artefacts, and not on the theoretical investigation of IS behaviour.

In the beginning, the genesis of BI and its early development were significantly influenced by the implementation and rapid expansion of IS in industrial organizations, as well as by the resulting demand for qualified IT personnel. Later, as a consequence of these early developments, increasingly more academic BI institutes and departments were founded, contributing to the successful institutionalization of the community (Heinrich, 2002; Heinrich *et al.*, 2011). Today, BI is an established field of study. Yet, discussions on the identity of the community have become more intensive, mainly as a consequence of the increasing influence of other IS communities, particularly that of North American IS research, which has its focus on behavioural research, and hence is substantially different from BI (e.g., Frank *et al.*, 2008; Heinrich *et al.*, 2011; Buhl *et al.*, 2012). Today, even though BI seems to be well prepared for the future challenges in the scientific landscape, the fundamental question of BI's future strategic focus needs to be discussed. This article seeks to contribute to this discussion, based on the investigation of the community's history.

Specifically, this article is based on an ongoing research project that investigates the history of BI. This project has been initiated and conducted by Lutz J. Heinrich, a well-known BI scholar who has helped to shape the field from its beginning (Frank *et al.*, 2008: 396), with the collaboration of historian Rudolf G. Ardelt at Johannes Kepler University Linz, Austria. A project documentation summarizing the project's motivation, methodology, data, and findings from the beginning of the project in February 2009 until March 2011 was published in a German-speaking monograph (Heinrich, 2011). The objective of this project is to study the genesis and development of BI – in short, to create a documentation of BI history that represents the first systematic investigation on this topic.

Despite the omission of a systematic enquiry into the history of BI in the research literature that is as comprehensive as the present project, a number of papers have addressed different aspects of BI's history (e.g., Resch and Schlögl, 2004; Heinrich, 2005; Heilmann and Heinrich, 2006; Wilde and Hess, 2007; Frank *et al.*, 2008; Steininger *et al.*, 2009; Buhl *et al.*, 2012). For example, a study by Heilmann and Heinrich (2006) illuminates the topics conventionally addressed in BI research, while the investigation by Wilde and Hess (2007) sheds light on the research methods used.

What is likely the most extensive investigation into important facets of BI's history was conducted by Frank and colleagues (Frank *et al.*, 2008), who interviewed eight scholars from the North American IS community and six scholars from the German-speaking BI community in order to identify differences in the communities' paths of development. Also, a recent paper by Buhl *et al.* (2012), which is organized along the history of BI's main publication outlet, the journal *WIRTSCHAFTSINFORMATIK*, outlines developments of BI history. However, though these works have made valuable contributions to the literature, the authors did not have an explicit intent to systematically reconstruct the community's history in its entirety, nor was that the result.[1]

This article, however, reports on an investigation that does have this explicit goal. In contrast to the ongoing research project, which is focused on BI's history in its entirety, this study targets historical events and developments that contribute to a better understanding of one specific yet highly important facet of contemporary IS research, namely the debate on the superiority of one of two research approaches – behaviouristic research and design-oriented research. While the former approach is focused on the development and testing of theories on IS behaviour of individuals, groups, and organizations, the latter concentrates on the development of artefacts (e.g., software prototypes or process models).

Recently, 10 well-known scholars from the BI field have published a 'memorandum on design-oriented information systems research', a document intended to 'propose principles' of this approach (Österle *et al.*, 2011: 7). The response by a group of prominent editors-in-chief of mainstream IS journals (*EJIS, JAIS, ISR, MISQ*), which 'disputes and expands several premises used to justify the main argument in the memorandum' (Baskerville *et al.*, 2011: 11), may serve as an example reflecting important positions in this debate.

In essence, Baskerville *et al.* 'welcome the intention behind the memorandum to emphasize relevancy in IS research and the quest to focus on the innovative and transformative role of information technology (IT) artifacts' (p. 11), but also stress that the characterization of Anglo-Saxon IS research as being based on a behaviouristic approach 'badly over-simplifies and stereotypes Anglo-American IS research' (p. 12). Importantly, because Österle *et al.* write that 'European IS research is in danger of shifting from a design-oriented discipline into a descriptive one', and further describe this shift as a 'quite questionable trend' (p. 8), there is reason to assume that the authors of the memorandum and, likely, a large number of the 111 supporters (all full professors) prefer the design-oriented research approach over the behaviouristic one, despite the fact that the memorandum states that 'while the memorandum's initiators and signers advocate the idea of design-oriented IS research, they also explicitly welcome behavioural research' (p. 8).[2]

Against the background of this debate, on which a number of relevant arguments have already been exchanged (i) in publications in related disciplines such as computer science (e.g., Newell and Simon, 1976; Wulf, 1995; Denning, 2005) and organization science (e.g., Simon, 1996); (ii) in discussions on rigour *vs* relevance in IS research (e.g., Benbasat and Zmud, 1999; Davenport and Markus, 1999; Lee, 1999); and (iii) in essays on the identity of the IS discipline (e.g., Benbasat and Zmud, 2003; Argarwal and Lucas, 2005; Lyytinen and King, 2006; Weber, 2006), this article seeks to contribute to a better understanding of the following research question:

What major historical events and developments have contributed to the dominance and advocacy of the design-oriented research approach in BI?

The main theoretical contribution is our intent to explain the dependent variable 'dominance and advocacy of the design-oriented research approach in BI' based on 'historical events and developments', the independent variables. Moreover, the research presented in this article is methodologically distinct from the existing literature. We applied an approach similar to *written autobiography*, of a kind pursued, for example, by the Mass Observation Archive, University of Sussex (for details, see www. massobs.org.uk). In an autobiography, typically, a person provides information about his or her own life, and in doing so often reveals details of specific aspects of the profession or field of study. In the application as used by the Mass Observation Archive, and as is similarly applied in this study, those data from the autobiographies are used to construct an anthropology of a society or community that looks not only to the past, but also to the future. This approach is established in history (e.g., Lejeune, 1989; Barros, 1998), and has been applied in such areas as research on the history of computing (e.g., Hall, 2000) and on the history of management (e.g., Chandler, 2009).

To address the research question at hand, in order to use autobiographies as data sources, an interpretive approach (e.g., Carr, 1961; Walsham, 1995, 2006) is applied in order to analyse the content of the autobiographies (Krippendorff, 2004). Because this approach is novel in BI, and different from the methods on which the existing studies are based (e.g., the interview in the case of Frank *et al.*, 2008; the analysis of published journal articles in the case of Heinrich, 2005), this research was designed to reveal new insights into the history of BI, thereby not only helping to create an understanding of the dominance and advocacy of the design-oriented research approach, but also providing insights into the successful future development of BI, because '[s]eeing the past can help one envision the future' (Neustadt and May, 1986: xv).

In line with this statement, Land (2010) argues that '[h] istory provides a richness in understanding which its neglect denies the IS researcher a vision of the whole story. And it is only with this understanding that we can learn lessons from past and current events' (p. 390). Similarly, Mason *et al.* (1997a: 307) write in their pioneering article on the significance of the historical method for IS research that '[h]istory helps one understand the sources of contemporary problems, how they arose and how their characteristics unfolded through time. It also identifies the solutions that worked in the past and those that did not'. Thus, studying the history of a scientific community, here BI, may serve the purpose of *critical self-reflection*, which makes possible a more informed preparation for future challenges (Ardelt, 2011).

Josef Schumpeter (1883–1950), the great Austrian-American economist, even argues that for a field of enquiry to earn the designation of 'scientific discipline', it is necessary to provide information about its history, because otherwise it is not possible to understand the field's paradigms, theories, data, and ethics (Mason *et al.*, 1997b). Consequently, any field of enquiry that does not investigate its own history is not only incomplete but, based on Schumpeter's notion, it is under-developed and premature, without any right to consider itself as a scientific discipline.

The remainder of this article is structured as follows: In the next section, we briefly outline background information on history research in BI, as well as the major characteristics of the research project. A discussion of our methodology follows, and this part also includes a description of the characteristics of the sample. Afterward, we present the results. The descriptive results (i.e., the major topics addressed in the personal narratives) are structured along 12 categories. The explanatory results (i.e., those that help to explain the dominance and advocacy of the design-oriented research approach in BI) are structured along a chronology of historical events and developments, and they are summarized in a sequence of phases. This is followed by a reflection on the results, which may, particularly for BI scholars, help in future decisions and actions to cope with upcoming challenges, thereby sustaining a competitive position in the scientific landscape. Finally, we provide concluding comments.

Background and research project characteristics

Introductory BI textbooks (e.g., Stahlknecht and Hasenkamp, 2010), as well as encyclopaedias, both in print (e.g., Back, 2001) and online (e.g., www.enzyklopaedie-der-wirtschaftsinformatik.de), sometimes give an account of chronologically sorted events with relevance for BI. However, because these accounts typically comprise only a small number of exemplary events (see also Frank *et al.*, 2008: 393), even their descriptive value is limited. More complete lists of events relevant for the genesis and development of BI are based on data collected and published by Heinrich (1988, 1992, 1996, 1999, 2002). One comprehensive chronology drawing upon these data, for example, has been published recently in a textbook (Heinrich *et al.*, 2011: 36–45).

Despite the fact that valuable work has been carried out in documenting events relevant for the history of BI, the nature of these studies is purely descriptive, and therefore their explanatory power is limited. History research, however, should not end up merely with lists of historical events, because history is 'more than a mere chronology and body of facts' and '[t]he assemblage of admissible and ordered facts must ... be interpreted and its meaning comprehended' (Mason *et al.*, 1997a: 315). Consequently, the study of history is a study of causes. The historian Carr (1961) writes: 'The historian ... continuously asks the question: Why?; and, so long as he hopes for an answer, he cannot rest' (p. 113).

Considering that (i) most of the research on the history of BI is descriptive rather than explanatory, and (ii) an established student's guide on the study of BI has eliminated a chapter on history in its most recent edition (Kurbel *et al.*, 2009), there is reason to assume that a considerable number of BI scholars have a poorly developed sense of history. Among the reasons for this situation are, first, that meta-research (i.e., research about research) does not play a significant role in BI, despite the few notable exceptions (e.g., König *et al.*, 1995; Resch and Schlögl, 2004; Heinrich, 2005; Frank *et al.*, 2008), and second, that the potential benefits of history research for the scientific community, such as the formation of a strong identity (Hirschheim and Klein, 2003; Klein and Hirschheim, 2008) and the ability to better cope with future challenges (Mason *et al.*, 1997a), are widely unknown.[3]

As a foundation for the discussion of our methodology in the section to follow, we briefly summarize here the major characteristics of this research project:

- The database consists of primary sources in the form of written autobiographies authored by 16 BI scholars.
- The perceptions and observations reported in the autobiographies are systemized and analysed along a set of 12 categories.

- Events significant for the history of BI are integrated into the most recent version of the chronology of BI history, namely that of Heinrich (2011).
- The entire history is described in the form of a sequence of phases.
- This sequence of phases enables the identification of possible causes for the dominance and advocacy of the design-oriented research approach in BI, because causality implies a difference in the temporal order of variables.

Methodology

Approach and procedure

Autobiography makes possible the collection and investigation of data about significant events in the past (e.g., Lejeune, 1989; Barros, 1998). Among the groups of people who contribute to the development of historical knowledge, contemporary witnesses (i.e., individuals who have made observations with respect to relevant events) are among the most valuable informants. Obviously, this method can only be applied in investigations on topics that are not too far in the past, but the history of BI is such a topic. The task is often that of the researcher to prompt written statements by informants, allowing the researchers to then generate documents that serve as a database for subsequent analyses. Specifically, the content of autobiographies can be analyzed by the investigator(s) to find an answer to the research question at hand. The approach of generating data on the basis of statements by contemporary witnesses has been appreciated in the IS literature. Mason *et al.* (1997a: 313), for example, write: '[M]any of the pioneers ... are still alive. They are sources of eye witness rather than hearsay evidence'. Access to such information may positively affect data reliability, because knowledge derived from the direct experience of these informants can provide a level of detail not otherwise available – particularly when gathered with respect to a specific object of study, as is done here for the history of BI.

In the context of this research project, a career autobiography is defined as a document in which an individual describes his or her perceptions of, and observations about, (i) historical events, (ii) artefacts such as institutions, curricula, and research projects, and (iii) persons with whom there had been personal involvement. Importantly, the description is developed and recorded at a later date. Thus, it is not simply a diary or journal written at the time of the experiences; rather, it is a documentation of current thoughts and reflections about past perceptions and observations (Krusenstjern, 1994).[4] To the best of our knowledge, at the beginning of this research project no such autobiographies were available. Consequently, we had to initiate the generation of such documents.

A decision had to be made about the group of people to be invited as informants. Instead of selectively picking potential informants, we invited all 18 persons on the editorial board of the journal *WIRTSCHAFTSINFORMATIK* at the time of its inaugural publication in 1990, all of whom were full professors in BI at a German, Austrian, or Swiss university.[5]

In March 2009, we invited the 18 scholars to contribute to the investigation of the history of BI. Specifically, we asked them to write autobiographies. The letter of invitation contained a brief description of what an autobiography is. Each informant received detailed information on the investigators' expectations regarding the autobiographies, particularly that their documents should conform to the following major criteria. First, each informant was to write the autobiography independently (i.e., co-authorships were discouraged). Second, informants were not to make enquiries in order to write the autobiographies. Rather, they were instructed to write the autobiographies 'from memory'. Third, informants were instructed to avoid the citation of related work, because it was the goal to reconstruct what knowledge informants carry in their minds, rather than what they are able to reconstruct based on additional enquiries into the literature. Although we did not provide guidelines for the formal creation of the documents, we suggested considering the style rules for essay writing (e.g., perform a Google search for 'essay writing'). We expected deliberate, yet smoothly formulated texts to result from these instructions.[6] As of 30 June 2010, we had obtained 16 autobiographies (in German), for a total of 150 pages (for details, see Table 22.2). Thus, the sample size of the present investigation is $N = 16$.

Because it was possible to rule out a belief that the genesis of BI took place before 1950, particularly due to the aftermath of the Nazi Era and World War II, we analysed the contents of 10 volumes of four German management journals, beginning with 1950 publications, and based on keywords that (i) are related to socio-technical systems and (ii) are typical for the scientific terminology during that time period; the term 'electronic data processing' may serve as an example.[7] Because we could not identify scientific BI articles in the four management journals, we dated the genesis of BI to 1961, when the first scientific monograph on the subject of BI was published (Hartmann, 1961).

Characteristics of the sample

The birth years of the 16 informants range from 1931 to 1951 (mean age: 70 years); 10 persons were born in the 1930s, five in the 1940s, and one in 1951. Eleven informants were emeritus professors in 2010. With respect to the academic backgrounds of the informants (i.e., their fields of study, Ph.D., and postdoctoral lecturer qualifications), we found a significant dominance of business administration (nine persons studied this subject, 13 held a corresponding Ph.D., and six had obtained their post-doctoral lecturer qualification). Altogether, the 16 informants made 45 statements about their academic origins, of which 28 pertained to business administration (62%).

Moreover, we also analysed the location and focus of the universities at which the informants completed their degree studies, and their Ph.D. and postdoctoral lecturer qualifications. Altogether, 18 universities were mentioned, of which 16 are located in Germany as well as one in Austria and one in Switzerland. Thirteen of the 18 universities are institutions with a focus on social and economic sciences (mainly management), while the remaining five are technical universities.

Results

Descriptive results

The perceptions and observations reported in the autobiographies were systemized and analysed along a set of 12 categories. Four of these categories are well-known characteristics of scientific disciplines (Wohlgenannt, 1969; Khazanchi and Munkvold, 2000; Wilson, 2000), namely subject matter, objectives of scientific enquiry, research and development methods, and professional organization (e.g., association or society). We selected an additional eight categories, because they were mentioned in at least two of the 16 autobiographies – namely, pioneers and founders, development facilitators and barriers, core areas in research and development, curricula and programmes of study, textbooks and journals, conferences, science and practice, and reference disciplines. Table 22.1 shows descriptive results that are structured along the 12 categories; the order is oriented towards the genesis and development of the community.[8]

Each autobiography was analysed by the first author of this article, based on the terms listed in Table 22.1 (e.g., research and development methods), as well as corresponding keywords (e. g., case study, laboratory experiment, modelling, prototyping) to identify corresponding

Table 22.1   Descriptive results structured along twelve categories

	Explicitly discussed	Mentioned	Not mentioned	Intensity of discussion
Pioneers and founders	3	2	11	5
Development facilitators and barriers	10	0	6	10
Subject matter	6	4	6	10
Objectives of scientific enquiry	5	5	6	10
Research and development methods	6	3	7	9
Core areas in research and development	5	6	5	11
Curricula and programmes of study	6	4	6	10
Textbooks and journals	2	6	8	8
Conferences	5	4	7	9
Professional organizations	4	4	8	8
Science and practice	8	5	3	13
Reference disciplines	3	7	6	10

Note: Intensity of discussion is the sum of 'Explicitly discussed' and 'Mentioned.'

statements. To this end, the search function of a word processing program was used. Because four categories already existed *before* data analysis started, while eight categories were developed *during* analysis, we applied a mixed approach to derive the categories. This approach includes deductive elements (four categories were derived based on existing literature) and inductive elements (eight categories were derived based on the data) (Krippendorff, 2004).

Importantly, data analysis was not solely based on keyword searches. Rather, the keywords were used in order to quickly identify text passages that are likely to be related to the four categories that we had defined *ex ante*. Because eight out of 12 categories emerged during the study of the autobiographies, the primary technique of investigation was *qualitative content analysis*. Accordingly, the informants' narrative statements were used to draw conclusions about the history of BI.

We employed the following schema to determine the intensity with which each category is discussed in the autobiographies (see Table 22.1):

• The category is discussed explicitly, either based on the terms listed in Table 22.1 or on corresponding keywords (denoted as *Explicitly discussed*).
• The category is not discussed explicitly, but is touched on in the context of an explicitly discussed category (*Mentioned*).

- Neither the category nor a corresponding keyword is mentioned, nor is the category touched on in the context of an explicitly discussed category (*Not mentioned*).

In order to determine the intensity of discussion, we combined the frequencies of the categories 'Explicitly discussed' and 'Mentioned'. Based on this metric, we identify 'Science and practice' (Σ 13) and 'Core areas in research and development' (Σ 11) as the two categories which were discussed most extensively, followed by five categories with Σ 10 (e.g., 'Subject matter'). In contrast, the category 'Pioneers and founders' was discussed least extensively (Σ 5).

Table 22.2 exhibits descriptive results structured along the 16 autobiographies; three documents (numbers 5, 10, and 16) explicitly discuss six of the 12 categories. In contrast, Autobiography 2 explicitly discusses one category. In order to determine the intensity of discussion, we again computed the sum of the frequencies of the categories 'Explicitly discussed' and 'Mentioned'. Using this metric, we find that Autobiography 16 discusses 11 out of 12 categories (the highest value), while Autobiography 4 discusses four categories (the lowest value). Altogether, we observe a moderate degree of variance across the 16 documents with respect to intensity of discussion, $SD = 1.9$ (M: 7.1, score range: 0 to 12). Moreover, the table shows the number of pages of each

Table 22.2 Descriptive results structured along the sixteen autobiographies

	Number of pages	Explicitly discussed	Mentioned	Not mentioned	Intensity of discussion
Autobiography 1	8	3	2	7	5
Autobiography 2	4	1	5	6	6
Autobiography 3	8	2	4	6	6
Autobiography 4	4	3	1	8	4
Autobiography 5	11	6	3	3	9
Autobiography 6	12	5	1	6	6
Autobiography 7	9	4	3	5	7
Autobiography 8	9	5	4	3	9
Autobiography 9	7	3	2	7	5
Autobiography 10	15	6	3	3	9
Autobiography 11	6	2	4	6	6
Autobiography 12	12	5	3	4	8
Autobiography 13	15	4	4	4	8
Autobiography 14	15	4	2	6	6
Autobiography 15	7	4	4	4	8
Autobiography 16	8	6	5	1	11

Note: Intensity of discussion is the sum of 'Explicitly discussed' and 'Mentioned.'

autobiography. We observe a medium degree of variance, $SD = 3.6$ ($M: 9.4/MIN: 4/MAX: 15$).

In the following, we discuss the descriptive findings along the 12 categories. We include example evidence from the informants, in the form of narrative statements that we extracted from the autobiographies.[9] The full-text autobiographies are published in Heinrich (2011, see chapter B). All page numbers indicated with the excerpts refer to this source.[10]

Pioneers and founders

Three informants explicitly discussed the topic of pioneers and founders, and two further persons touched on this. Business administration professors played the most significant role, as indicated by the statement below. The next level of importance was that of scholars from applied mathematics, particularly from operations research, and from computer science:

> At the end of the 1960s, there existed no more than 40 to 50 business administration professors in the German-speaking region who were interested in electronic data processing, and typically these academics were 'lone fighters' and their scholarly work was a 'foreign body' in institutes with completely different scientific foci. In the beginning, there actually were only two institutes with an explicit focus on the design of management information systems, the one in Linz founded by Peter Mertens and later in Erlangen-Nürnberg, as well as the Business Administration Institute for Organization and Automation at the University of Cologne ... which was the first institute with several professorships related to electronic data processing .... (Autobiography 3, p. 73)

Moreover, the development of artefacts such as methods, concepts, or strategies (e.g., costing methods), rather than empirical research, was a core activity in the academic work of the pioneers and founders. As a consequence, their works were seldom published in top journals. Also, we found that management consulting has been a significant activity for business administration professors since the 1950s. Altogether, the impact of the business administration community on the genesis and development of BI was significant. Subjects like industrial management, organization theory, and accounting were of paramount importance.

Development facilitators and barriers

Ten informants explicitly discussed facilitators and barriers, reporting on organizations and individuals that positively affected the history of BI.

The genesis and development of BI was significantly supported by computer companies (e.g., IBM Germany), software houses (e.g., mbp, Europe's first software house), as well as the top management of large companies with a need to operate IT systems (e.g., Siemens, DSL Bank, Kaufhof).[11] The strongest influence was exerted by IBM via trainee programmes, research fellowships for young scholars (e.g., IBM University, New York), postdoc programmes (e.g., in Yorktown Heights and San Jose), endowments of hardware and software, as well as funding of IT institutes and departments. Altogether, the computer industry had a significant impact on the history of BI.

Four out of the 10 autobiographies contain explicit statements about institutions and persons that impeded the genesis and development of BI. The Society for Informatics (Gesellschaft für Informatik, www.gi.de), as well as individual computer science professors, are mentioned as barriers. A major motivation for this behaviour was the intention to incorporate BI into informatics, as one specific form of applied informatics. The same goal, although to a lesser extent, was pursued by the German Academic Association for Business Research (Verband der Hochschullehrer für Betriebswirtschaft, www.vhbonline.org), which had the intention to incorporate BI as a specific management discipline. Both organizations made these attempts in order to incorporate the increasing teaching and research potential (e.g., new institutes and departments) into their own institutions. Also, these two organizations sought to avoid the reallocation of resources to BI institutes; particularly, they worked against the reduction of business administration and operations research resources. One informant tellingly described BI's fight against barriers, and also stated important reasons for the existence of these barriers:

> Despite the success of BI, especially during the last 25 years, a number of barriers had to be overcome in order to, first, introduce data processing on a grand scale in the early stages, and second, to establish BI as an autonomous discipline. These barriers were based on lack of knowledge and lack of understanding, inaccurate evaluations, skepticism and reservation, or intentional rejection. (Autobiography 13, p. 165)

Subject matter

Six informants explicitly discussed the topic of subject matter. In two of the six autobiographies the subject matter is not distinguished from the contents of curricula, indicating that BI legitimizes itself primarily via curricula. Hence, supplying practice with well-educated staff, rather than scientific research, was a major objective of scientific activity. Four further autobiographies touch on this topic (e.g., by stating objects that pertain to the subject matter of BI). The prevailing opinion among the informants is that the subject matter of BI is 'information and communication systems in business and administration'. One informant, for example, wrote:

> The organization [as a whole] has always been at the core of research interest in the BI discipline. As in any other research domain, diverse perspectives emerged in the field, all of which addressed existing questions from their own points of view. (Autobiography 7, p. 107)

The finding that organizational information and communication systems are at the core of BI research is in line with a position paper on the nature of BI published in the 1990s (WKWI, 1994). Moreover, three informants discussed the importance of an ongoing discourse on the subject matter. Specifically, these persons indicated the necessity to enlarge the subject matter in the future, for example, by addressing topics pertaining to various levels of analysis, and not only those on the organizational level.

Objectives of scientific enquiry

Five informants explicitly discussed the objectives of scientific enquiry, and five others touched on it. Most important, no autobiography deals with a theory of BI or with explanatory models related to IS theorizing. In contrast, several informants explained BI's strong design and engineering focus, as exemplified in the following statement:

> In the beginning, most BI scholars were design-oriented. The apparent success of BI research was based on an engineering approach ... From my point of view, the majority of BI scholars are still engineering-oriented today. (Autobiography 8, p. 122)

However, two autobiographies contain information about the use of theories from reference disciplines, and specifically mention systems theory and organization theory. This lack of awareness of the importance of theoretical research (i.e., the identification and test of cause-effect relationships) characterizes the founding generation of BI, as well as their successors.

Another major finding of the analysis is the 'glorification' of past achievements, with respect to design and action; a significant strength of BI has always been the distinct orientation towards the development of IT artefacts. Importantly, complementing the design and engineering focus by an emphasis on theory is considered a threat for the future development of the community (e.g., because this may result in a reduction of the community's success potential). However, this prevailing opinion stands in contradiction to the previously mentioned position paper (WKWI, 1994), because this document explicitly indicates theoretical research *and* design science research as objectives of scientific enquiry. According to one informant, contribution to theory had long been an important factor in BI research:

> In the midst of the 1990s, the theoretical foundation of articles was introduced as an explicit evaluation criterion: What is the state-of-the-art with respect to a specific object of research, and how does the paper at hand make a theoretical contribution? (Autobiography 6, p. 99)

A review of the overall group of commentaries, however, reveals that only two informants considered a theoretical focus to be an essential complement to the design-oriented research approach.

Research and development methods

Six informants explicitly discussed research and development methods, and three others touched on these topics (e. g., by stating specific research methods such as the case study). Such remarks notwithstanding, a detailed look at the data makes clear that most of the methods mentioned are not empirical research methods; rather, they are techniques for modelling business processes or development methods (e.g., prototyping), as is specifically noted by one of the informants:

> It became clear that not only is value added to a firm's products or services by activities that are directly related to those products or services, but supporting communication and information structures add value, also, to an organization. Based on this insight, an approach for communication structure analysis emerged. This approach is part of BONAPART, a tool for graphical modeling, documentation, and analysis of business processes, organizations, and information systems. (Autobiography 7, pp. 108–109)

Interestingly, the term 'development method' was not mentioned in any of the autobiographies, although BI has its primary focus on design-oriented research. Moreover, the method of 'research by development' (e.g., Szyperski and Müller-Böling, 1981), which thwarts an approach that considers findings of theoretical research in the development of artefacts (in other words: research first, development second), is mentioned in only two autobiographies. The following statement is a clear example:

> Our research efforts were based on the explicit belief that we cannot investigate our objects of study in the laboratory. Rather, we believed in investigations in the real world of existing organizations; that is, we pursued the strategy we preached – 'research by development,' thwarting the sequence 'research first, development second'. (Autobiography 16, p. 294)

Core areas in research and development

Five autobiographies include explicit discussions about research projects funded by the German Federal Ministry of Research and Technology or the German Research Foundation. Almost all of the mentioned projects are development projects, for which the outcome was the development of prototype software systems, as exemplified in the following statement:

> The apparent achievements of BI research were based on a construction-oriented approach. The above-mentioned program of the German Research Foundation in the period from 1985 to 1990 [Interactive Corporate Information and Controlling Systems] was characterized by modeling, development, and software prototype construction projects. In my view, the majority of BI scholars working today remain construction-oriented in their approach. (Autobiography 8, p. 122)

Thus, the explicit goal was the design and implementation of IT artefacts, and not theory development and testing, respectively. Most autobiographies do not contain discussions about specific themes addressed in the projects. However, six informants mentioned topics, particularly query-reply systems, executive IS, and computer integrated manufacturing. Basic research, as a significant and enduring source of technological innovation, is not mentioned in any of the autobiographies. Two informants discussed the tendency of BI to dwell on recent topics, so-called fads (Mertens, 1995; Steininger et al., 2009). Such a focus may negatively affect a cumulative research tradition, as well as direct comparisons of research quality, as is effectively exemplified in the following remark:

> In fact, a strategy could be observed which aimed at the establishment of local and small research domains and publication markets that are virtually unconnected, thereby impeding national and global quality comparisons in a putative intelligent way. (Autobiography 6, p. 101)

Also, it is discussed that BI should continuously scrutinize its core areas in research and development, thereby identifying promising new areas of enquiry. One informant, however, indicated that despite the large variety of possible topics, the fundamental question in BI is how IT systems can be effectively and efficiently designed, implemented, used, maintained, and renewed.

Curricula and programmes of study

Six informants explicitly addressed the topic of curricula and programmes of study, and another four autobiographies touch on the subject. The informants' narratives mention that the first BI courses were instituted in the mid-1960s, remaining part of business administration programmes until the 1970s. After that time, an increasing number of autonomous BI programmes have been established. The first specification of requirements for education in BI was developed in 1984, and this document was later continually updated. Importantly, not only academics but also practitioners contributed significantly to these specifications, particularly in the 1980s, as is explained by one informant:

> After I had expressed interest in this topic [participation in a curriculum committee], I was assigned the task of forming and chairing the next committee ... Then, I have repeatedly worked out curriculum recommendations together with colleagues and practitioners since 1988, in which the major BI topics were documented, at least those topics that were considered to have useful teaching content. (Autobiography 8, p. 121)

The predominant group of contributors from practice were computer companies (e.g., Honeywell Bull, IBM), as well as large firms with a need to run IT systems (e.g., Hoesch, Siemens). The development of the specifications came about in the hope of implementation at all universities in the German-speaking countries. However, this hope was not always fulfilled, due to varying situational preferences (e.g., as a result of budget restrictions). It is also important to note that two informants mentioned that the specifications reflected BI's self-conception as academic field of study, and not as science.

Textbooks and journals

Two informants explicitly discussed textbooks and journals, and six other persons touched on this. One informant stressed that textbooks are a manifestation of an emerging discipline, and this person explicitly mentioned examples (Hartmann, 1961; Grochla, 1966; Mertens, 1966). The moment of the genesis of BI was dated to 1961, when a substantial monograph on the subject of BI was published by Hartmann, even though the publication was descriptive in nature (thereby making no claim to be a theoretical contribution) (Hartmann, 1961). With respect to BI journals, only *WIRTSCHAFTSINFORMATIK*, which published its inaugural issue in 1990, was mentioned (in seven autobiographies). One informant clearly expressed the significance of this journal:

> The most important German-language journal is *WIRTSCHAFTSINFORMATIK*. It is based on a tradition over 50 years long, at first under the name of *elektronische datenverarbeitung [electronic data processing]* ... later *Angewandte Informatik [Applied Informatics]* ... the renaming to *WIRTSCHAFTSINFORMATIK* in the 1990 volume constitutes a milestone in the history of BI. (Autobiography 4, p. 81)

Conferences

Nine informants either explicitly discussed or mentioned conferences attended by BI scholars and IT practitioners, such as the 1978 event 'Computer-Based Information Systems and Organization' ('Rechnergestützte Informationssysteme und Organisation'). Most of these conferences were focused on the description and design of systems. Consequently, theoretical research was rarely made the subject of discussion. From the early 1960s, many conferences were initiated and supported by practitioners, mainly by associations that were founded by computer companies. Examples include conferences organized by the Consortium Data Processing, which was founded in 1959 in Vienna (ADV – Arbeitsgemeinschaft Datenverarbeitung, www.adv.at) and whose first congress in 1966 attracted more than 700 participants, as well as BI symposia organized by IBM Germany starting in 1972.

The breakthrough for the community occurred in 1993 when the International Conference on Business Informatics was organized for the first time (Internationale Tagung Wirtschaftsinformatik); the conference attracted 560 participants, including both academics and practitioners

(Kurbel, 1993). One informant tellingly described his motivation to help establish this conference:

> Annual conferences such as the International Conference on Information Systems (ICIS) or the Hawaii International Conference on System Sciences (HICSS) serve the purpose of discussing scientific progress. As well, based on corresponding doctoral consortiums, the conferences contribute to the qualification of young academics. This prompted me to assist in the establishment of similar competitive mechanisms in the German-speaking and European regions. (Autobiography 2, p. 68)

Since 1993, the conference has been organized every 2 years, and is now the largest and most prestigious scientific gathering in BI, thereby contributing significantly to BI's identity.

Professional organizations

The institutional integration of BI into the German Academic Association for Business Research, in the form of the designation as a specialized area, as well as the integration into the Society for Informatics as an interest group, was mentioned positively in three autobiographies. In a fourth document, however, this is viewed more sceptically. Four other informants mentioned both organizations, and one of those also referred to the German Society for Operations Research (Deutsche Gesellschaft für Operations Research, https://gor. uni-paderborn.de), which founded a BI working group in the 1970s. Importantly, one informant put forth the view that BI's lack of an independent professional organization is evidence of the weak scientific identity of the community:

> A remarkable detail ... is the unsuccessful attempt of the establishment ... of a BI association or society. In the early 1990s, criticism on the German Academic Association for Business Research and the Society for Informatics emerged in the scientific community ... BI scholars expected an adequate representation, based on the discipline's gained significance. (Autobiography 5, p. 89)

Another informant argued that the goal of becoming perceived as an independent discipline, and of being accepted in that role, was a major motive for the establishment of an own association:

> Given the attempts of several computer scientists to deny the autonomy of BI in the 1980s, and to define it as a part of computer science, serious attempts were made to found an association for BI,

in parallel and to compete with the Society for Informatics. As soon as influential computer scientists acknowledged the autonomy of BI, these plans were stopped. (Autobiography 4, p. 80)

However, there is agreement among most informants that BI's integration into the German Academic Association for Business Research and the Society for Informatics is adequate, with the implication that the development of an independent professional organization comparable to the Association for IS is hardly worth pursuing.[12]

Science and practice

The topic of science and practice is explicitly discussed in eight autobiographies, and five further informants mentioned it. In general, most informants indicated that there have always been close and fruitful relationships with practice, as exemplified in the following statement:

As a consequence of the joint responsibility for the success in research by development, faithful and competent relationships with organizations and their executives have emerged during these times. As well, successful technological and organizational implementations and the stable use of the created systems contributed to the establishment of these relationships, which were effective much longer than the project duration .... (Autobiography 16, p. 204)

There is agreement among the informants that the demand for academically educated and trained staff was a major driver of the development of BI as a programme of study, and that the demand has positively affected the scientific development of the community. Moreover, the autobiographies indicate that time-consuming consulting activities in practice not only served the purpose of knowledge transfer, but also contributed significantly to a scholar's income:

Another phenomenon also became visible, one which occurs in all scientific disciplines that have practical relevance ... some peers did not overcome the temptation of time-consuming and financially alluring additional activities in practice .... (Autobiography 2, p. 67)

A majority of the informants hold the opinion that both research and teaching benefited from consulting activities; only one informant did not explicitly agree. This sceptical view is shared by stakeholders from outside the community (e.g., professors from other disciplines).

Knowledge transfer from science to practice started early. For example, many master and doctoral theses were written in collaboration with the computer industry (e.g., SAP). This form of liaison typically entails close relationships between practitioners and students, thereby stimulating mutual learning processes. Moreover, knowledge transfer from practice to science also occurred by way of lectureships, through which practitioners shared their experiences with faculty and students. As well, practitioners were appointed as professors, thereby ensuring transfer of knowledge from practice to academia. Such professors were typically former personnel from IT companies, management consultancies, or software houses, who had experience in academic teaching through lectureships (e.g., IBM staff members).

Reference disciplines

Reference disciplines were discussed directly by three informants, while another seven acknowledged the topic by mentioning specific disciplines. Two informants considered business administration as the 'mother' discipline, and one referred to the field as a 'sister' discipline. In two autobiographies the IS discipline is mentioned as a 'sister' discipline. Altogether, business administration is discussed more intensively in the autobiographies than is applied informatics and the IS discipline. There is, notably, general agreement among the informants that BI has its origins in business administration, from the standpoint that in the beginning business administration was BI's 'mother':

> Because the pioneers and supporters of BI – like most members of the successive founding generations – have been scholars from business administration, particularly management researchers and industrial engineers who were active in academic teaching and research, the question of the mother discipline is answered. It is business administration. (Autobiography 5, p. 86)

However, as time progressed and BI became increasingly more independent, this relationship with business administration changed, leading to the view, today, that business administration is BI's 'sister'. Applied informatics, in contrast, has always been a 'sister'. With respect to BI's relationship with the IS discipline, there is agreement among the informants that both are 'sisters', despite the insightful observation that they are perceived to be 'dissimilar sisters' because, although their subject matters are similar, their research approaches are significantly different, as is reflected by actual journal publications rather than journal policy statements (e.g., Chen and Hirschheim, 2004; Wilde and Hess, 2007).

Identification of patterns

Despite occasional disagreements with respect to specific facets, the prevailing opinion among the informants is that BI has gone through a successful development during the past five decades. Specifically, BI became independent from other disciplines, especially from business administration, and is now established in the scientific arena as well as in the broader society. The specific subject matter of BI developed primarily as a consequence of the increasing adoption of IT systems in organizations. This, in turn, created problems associated with IT design, implementation, use, and maintenance, as well as renewal. Consequently, the need for academically educated and trained personnel emerged – personnel who conceived that the effective and efficient design and management of IT systems implies a socio-technical perspective. With respect to the focus of scientific activity, design and implementation of IT artefacts, rather than theory-based explanation of IS behaviour, has dominated in BI. This fact, however, conflicts with the community's explicit commitment (WKWI, 1994) to consider theoretical and design science research as equal objectives.

Against this background, in the following section we seek to explain the dominance and advocacy of the design-oriented research approach in BI. Events important in the history of BI are integrated into the most recent version of the chronology of BI history, namely that of Heinrich (2011). Moreover, the historical development is described in a *sequence of phases* (see Figure 22.1). Because the phases reveal the temporal order of important events during the past five decades, both within each phase and among them, this concept is designed to 'determine patterns' (Mason *et al.*, 1997a: 315) that may explain the dominance and advocacy of the design-oriented research approach in BI. Importantly, the phases of the history have been generated inductively, based on the evidence provided by the informants, while the identification of patterns is based on the authors' deliberations. In the following section, we again include exemplary evidence from the autobiographies in the form of narrative statements.

1950s–1960s: becoming aware of a specific problem area

A specific configuration of circumstances, at a particular point of time, may result in the perception of a new problem area by scholars in existing disciplines. In the 1950s, business administration professors

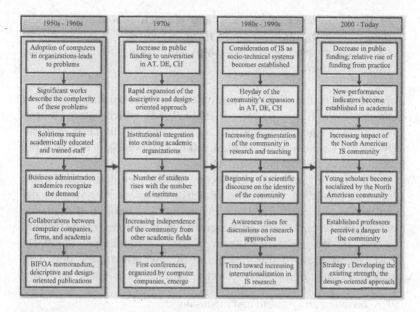

1950s - 1960s	1970s	1980s - 1990s	2000 - Today
Adoption of computers in organizations-leads to problems	Increase in public funding to universities in AT, DE, CH	Consideration of IS as socio-technical systems becomes established	Decrease in public funding; relative rise of funding from practice
Significant works describe the complexity of these problems	Rapid expansion of the descriptive and design-oriented approach	Heyday of the community's expansion in AT, DE, CH	New performance indicators become established in academia
Solutions require academically educated and trained staff	Institutional integration into existing academic organizations	Increasing fragmentation of the community in research and teaching	Increasing impact of the North American IS community
Business administration academics recognize the demand	Number of students rises with the number of institutes	Beginning of a scientific discourse on the identity of the community	Young scholars become socialized by the North American community
Collaborations between computer companies, firms, and academia	Increasing independence of the community from other academic fields	Awareness rises for discussions on research approaches	Established professors perceive a danger to the community
BIFOA memorandum, descriptive and design-oriented publications	First conferences, organized by computer companies, emerge	Trend toward increasing internationalization in IS research	Strategy : Developing the existing strength, the design-oriented approach

Figure 22.1 Sequence of phases on the history of BI

Note: International Organization for Standardization (ISO) country codes: AT (Austria), DE (Germany), CH (Switzerland); BIFOA = Betriebswirtschaftliches Institut für Organisation und Automation an der Universität zu Köln (Business Administration Institute for Organization and Automation at the University of Cologne), IS = information systems.

perceived the adoption of computers in organizations as significant – as a new and complex problem. As specific manifestations of this problem, the alignment of the organization to computer technology, as well as the customization of technology to organizational requirements, constituted a major challenge. Moreover, the significant differences in thinking and action between computer companies and client firms were another challenge. Hence, the exploration of the potential of computer system adoption in organizations was fuelled by interaction and cooperation among computer companies, client firms, and academics. These interactions were successfully established. One informant, for example, explained the situation as follows:

> Education and advanced training of clients became both a significant cost factor and bottleneck in the 1960s, which increasingly negatively affected tapping of market potential related to electronic data processing. As a consequence, computer firms developed a strategy that aimed to convince universities and technical colleges

of the importance of teaching and research related to electronic data processing. As well, these firms supported the establishment of computer science professorships and corresponding curricula. (Autobiography 3, p. 71)

Also, the publication of significant works such as *Automation: The Advent of the Automatic Factory* by John Diebold (1952), which became a bestseller and had considerable impact on the scientific discourse (particularly among German business administration scholars), accelerated the fruitful genesis and development of BI.

At the end of this phase, the second BIFOA memorandum (BIFOA, 1969) was published.[13] This was the first document to systematically describe 'Organization and Data Processing' as a subject of academic teaching and research. Moreover, increasing public notice of the method 'research by development' advanced the design-oriented approach. Hence, in addition to the description of phenomena, the design of artefacts became an important objective of scientific enquiry.

1970s: becoming independent and expansion

Neither epistemological discourse, particularly discourse on the nature of BI, nor its establishment as an accepted scientific field, increased noticeably (Heinrich, 1975). Despite this, however, public funding to universities increased, leading to the introduction of more BI programmes, and thereby positively affecting the independence of the community. Moreover, the rapid and prosperous development of the computer industry (e.g., IBM), as well as aspired improvements in organizational productivity, had a positive influence on the development of BI. One informant unequivocally described the significant influence of IBM on the BI community:

A factor that should not to be sneezed at was the impact of the IBM postdoc program on the emerging discipline of BI in the 1970s and 1980s. Several of today's BI professors were involved in one-year-long fundamental research projects in Yorktown Heights or San Jose, providing a basis for their habilitation treatises. (Autobiography 4, p. 81)

Altogether, there was a notable growth of BI (in terms of the number of students and of institutes). As a result of the creation of an independent section in the German Academic Association for Business Research, and an interest group in the Society for Informatics, initiation of the community's institutionalization outside of universities took place. By the end of the 1970s, the first conferences were organized, mainly by computer companies, resulting in a higher degree of proliferation of the design-oriented research approach.

1980s–1990s: becoming a brand

By the late 20th century, computers had become pervasive in almost all organizations, and IS were increasingly considered to be socio-technical systems (e.g., Heinrich, 1986). Therefore, the demand for teaching and research increased. In particular, the development of artefacts played a significant role. In this era, BI experienced its heyday, and the term *Wirtschaftsinformatik* became a brand, both at universities and in practice. At this stage, most BI institutes were part of schools of business and social science.

As a consequence of the rapid expansion of BI, however, the community became increasingly more fragmented, and this, in turn, was often perceived as a threat to the community's identity (see, for example, Benbasat and Zmud, 2003; Hirschheim and Klein, 2003). One informant, for example, tellingly described the situation:

> There was too little concentration on a few primary streams, as well as partial divergence from the approaches of German-language BI research and international IS research. Against this background, I welcome the slow, yet permanently progressing development towards a reduction of interdisciplinary domains, which may be characterized best by 'nice to have'. (Autobiography 6, p. 103)

Also, an increasing degree of specialization in teaching and research impeded a holistic research approach, so that theoretical research and the design of IT artefacts were seldom combined. Some researchers began to investigate the community's self-conception. Specifically, the objectives of scientific enquiry, especially the questions of whether there should be a theory or engineering focus, and what research and development methods would be appropriate, became the subject of discussion (a Delphi study conducted in the 1990s by König, Heinzl, and colleagues may serve as an example; König *et al.*, 1995). This development indicated the necessity to discuss the community's academic legitimation, which was further substantiated by an increasing internationalization. Consequently, influences from the IS discipline, particularly from the North American community, increasingly affected the work of BI scholars. In 1997, five prominent BI scholars presented and discussed the 'German perspective on information systems' at the

International Conference on Information Systems (ICIS panel; Frank *et al.*, 1997), signifying the increasing awareness within BI of the influences of other IS communities.

2000 – today: in the age of globalization

The increasing internationalization of the current era has become a major challenge, because research standards, in particular those from North America, differ significantly from established norms in BI. The BI community recognizes the influence of other regions, but it is now clear that BI itself has begun to affect other research communities. Notably, BI has been exerting influence on communities in the former Eastern Bloc, in Asia, and in Australia, 'exporting' the design-oriented research approach into these regions. Despite this development, however, the continuous decrease in public funding has necessitated that BI institutes keep their focus on applied research projects for which, in many cases, the theoretical bases are often not well-developed (e.g., Heinrich, 2005). Furthermore, new performance indicators have been instituted (e.g., requirements for numbers of publications in highly ranked journals).

Within BI, young scientists have increasingly sought opportunities to apply a behaviouristic research approach, with the result that ever more BI scholars have become socialized by other IS communities, especially by North America. A major reason for this development is the increasing pressure within academia to publish in top-tier journals, many of which are deeply rooted in the North American research tradition (e.g., *ISR*, *MISQ*). In combination with an emphasis on quantitative research methods, that tradition has been characterized as being based on behaviourism (e.g., Chen and Hirschheim, 2004).[14] One informant remarked pointedly on this issue:

> Most notably, the domain that is now referred to as an 'engineering-oriented approach' ... is eclipsed unfairly. Because scholars in this domain have few counterparts in the US sister discipline Information Systems (IS), which pursues a strong behaviouristic approach, it is difficult for engineering-oriented scholars to publish papers in highly ranked US journals. The anonymous reviewers have dubious objections against the solution of practical IT tasks during various phases. (Autobiography 9, p. 129)

This development has led to an 'importing' of different views on the concept of science which, in turn, raises major questions: What is science, and what is it not? What research approach is best suited to BI? Established BI scholars, who are themselves proponents of the design-oriented research approach, have been forced into a defensive posture by these and similar questions. The major strategy these scholars perceive for resisting this trend is the development of the existing strength – the design-oriented research approach (Österle *et al.*, 2011). In line with this development, a paper was recently published in *JAIS* in which BI scholars 'give recommendations on how the NAIS [North American Information Systems] community can mitigate some of its weaknesses ... [by providing] insights into the traditional strength of the [BI] community' (Buhl *et al.*, 2012: 236). This response confirms that BI scholars are not passive observers of the development towards a behaviouristic research paradigm. Rather, they seek to actively inform those IS scholars who are not design-oriented about (i) the opportunities associated with design orientation (e.g., practical utility) and (ii) the risks related to a purely behaviouristic orientation (e.g., decreasing student numbers).

From the past to the future

History research should not only describe historical facts and patterns of development, but should also provide 'wisdom that can be used effectively by leaders and decision makers' (Mason *et al.*, 1997b: 259). Thus, history research should outline, at least to some degree, insights into possible future developments. One pivotal question for BI is whether the community should continue in its current direction, and if so, whether there are specific forms it should take.

Should BI continue the design-oriented research approach?

Although more than one hundred BI scholars, several of them ranked among the most established academics in the community, have signed the 'memorandum on design-oriented information systems research', many prominent BI scholars do not support the memorandum.[15] However, we do not believe that the lack of support for the document is because the scholars consider design-oriented research to be unimportant. Rather, evidence based on personal communication reveals that at least some of these scholars are of the opinion that the explicit accentuation of the design component is not necessary, because IS research consists *expressis verbis* (see, e.g., WKWI, 1994) of both theoretical *and* design-science research. We are not aware of well-founded arguments why one approach should dominate the other.

The genesis of BI has been driven by the practical problem of handling the complexity of computer systems in organizations. Afterward, throughout the history of BI, there has always been a close relationship with practice, so that the major stakeholder group to which BI has felt obliged was practice rather than other groups (e.g., researchers in or outside BI's own community). As a consequence, addressing 'How' questions has traditionally been more important than addressing 'Why' questions; the former is mainly associated with the design-science approach, while the latter is primarily related to theoretical research (König *et al.*, 1996).

Developments during the past two decades, taking place outside the community, have both promoted and impeded the design-oriented research approach. On the one hand, decreases in public funding of scientific research necessitated an orientation towards practice in order to increase funding from this stakeholder group; BI's performance in acquiring funds from practice in order to conduct applied research has always been excellent. On the other hand, internationalization and new performance indicators (e.g., publications in highly ranked journals) have changed the behaviour of BI scholars, especially those of the younger generation. They are moving towards a behaviouristic and more theory-focused approach, because this is expected to provide a better chance for publishing in mainstream IS journals.

However, considering BI's significant past achievements in design-oriented IS research, as signified, for example, by the innovations of software companies developing enterprise-wide systems (e.g., SAP), as well as contributions to the development of modelling notations (e.g., ARIS, Architecture of Integrated Information Systems), it is unlikely that the community will weaken its design focus. This appraisal is based on predictions of path dependence theory, which explains that current decision and action alternatives are dependent on past decisions and developments, even though past circumstances may no longer be relevant (Liebowitz and Margolis, 1995; Mahoney, 2000).

Should BI choose another form of its current approach?

Considering BI's historical development, it appears almost impossible for the community to give up the design focus for a concentration on theoretical research. At the very least, such a shift could take many years or even decades before the community's productivity would be comparable to the current status.[16]

But is the explicit preference for design-oriented research in the current form the only option for BI? We think *not*. One major alternative, or complement, would be to consequently pursue a *theory-driven design approach*. Although pioneering work on this approach was carried out in the 1980s and 1990s (e.g., Weber, 1987; Walls *et al.*, 1992; March and

Smith, 1995), renewed calls for theory-driven IS design were made in the recent past, both within the IS discipline (e.g., Markus *et al.*, 2002; Gregor and Jones, 2007; Arazy *et al.*, 2010) and in other fields such as psychology (e.g., Carroll, 1997) and human-computer interaction (e.g., Briggs, 2006).[17]

One fundamental assumption underlying the utility of this approach, however, is that the design of high-quality artefacts requires the explicit consideration of theoretical findings from behavioural research.[18] Although this assumption seems to be intuitively plausible, we are not aware of scientific research reporting empirical evidence that confirms such a notion. Thus, the provision of empirical evidence for this assumption should be a major endeavour in future IS research. A look at the possible outcome of such enquiries reveals two scenarios.

If empirical evidence was found (scenario 1), a 'theory-driven design approach' would constitute a fruitful direction for future BI research, because a historical strength would be further developed, and a traditional deficit, the theory focus (e.g., Heinrich, 2005), would be mitigated or even eliminated. The mentioned articles (e.g., Walls *et al.*, 1992; Markus *et al.*, 2002; Briggs, 2006; Gregor and Jones, 2007; Arazy *et al.*, 2010) are promising starting points to establish a cumulative tradition in this field. Also, a chapter in the most recent edition of an established BI textbook illustrates, based on the example of the development of online shops and theories from cognitive decision making, how behavioural theories can be applied to design user-friendly systems (Heinrich *et al.*, 2011: 395–403). In general, if this scenario was proven, the practical design value of behavioural IS research would be confirmed.

A major decision in scenario 1 is whether BI should focus on the application of theories, or on theory development *and* application. A pure application strategy would imply that BI scholars draw their design works upon theories developed by other IS communities (e.g., the North American or Scandinavian communities) or disciplines (e. g., psychology). This could be advantageous from a division of labour viewpoint, due to specialization effects. Also, increasing differentiation in a discipline indicates a rising degree of maturity (e.g., in physics various communities such as theoretical or applied physics coexist). However, it is also possible that BI not only applies theories on IS behaviour, but also contributes to their development, a strategy that has been touched on recently in the BI literature (Winter *et al.*, 2009). Importantly, the journal *WIRTSCHAFTSINFORMATIK*, as well as the English-speaking equivalent *Business & Information Systems Engineering* (BISE), has recently established a department entitled 'Theories for BISE', signifying the increasing importance of theoretical research in BI, as well as the fact that BI seeks to contribute to both theoretical and design-science research.[19]

If no empirical evidence was found (scenario 2), however, the question arises of whether theoretical research based on behaviourism has more to offer than predictive value. Specifically, doubts will emerge about whether theories focused on IS behaviour at the individual, group, and organizational level are actually necessary for the design and implementation of artefacts. Because the identification of relevant theories and their goal-oriented application in a specific engineering context may be associated with significant investments, design and implementation could be managed more effectively and efficiently based on intuition, speculation, and an engineer's implicit know-how. Therefore, if evidence was found for this scenario, the current approach in BI is likely to result in a prosperous future. In contrast to scenario 1, no significant changes would be necessary.

Concluding comments

The objective of this article was to explain, on the basis of history research, the dominance and advocacy of the design-oriented research approach in BI, one of the largest IS communities worldwide. To this end, we applied an innovative research approach, namely autobiography, in order to explain what happened (see the descriptive results) and why (see the patterns, Figure 22.1). Because history research should also provide insight into possible future developments, we discussed whether BI should continue the current orientation towards the design of artefacts, and if so, whether there are specific forms of this orientation. Considering BI's achievements in design-oriented IS research during the past five decades, we argued, based on path dependence theory, that it is unlikely that the community will weaken its design orientation. Moreover, we explained that a focus on a 'theory-driven design approach' could constitute a viable direction for future BI research, because it makes possible the combination of scientific rigor and practical relevance. First, however, replicable empirical evidence must be found for a fundamental, yet hardly explored, assumption – namely that the design of high-quality artefacts requires the explicit consideration of theoretical findings from behavioural research. This research call is directed towards the entire IS community.

This investigation systematically reconstructs an important aspect of BI's history. However, we do not yet see this work as complete, nor do we consider it to be without limitations. First, it is possible that future history research will reveal further descriptive facts about BI.[20]

Obviously, new facts may lead to the identification of new patterns. Second, the presented interpretation of the facts and the resulting patterns cannot be free from our own, sometimes even unconscious, beliefs. In this context, the Hungarian-British polymath Michael Polanyi (1891–1976) argues in his book *Personal Knowledge* that objectivity is a false ideal, because all knowledge claims rely, at least to some extent, on personal judgments (Polanyi, 1958). Similar notions can be found in the IS literature. Mason *et al.* (1997a), for example, write that '[s]ometimes a history serves as a mirror of the researcher's beliefs' (p. 310), and Walsham (2006), citing the American anthropologist Clifford Geertz (1926–2006), writes: 'What we call our data are really our own constructions of other people's constructions of what they and their compatriots are up to' (p. 320).

History research is typically deeply rooted in a hermeneutic tradition, thereby being of a fundamentally idiographic nature. Such research, therefore, has the objective of providing 'richness in reality', and not 'tightness of control' (Mason *et al.* 1997a: 308). The entirety of the database underlying our analyses and interpretations (i.e., the sixteen autobiographies) is published in Heinrich (2011, chapter B). Other BI scholars may use this database to conduct their own analyses and develop their own interpretations. It will be rewarding to see what insights these potential studies will reveal.

Acknowledgements

We would like to thank the senior editors (Antony Bryant, Alistair Black, Frank Land, and Jaana Porra) for their excellent guidance that has significantly improved the quality of this article. Moreover, we thank three anonymous reviewers for their developmental feedback and suggestions that enhanced the paper's presentation and contribution. Also, we are grateful to Rudolf G. Ardelt and Thiemo Gaisbauer for their excellent work in providing guidance on ways to improve an earlier version of this manuscript. As well, we would like to thank the participants of the event '50 Jahre Wirtschaftsinformatik' (13th October, 2011; Johannes Kepler University Linz) for their valuable comments on this work. Finally, we thank Deborah C. Nester for proof-reading.

Notes

1. This fact is confirmed in the papers themselves. Frank *et al.* (2008), for example, write that '[w]e do not intend to provide a complete description of important historical events' (p. 393). The paper by Buhl and colleagues

makes reference to the Ardelt and Heinrich project described in this article; Buhl *et al.* (2012) write that '[r]eaders who are interested in more comprehensive information about the ... community's history and are familiar with the German language are referred to Ardelt and Heinrich' (p. 239).

2. Note that Österle *et al.* (2011) use the word 'descriptive' in a broad sense. Thus, their definition includes both the description of phenomena *and* theoretical research (i.e., the identification and testing of cause-effect relationships). According to a survey by Frank *et al.* (2008, p. 391), BI comprises 208 full professors.

3. It is important to note that contributors to the history of computing include historians (e.g., Mahoney, 2005; Schlombs, 2010), computing and IS researchers (e.g., Land, 2000; Cortada, 2004, 2008; Campbell-Kelly, 2009) and, occasionally, BI practitioners (e.g., Leimbach, 2008). These contributions, along with many related publications that appear in specialized journals such as *IEEE Annals of the History of Computing*, are a valuable base for future studies on the history of BI.

4. The German translation of autobiography is *Selbstzeugnis*.

5. The names of the 18 persons are indicated on page 1 of the inaugural issue. Given the listing of the 18 people, it was not possible to hide the names of those we approached, nor were we able to preclude some or add others.

6. The original German-language instructions may be obtained in electronic form by request from the corresponding author.

7. The four journals are: *Zeitschrift für handelswissenschaftliche Forschung (ZfhF)*, *Zeitschrift für Betriebswirtschaft (ZfB)*, *Zeitschrift Betriebswirtschaftliche Forschung und Praxis (BFuP)*, and *Zeitschrift Organisation und Betrieb*.

8. Despite the fact that we do not claim that the 12 categories are completely disjointed, a requirement that is virtually impossible to meet because several of the categories are interrelated (e.g., perceptions regarding research and development methods might present implications of perceptions concerning objectives of scientific enquiry, such as explanation or design), we believe that the 12 categories have a level of abstraction that is appropriate for the analysis of the data, as well as for the presentation of the results.

9. The narrative statements are literal translations of the original German-language statements.

10. The autobiographies may be obtained in electronic form by request from the corresponding author.

11. mpb denotes Mathematischer Beratungs und Programmierungsdienst (Mathematical Consulting and Programming Service), a software house founded in Dortmund (Germany) in 1957 by 14 companies; mpb was bought by EDS (Electronic Data Systems) in 1992 (Source: www.wikipedia.org).

12. The Business Informatics Association for Academia and Practice in Europe (Wirtschaftsinformatik-Verband für Hochschule und Praxis in Europa e. V.), which was founded in 1994, could not be established successfully and was therefore closed in 1995 (Heinrich, 2011: 268).

13. BIFOA = Betriebswirtschaftliches Institut für Organisation und Automation an der Universität zu Köln (Business Administration Institute for Organization and Automation at the University of Cologne).

14. It is important to note, as we have done in the introduction through arguments provided in Baskerville *et al.* (2011), that characterizing Anglo-Saxon

IS research as being based on a behaviouristic approach over-simplifies the current situation. In particular, it is important to stress that policies of journals from this region do not dismiss research simply due to its approach.

15. For example, among the scholars who have not signed the memorandum are the current and a former editors-in-chief of the journal *WIRTSCHAFTSINFORMATIK*, as well as former spokespersons of the BI section in the German Academic Association for Business Research.

16. Metrics to measure productivity in a community with a focus on theoretical research are, for example, the number of publications in highly ranked journals or citations. In a community with a focus on design-oriented research, the number of patents or innovations adopted in practice may serve as examples for productivity measures.

17. See also a special issue on design science research (*MISQ*, Vol. 32, Issue 4, December 2008), as well as an article by King and Lyytinen (2004).

18. High quality could be measured, for example, based on technology acceptance or user satisfaction, as well as productivity parameters.

19. The current department editors are Armin Heinzl and Dorothy E. Leidner (September 2012, see www.wirtschaftsinformatik.de).

20. One promising avenue for future research is to select different samples; possibilities are choosing (i) other BI scholars of the founding generation, and/ or (ii) scholars of younger generations. Another avenue is to select samples that provide insights from outside the community (e.g., scholars from other disciplines such as business administration or computer science). Moreover, it could be a fruitful avenue for future research to extend the focus of the investigation from '*who* says *what*' to '*who* says *what*, and *why*.' Because the entire data set underlying this article is published in Heinrich (2011), future research could draw directly upon these data to address this 'why' question.

References

Arazy, O., Kumar, N. and Shapira, B. (2010). A Theory-Driven Design Framework for Social Recommender Systems, *Journal of the Association for Information Systems* 11(9): 455–490.

Ardelt, R.G. (2011). Geschichte der Wirtschaftsinformatik: Ein Instrument kritischer Selbstreflexion? Working Paper, Johannes Kepler University Linz.

Argarwal, R. and Lucas, H.C. (2005). The Information Systems Identity Crisis: Focusing on high-visibility and high-impact research, *MIS Quarterly* 29(3): 381–398.

Back, A. (2001). *Lexikon der Wirtschaftsinformatik*, 4th edn, Berlin: Springer.

Barros, C.A. (1998). *Autobiography: Narrative of transformation*, Michigan: University of Michigan Press.

Baskerville, R., Lyytinen, K., Sambamurthy, V. and Straub, D. (2011). A Response to the Design-oriented Information Systems Research Memorandum, *European Journal of Information Systems* 20(1): 11–15.

Benbasat, I. and Zmud, R.W. (1999). Empirical Research in Information Systems: The practice of relevance, *MIS Quarterly* 23(1): 3–16.

Benbasat, I. and Zmud, R.W. (2003). The Identity Crisis within the IS Discipline: Defining and communicating the discipline's core properties, *MIS Quarterly* 27(2): 183–194.

BIFOA (1969). Zweites Memorandum Betriebsinformatik und Wirtschaftsinformatik als notwendige anwendungsbezogene Ergänzung einer Allgemeinen Informatik, *elektronische datenverarbeitung* **11**(11): 544–548 (Reprinted in *Wirtschaftsinformatik* 2009, 51(1): 104–109).

Briggs, R.O. (2006). On Theory-driven Design and Deployment of Collaboration Systems, *International Journal of Human-Computer Studies* **64**(7): 573–582.

Buhl, H.U., Müller, G., Fridgen, G. and Röglinger, M. (2012). Business and Information Systems Engineering: A complementary approach to information systems – What we can learn from the past and may conclude from present reflection on the future, *Journal of the Association for Information Systems* **13**(4): 236–253.

Campbell-Kelly, M. (2009). Origin of Computing, *Scientific American* **301**(3): 62–69.

Carr, E.H. (1961). *What is History?* Cambridge: University of Cambridge & Penguin Books.

Carroll, J.M. (1997). Human-Computer Interaction: Psychology as a science of design, *Annual Review of Psychology* **48**: 61–83.

Chandler, A.D.Jr. (2009). History and Management Practice and Thought: An autobiography, *Journal of Management History* **15**(3): 236–260.

Chen, W.S. and Hirschheim, R. (2004). A Paradigmatic and Methodological Examination of Information Systems Research from 1991–2001, *Information Systems Journal* **14**(3): 197–235.

Cortada, J.W. (2004). How Did Computing Go Global? The Need for an Answer and a Research Agenda, *IEEE Annals of the History of Computing* **26**(1): 53–58.

Cortada, J.W. (2008). Patterns and Practices in How Information Technology Spread around the World, *IEEE Annals of the History of Computing* **30**(4): 4–25.

Davenport, T.H. and Markus, M.L. (1999). Rigor *vs* Relevance Revisited: Response to Benbasat and Zmud, *MIS Quarterly* **23**(1): 19–23.

Denning, P.J. (2005). Is Computer Science Science? *Communications of the ACM* **48**(4): 27–31.

Diebold, J. (1952). *Automation: The advent of the automatic factory*, Princeton: Van Nostrand.

Frank, U., Buhl, H.U., König, W., Krcmar, H., Mertens, P., Zmud, B. and Klein, H.K. (1997). German Perspectives on Information Systems: Research topics, methodological challenges, and patterns of exchange with IS practice, *ICIS 1997 Proceedings*, Paper 75.

Frank, U., Schauer, C. and Wigand, R. (2008). Different Paths of Development of Two Information Systems Communities: A comparative study based on peer interviews, *Communications of the Association for Information Systems* **22**(21): 391–412.

Gregor, S. and Jones, D. (2007). The Anatomy of a Design Theory, *Journal of the Association for Information Systems* **8**(5): 312–335.

Grochla, E. (1966). *Automation und Organisation*, Wiesbaden: Gabler.

Hall, E.C. (2000). From the Farm to Pioneering with Digital Control Computers: An autobiography, *IEEE Annals of the History of Computing* **22**(2): 22–31.

Hartmann, B. (1961). *Betriebswirtschaftliche Grundlagen der Automatisierten Datenverarbeitung*, Freiburg i. Br.: Haufe.

Heilmann, H. and Heinrich, L.J. (2006). Erkenntnisobjekte der Wirtschaftsinformatik, *HMD – Praxis der Wirtschaftsinformatik* **43**(250): 99–108.

Heinrich, L.J. (1975). Zum wissenschaftlichen Standort einer Betriebs- und Verwaltungsinformatik, *Angewandte Informatik* **17**(7): 265–268.

Heinrich, L.J. (1986). Wirtschaftsinformatik in Forschung und Ausbildung, *Information Management* **1**(1): 63–69.

Heinrich, L.J. (1988). Zeittafel zur Entwicklung der Wirtschaftsinformatik, in L. J. Heinrich and K. Kurbel (eds.) *Studien- und Forschungsführer Wirtschaftsinformatik*, 3rd edn, Berlin *et al*.: Springer, pp. 50–54.

Heinrich, L.J. (1992). Zeittafel zur Entwicklung der Wirtschaftsinformatik, in P. Mertens *et al*. (eds.) *Studien- und Forschungsführer Wirtschaftsinformatik*, 4th edn, Berlin *et al*.: Springer, pp. 63–68.

Heinrich, L.J. (1996). Geschichte der Wirtschaftsinformatik, in P. Mertens, D. Ehrenberg, J. Griese, L. J. Heinrich, K. Kurbel and P. Stahlknecht (eds.) *Studienführer Wirtschaftsinformatik*, Braunschweig/Wiesbaden: Vieweg, pp. 48–53.

Heinrich, L.J. (1999). Geschichte der Wirtschaftsinformatik, in P. Mertens, D. Ehrenberg, P. Chamoni. J. Griese, L.J. Heinrich and K. Kurbel (eds.) *Studienführer Wirtschaftsinformatik*, 2nd edn, Braunschweig/Wiesbaden: Vieweg, pp. 47–52.

Heinrich, L.J. (2002). Geschichte der Wirtschaftsinformatik, in P. Mertens, P. Chamoni, D. Ehrenberg, L. J. Heinrich, K. Kurbel (eds.) *Studienführer Wirtschaftsinformatik*, 3rd edn, Braunschweig/Wiesbaden: Vieweg, pp. 45–52.

Heinrich, L.J. (2005). Forschungsmethodik einer Integrationsdisziplin: Ein Beitrag zur Geschichte der Wirtschaftsinformatik, *NTM – Internationale Zeitschrift für Geschichte und Ethik der Naturwissenschaften, Technik und Medizin* **13**(2): 104–117.

Heinrich, L.J. (2011). *Geschichte der Wirtschaftsinformatik: Entstehung und Entwicklung einer Wissenschaftsdisziplin*, Heidelberg *et al*.: Springer.

Heinrich, L.J., Heinzl, A. and Riedl, R. (2011). *Wirtschaftsinformatik – Einführung und Grundlegung*, 4th edn, Heidelberg *et al*.: Springer.

Hirschheim, R. and Klein, H.K. (2003). Crisis in the IS Field? A Critical Reflection on the State of the Discipline, *Journal of the Association for Information Systems* **4**(10): 237–293.

Khazanchi, D. and Munkvold, B.E. (2000). Is Information Systems a Science? An Inquiry into the Nature of the Information Systems Discipline, *The DATA BASE for Advances in Information Systems* **31**(3): 24–42.

King, J.L. and Lyytinen, K. (2004). Reach and Grasp, *MIS Quarterly* **28**(4): 539–551.

Klein, H.K. and Hirschheim, R. (2008). The Structure of the IS Discipline Reconsidered: Implications and reflections from a community of practice perspective, *Information and Organization* **18**(4): 280–302.

König, W., Heinzl, A. and Poblotzki, A.von (1995). Die zentralen Forschungsgegenstände der Wirtschaftsinformatik in den nächsten zehn Jahren, *Wirtschaftsinformatik* **37**(6): 558–569.

König, W., Heinzl, A., Rumpf, M.-J. and Poblotzki, A.von (1996). Zur Entwicklung der Forschungsmethoden und Theoriekerne der Wirtschaftsinformatik: Eine kombinierte Delphi- und AHP-Untersuchung, in H. Heilmann, L.J. Heinrich and F. Roithmayr (eds.) *Information Engineering*, München/Wien: Oldenbourg, pp. 35–65.

Krippendorff, K. (2004). *Content Analysis: Introduction to its methodology*, 2nd edn, Thousand Oaks/CA: Sage Publications.

Krusenstjern, B. von (1994). Was sind Selbstzeugnisse? Begriffskritische und quellenkundliche Überlegungen anhand von Beispielen aus dem 17. Jahrhundert, *Historische Anthropologie/Kultur, Gesellschaft, Alltag* **2**(2): 462–471.

Kurbel, K. (ed.) (1993). *Wirtschaftsinformatik '93: Innovative Anwendungen, Technologie, integration*, Berlin *et al*.: Springer.

Kurbel, K., Brenner, W., Chamoni, P., Frank, U., Mertens, P. and Roithmayr, F. (eds.) (2009). *Studienführer Wirtschaftsinformatik 2009/2010*, Wiesbaden: Gabler.

Land, F. (2000). The First Business Computer: A case study in user-driven innovation, *IEEE Annals of the History of Computing* 22(3): 16–26.

Land, F. (2010). The Use of History in IS research: An opportunity missed, *Journal of Information Technology* 25(4): 385–394.

Lee, A.S. (1999). Rigor and Relevance in MIS Research: Beyond the approach of positivism alone, *MIS Quarterly* 23(1): 293–307.

Leimbach, T. (2008). The SAP Story: Evolution of SAP within the German software industry, *IEEE Annals of the History of Computing* 30(4): 60–76.

Lejeune, P. (1989). *On Autobiography*, Minnesota: University of Minnesota Press.

Liebowitz, S.J. and Margolis, S.E. (1995). Path Dependence, Lock-in, and History, *Journal of Law, Economics and Organization* 11(1): 205–226.

Lyytinen, K. and King, J.L. (2006). The Theoretical and Academic Legitimacy: A response to Professor Weber, *Journal of the Association for Information Systems* 7(11): 714–721.

Mahoney, J. (2000). Path Dependence in Historical Sociology, *Theory and Society* 29(4): 507–548.

Mahoney, M.S. (2005). The Histories of Computing(s), *Interdisciplinary Science Reviews* 30(2): 119–135.

March, S.T. and Smith, G.F. (1995). Design and Natural Science Research on Information Technology, *Decision Support Systems* 15(4): 251–266.

Markus, M.L., Majchrzak, A. and Gasser, L. (2002). A Design Theory for Systems That Support Emergent Knowledge Processes, *MIS Quarterly* 26(3): 179–212.

Mason, R.O., KcKenney, J.L. and Copeland, D.G. (1997a). An Historical Method for MIS Research: Steps and assumptions, *MIS Quarterly* 21(3): 307–320.

Mason, R.O., KcKenney, J.L. and Copeland, D.G. (1997b). Developing an Historical Tradition in MIS Research, *MIS Quarterly* 21(3): 257–278.

Mertens, P. (1966). *Die zwischenbetriebliche Kooperation und Integration bei der automatisierten Datenverarbeitung*, Meisenheim am Glan: Hain.

Mertens, P. (1995). Wirtschaftsinformatik – Von den Moden zum trend, in König W. (ed.) *Wirtschaftsinformatik '95, Wettbewerbsfähigkeit – Innovation – Wirtschaftlichkeit*, Heidelberg *et al*: Springer, pp. 25–64.

Neustadt, R.E. and May, E.R. (1986). *Thinking in Time: The uses of history for decision makers*, New York: The Free Press.

Newell, A. and Simon, H.A. (1976). Computer Science as Empirical Inquiry: Symbols and search, *Communications of the ACM* 19(3): 113–126.

Österle, H., Becker, J., Frank, U., Hess, T., Karagiannis, D., Krcmar, H., Loos, P., Mertens, P., Oberweis, A. and Sinz, E.J. (2011). Memorandum on Design-oriented Information Systems Research, *European Journal of Information Systems* 20(1): 7–10.

Polanyi, M. (1958). *Personal Knowledge: Towards a post-critical philosophy*, Chicago: University of Chicago Press.

Resch, A. and Schlögl, C. (2004). Die Wirtschaftsinformatik aus der Sicht ihres Hauptpublikationsorgans: Eine szientometrische Analyse der Zeitschrift Wirtschaftsinformatik/Angewandte Informatik, *Wirtschaftsinformatik* 46(4): 302–310.

Schlombs, C. (2010). Productivity Machines: Transatlantic transfers of computing technology and culture in the cold war, Dissertations available from ProQuest. Paper AAI3414208.

Simon, H.A. (1996). *The Sciences of the Artificial*, 3rd edn, Massachusetts, MIT Press.

Stahlknecht, P. and Hasenkamp, U. (2010). *Einführung in die Wirtschaftsinformatik*, 12th edn, Berlin *et al.*: Springer.

Steininger, K., Riedl, R., Roithmayr, F. and Mertens, P. (2009). Fads and Trends in Business and Information Systems Engineering and Information Systems Research: A comparative literature analysis, *Business & Information Systems Engineering* 1(6): 411–428.

Szyperski, N. and Müller-Böling, D. (1981). Zur technologischen Orientierung der empirischen Forschung, in E. Witte (ed.) *Der praktische Nutzen empirischer Forschung*, Tübingen: Mohr, pp. 159–188.

Walls, J.G., Widmeyer, G.R. and El Sawy, O.A. (1992). Building an Information System Design Theory for Vigilant EIS, *Information Systems Research* 3(1): 36–59.

Walsham, G. (1995). The Emergence of Interpretivism in IS Research, *Information Systems Research* 6(4): 376–394.

Walsham, G. (2006). Doing Interpretive Research, *European Journal of Information Systems* 15(3): 320–330.

Weber, R. (1987). Toward a Theory of Artifacts: A paradigmatic base for information systems research, *Journal of Information Systems* 1(2): 3–19.

Weber, R. (2006). Reach and Grasp in the Debate over the IS Core: An empty hand? *Journal of the Association for Information Systems* 7(10): 703–713.

Wilde, T. and Hess, T. (2007). Forschungsmethoden der Wirtschaftsinformatik: Eine empirische Untersuchung, *Wirtschaftsinformatik* 49(4): 280–287.

Wilson, F. (2000). *The Logic and Methodology of Science and Pseudoscience*, Toronto: Canadian Scholars Press.

Winter, R., Krcmar, H., Sinz, E.J., Zelewski, S. and Hevner, A.R. (2009). What in Fact is Fundamental Research in Business and Information Systems Engineering, *Business & Information Systems Engineering* 1(2): 192–198.

WKWI, (ed.) (1994). Profil der Wirtschaftsinformatik, *Wirtschaftsinformatik* 36(1): 80–82.

Wohlgenannt, R. (1969). *Was ist Wissenschaft?*, Braunschweig: Vieweg.

Wulf, W.A. (1995). Are We Scientists or Engineers? *ACM Computing Surveys* 27(1): 55–57.

23

Analysing Business Losses Caused by Information Systems Risk: A Business Process Analysis Approach

Hannu Salmela
Turku School of Economics, Information Systems Science, Finland

Introduction

The widespread use of computers has enabled both private and public organisations to streamline their operative and managerial processes. Simultaneously, the new processes have become critically dependent on information systems (IS) and IS have become a significant operational risk to these organisations. Increased complexity of systems themselves, combined with increased penetration of computers in user organisations, means that the nature of threats and consequences is more diverse than ever. Systematic analysis of IS risk has become both more significant and more difficult.

Because the phenomenon as such is not new, well-established methods for investigating IS risks exist. The traditional approach to analysis begins with a systematic review of threats, vulnerabilities and risks in the computerised information systems (Stewart, 2004). Auditing provides methods to assess whether the organisation has sufficiently protected its systems against these threats (Eloff and von Solms, 2000; Nearon, 2000; Stevenson-Smith, 2004). Sophisticated methods can be employed to calculate probabilities for individual systems risks and potential business losses (Pate-Cornell, 1996; Baskerville and Portougal, 2003). Return on Security Investments techniques assist in comparing the cost of investing in additional protection with the savings that are achieved through such investments (Gordon and Loeb, 2002; Baskerville and Portougal, 2003; Cavusoglu *et al.*, 2004). These methods constitute the primary means through which IS professionals and auditors have identified and reduced IS risks.

The focus in this paper is on the methods that can be used to analyse potential business losses in the user organisation resulting from IS risk. It is argued that in addition to the traditional technology-centred analyses, companies need to employ business analysis methods to provide a more comprehensive view about potential business losses in the user organisations. Reports from these analyses can support traditional analysis in identifying potential consequences in the user organisation. Perhaps more importantly, such reports can be used to inform business managers and owners about the potential business losses that IS risks can cause for their company.

This paper reviewed prior literature in order to identify methods that can be used to systematically analyse losses in the user organisation. Methods such as Labour Cost Analysis (Toigo, 1989; Stevenson-Smith, 2004), Lost Profit Analysis (Stevenson-Smith, 2004), Information Asset Value Analysis (Palmer *et al.*, 2001), Business Process Analysis (Mooney *et al.*, 1996; Kettinger *et al.*, 1997; Macfarlane and Rudd, 2005) and Stock Market Reaction Analysis (Garg *et al.*, 2003a, b) all provide estimates of potential business losses resulting from information availability, integrity, confidentiality and/or authenticity problems. The methods are, however, usually published in practitioner-oriented computer or information security journals. In particular, if compared to the vast amount of literature on the causes for IS risks, the attention to the analysis of potential losses is very limited.

One reason for limited attention to the analysis of losses may be that the background theories required in traditional *vs* business loss-oriented analyses are fundamentally different. The research on threats, vulnerabilities and security methods is based on the traditions and theories of computer science and rigorous mathematical models. The analysis of diverse adverse consequences in the user organisations, however, requires organisational and business analysis skills and the employment of methods and theories drawn from social sciences. Hence, the latter topic would be better positioned in IS research than in computer science-oriented IS security research. IS science has, however, been slow in recognising the analysis of potential business losses as a legitimate research topic (Ciborra, 2004).

In this study, action research was applied to examine the potential of using business process analysis as a method to associate information availability risk with adverse business consequences and losses. The analysis was carried out in two different companies, one operating in the forest industry and the other one in the finance sector. In both cases, key business processes were identified and described. These business process descriptions were used for interviewing users and assessing the business consequences of computer breakdowns. Both studies produced a risk report that identified and described the adverse consequences of IS risks in the client company's core business processes. The results from these two studies suggest that business process analysis assisted in making business managers more aware of part of the business risks caused by systems risks.

This paper begins with a review of IS risks and the traditional methods used in managing these risks. It then continues to review prior literature on methods that can be employed to systematically evaluate potential business losses. The uses of reports from both traditional and business loss-oriented analyses are discussed in order to illustrate ways how analyses in the user organisation complement traditional analyses. The paper then continues to describe the method used in this study, the nature of risk findings in the two empirical cases, and the immediate feedback that was received. The contribution of business loss centred methods to prior methods is discussed in the contributions for research section. In addition, contributions for practice and suggestions for further research are presented.

From systems risk to business losses

Systems risk has been defined as the uncertainty related to using computer-based systems for delivering information (Straub and Welke, 1998). It can be broadly construed to mean modification, destruction, theft or lack of availability of computer assets, such as hardware, software, data, records and files. Causes for systems risk can vary from natural disasters to intentional abuse of computers by own employees or external parties. Like the definitions of risk in general, also systems risk comprises two dimensions: (1) the probability associated with an undesirable event, and (2) the adverse consequences (usually financial) of the occurrence of this event (Barki *et al.*, 1993; Straub and Welke, 1998). In this article, the latter dimension is also referred to as business loss.

Systems security risk has been defined as 'the risk that the firm's information and/or IS are not sufficiently protected against certain kind of damage or loss' (Straub and Welke, 1998). Technology itself provides solutions to prevent, detect, respond to and support recovery from systems risk. Passwords, media backup and virus protection software are examples of commonly used technical measures (Whitman, 2003). Administrative security measures can be used to restrict the behaviour of IS professionals and users so that sufficient level of IS security can be guaranteed (Straub and Welke, 1998; Tryfonas *et al.*, 2001).

Information risk refers to the threat for the authenticity, confidentiality, integrity and availability of business information and documents (Gordon and Loeb, 2002). The pervasive role of computers in current enterprises has made the technology itself a major threat for business information and documents. Ensuring reliable processing of information in computerised systems is naturally essential for reducing these risks. Information risks do, however, comprise also traditional risks related to how employees discuss corporate affairs and manage printed documents (Dhillon, 2004; Stewart, 2004).

Business loss, as used in this article, refers to the negative business consequences that follow from a realised system risk. While some of the losses are easily expressed in monetary terms, there are also losses that are difficult to quantify. The exact content of potential business losses has not been a primary interest in prior research. Some researchers have, however, considered the nature of business losses in more detail as a secondary task in their research when formulating questionnaires or checklists for managers. Table 23.1 lists typical business losses that prior research has associated with systems risks (Moulton and Moulton, 1996; Straub and Welke, 1998; Stevenson-Smith, 2004).

The categories listed in Table 23.1 are not necessarily exhaustive. Still, even these nine categories reflect the diverse nature of potential negative consequences. In principle, a single realised systems risk, for example, a mistake in the IS service provider side, can result to losses in all categories.

Table 23.1 Categories of business losses

#1 Operative business losses (additional labour, material or capital cost)
#2 Lost revenues due to problems in operative or customer service processes
#3 Opportunity losses or costs resulting from wrong management decisions
#4 Competitive losses resulting from theft of confidential information
#5 Business losses resulting from theft of money or goods
#6 Company image losses: losses resulting from negative media exposure
#7 Shareholder losses: negative impact on company's share price
#8 Losses resulting from legal processes and punishments against the company
#9 IT losses: lost value of IT assets or significant unbudgeted IT costs

---

Analysis of systems risks

The traditional approach to the analysis of IS risk begins with a systematic analysis of vulnerabilities and threats. Literature provides several exhaustive lists of typical threats and vulnerabilities related to the use of computers (Loch *et al.*, 1992; Neumann, 1995; Whitman, 2003). In order to cover all threats and vulnerabilities, the analysis typically comprises both the technical infrastructure and the IS service, development and use processes (Toigo, 1989; Loch *et al.*, 1992; Collins and Mathews, 1993; DeMaio, 1995; Fitzgerald, 1995; Kokolakis *et al.*, 2000; Im and Baskerville, 2005).

The analysis of whether the company has built sufficient protection against threats is typically made in audits. To ensure completeness of audits, the internal auditors and IS managers can not only draw from well-established codes of practice (Royal Canadian Mounted Police, 1981; British Standard Institution, 1993) but also from information security policy frameworks, baselines and checklists suggested in research (Fitzgerald, 1995; Moulton and Moulton, 1996; Palmer *et al.*, 2001; Vermeulen and von Solms, 2002). IS managers can also invite external IT auditors, certification professionals or rating agents from insurance companies to critically assess their security policies and measures (Eloff and von Solms, 2000; Nearon, 2000; Stevenson-Smith, 2004).

In order to estimate the likelihood of risk, the analysis can employ mathematical models of risk probabilities (Pate-Cornell, 1996). Analysts can choose from different treatments of risk (e.g. probabilistic or deterministic methods) depending on the completeness of historical information that exist for estimating uncertainties (Pate-Cornell, 1996). They may also choose between different levels of sophistication of uncertainties (Pate-Cornell, 1996). The use of possibility measures instead of probabilistic expressions may provide a more sensible method for cases where historical data is very limited (Baskerville and Portougal, 2003).

Finally, the analysis may comprise economic modelling, which also addresses the problem of estimating losses. The idea behind economic modelling is to identify the potential risks, expected losses and their likelihoods and to compute the expected loss (Cavusoglu *et al.*, 2004). Decision trees can provide a framework for analysing the role of risk factors and the sensitivity of final outcomes. Return on Security Investment (ROSI) analysis provides rigorous methods for making comparisons in situations when additional security investments are considered (Gordon and Loeb, 2002; Baskerville and Portougal, 2003; Cavusoglu *et al.*, 2004). ROSI analysis requires estimates about the reduced probability for systems risk and business loss if a security investment is made. Accounting techniques, such as internal rate of return and net present value, can be used to compare initial security investments with the reduction in expected business losses in future years (Gordon and Loeb, 2002).

These methods provide sound principles for chief information officer's (CIOs), IS professionals and IT auditors to manage IS risks. Growing awareness of both risks related to complex IT infrastructures and to the significance of potential business losses has resulted in the increased use of these methods. The main response to mandatory requirements stated by Sarbanes–Oxley and Basel documents in the banking sector has been a more intensified use of traditional risk analysis methods (Damianides, 2005).

The ability of traditional methods to establish an overall view of potential consequences in the user organisation is, however, limited (Ciborra, 2004; Stewart, 2004). Increased complexity of IT infrastructures means that even in a medium-sized organisation the number of potential vulnerabilities and threats is often calculated in hundreds (Stewart, 2004). Developing an overall view of potential adverse consequences in the user organisation by projecting the consequences of each identified risk is usually not a feasible option. Limiting the analysis to high-probability risks hides low–probability–high-impact risks (Renn, 1998; Ciborra, 2004). Hence, prior research has called for holistic methods that analyse risks from the perspective of business operations instead of technology (Olson, 2005).

Analysis of business losses

The interest in this paper is in methods that assist systematic analysis of potential losses in the user organisation. Rather than looking at specific risks in computerised environment and in security measures, such analysis starts from the level of information risks. The point of departure in the analysis is that the availability, integrity, confidentiality or authenticity of information can be violated. The objective and the challenge for the analyst is to identify the diverse business losses (e.g. operative, competitive, legal and managerial consequences and losses) that such violation can cause in the user organisation.

Even the traditional methods assume some analysis of potential losses. This is, however, the part that is generally perceived as difficult. In methods like ROSI, the challenge is not only the estimation of loss probabilities, or the correct use of accounting techniques and metrics, but also the identification of the actual losses. One article summarises the problems of economic models by saying that they can only be imperfectly applied to computer security because one has to wrestle with defining what is meant by the notion of 'return'.

In research, systematic analysis of potential business losses has, however, received only modest attention. Prior research has created a rich picture about potential vulnerabilities and threats. In comparison to this, the other side of risk – the estimation of financial consequences of risks – has received very limited attention. The methods described below, published usually in practitioner-oriented computer or information security journals, illustrate typical approaches that have been employed in different settings.

Labour cost analysis provides a simple and widely used method for analysing business losses associated with systems risks (Stevenson-Smith, 2004). The analysis comprises both the extra time needed from IT employees in recovering the systems (e.g. after a hack attack) and the lost worker productivity during the time when company operations were diminished or shut down. The business loss is evaluated by calculating the average overtime salary of all IS employees and users (Toigo, 1989). While such calculations are simple to make and they produce compelling figures, business managers may question the logic used. The relationship between systems shutdown and labour cost is rarely as straightforward as the formula assumes. Furthermore, managers might believe the potential indirect costs – for example, customer dissatisfaction and missed sales inquiries – to be more significant. Nevertheless, labour cost analysis provides the primary means to evaluate additional labour costs, which often represents a significant proportion of total loss.

Lost profits analysis can be used to estimate part of the intangible losses resulting from systems risk (Stevenson-Smith, 2004). A crash of a web-site or problems in point-of-sale systems can lead to a situation where customers cannot place new orders or make purchases. By using statistics from marketing and sales databases it is possible to provide an estimate of lost sales and profits associated with the incident. However, the long-term losses resulting from negative media exposure and customer inconvenience are usually impossible to quantify.

Information asset value analysis aims to classify information assets relative to their criticality, sensitivity and value to the organisation. A typical result is the classification of information according to a predefined typology, for example, restricted, confidential, internal use only and public (Palmer *et al.*, 2001). The classification is normally based on an analysis of consequences of confidentiality violations for each information asset. In terms of business losses, the primary emphasis is on IT losses, competitive losses and/or legal processes that can result if confidential information is lost or stolen (Stevenson-Smith, 2004). In addition to information assets, the value of hardware and software can also be included in such analysis (Kokolakis *et al.*, 2000).

Business process analysis is a widely used technique in the field IS. It is commonly used, for instance, in IS development projects to reengineer user processes, to define user requirements for new systems, to guide systems configuration in ERP implementation projects and to measure the business benefits associated with implementing new IS (Mooney *et al.*, 1996; Kettinger *et al.*, 1997). Business process analysis, or transaction walkthrough, is also one of the methods that auditors frequently use to identify threats and vulnerabilities in the IS use processes (Collins and Millen, 1995; DeMaio, 1995; Kokolakis *et al.*, 2000).

The Information Technology Infrastructure Library, and its description of 'business impact analysis', provides a good overall prescription for the use of business process analysis in the analysis of losses. Business Impact Analysis constitutes the first phase in the IT Service Continuity Management process and it is recommended to be done before risk assessment and formulation of business continuity strategy (Leopoldi, 2002; Macfarlane and Rudd, 2005). It should comprise the identification of critical business processes, and the potential damage or loss that may be caused to the organisation resulting from a disruption to those processes. The process should result in identification of, for example, the form the loss or damage will take, the escalation of damage with time following an incident, the minimum staffing and facilities and services needed to enable business processes to continue to operate at a minimum acceptable level (Department of Trade and Industry, 2007).

Literature provides only few descriptions of the use of business process analysis to identify losses. Research on health care IS provides two cases that report the use of systematic business process analysis to detect potential adverse consequences resulting from IS risks. A study conducted by Smith and Eloff (2002) applied process techniques to assess IT risks in hospital operations. The assessment identified critical patient routes in a health care institution and assigned risk values for each phase along a specific patient route. Another study, also in health care context, investigated whether information delivery problems can lead to longer queues and/or adverse events for patients (Lederman, 2004; Lederman, 2005).

Stock market reaction analysis is a relatively new approach for estimating the financial impact of IT security breaches (Ott, 2003; Garg *et al.*,

2003a, b; Hovav and D'Arcy, 2004). The basic assumption is that if the stock markets are efficient, then all present and future effects of a publicly reported security breach are captured in stock price. By using event-study methodologies to analyse the stock prices after public reporting of security breaches, researchers have been able to show that the actual losses on a per-incident basis are substantially greater (e.g. $17 and 28$ million per incident) than previous studies indicate. The results also capture genuine heterogeneity in market reaction to different types of information breaches (Garg *et al.*, 2003a). The analysis establishes a connection between public exposure of realised systems risk and the negative impact of such exposure on company's share price.

Table 23.2 provides a summary of methods documented in prior research. While each of these methods produces estimates about potential business losses, they are different in terms of assumptions about information risks, the content of analysis and the nature of business losses detected.

A common feature in the methods is that none of them requires an in-depth analysis of vulnerabilities in the computerised environment. The analysis starts from information risks and proceeds to the analysis of their consequences in the business environment. Labour cost, lost sales and business process analyses focus primarily on losses resulting from information availability problems. Both information asset value analysis and stock market reaction analysis address losses resulting from information confidentiality problems. Current methods do not, however, provide much support for an analyst who is trying to address losses resulting from potential information integrity or authenticity problems.

The actual analysis of events in the user organisation is based on organisational and/or economic analyses. In the Labour Cost and Lost Sales Analyses, calculation of losses is based on a few summary figures, for example, the amount of users or business sales volumes. An obvious advantage is that the analyses are fairly easy to make. Information Asset Value Analysis starts from comprehensive identification of information assets, which provide a natural basis for identifying potential losses. Business Process Analysis and Stock Market Reaction Analysis are both based on applying well-established analysis methods to the analysis of losses. Business process analysis is a common organisational analysis method. Event-study method, on the other hand, has been used extensively in management science and finance to measure the impact of various corporate events on shareholder value.

In terms of detecting potential losses, none of the methods appear to be sufficient alone, but in combination the methods cover most of the

Table 23.2 Assumptions about risks and losses in loss evaluation methods (shaded area represents the method employed in this study)

	Labour cost analysis	Lost profit analysis	Information asset value analysis	Business process analysis	Stock market analysis
Information risk that causes losses	Information availability problem	Information availability problem	Information confidentiality problem	Information availability problem	Information confidentiality problem (and its public exposure)
Content of analysis	Estimation of the number of users affected by computer problems and calculation of associated labour cost	Estimation of sales volumes, that is, number of orders that are typically placed in a given time frame	Analysis and classification of organization's business documents and other information assets	Analysis of information use in different phases of the process, identification of consequences in each step	Analysis of stock market reaction on public exposure of a realised risk
Category of business losses detected	Reports potential for losses in user productivity (#1) and extra time of IS personnel (#9)	Reports potential for lost revenues due to missed sales (#2)	Reports potential for operative losses (#1) competitive losses (#4) losses resulting from legal processes (#8), and losses in the value of computer assets (#9).	Reports potential for operative losses (#1) and lost sales (#2)	Reports potential for shareholder value losses (#7). Share price also reflects the damage to company image (#6)
Advantage	Easy to use: estimate of losses is easy to calculate	Easy to use: estimate of losses is easy to calculate	Comprehensive: can potentially addresses all risks, all information assets and all potential losses	Focused and detailed: a detailed view of potential losses in core business processes; losses reported in a framework that managers are familiar with.	Convincing: provides an evidence based figure of potential shareholder loss
Limitation	Labour cost is only one potential loss	Direct lost sales is only one potential loss	Time consuming due to large number of information assets and processes where each asset is used	Omits losses in other processes than those selected to analysis	Analysis does not address organization's own risks/losses; limited to risks that receive attention in media

potential losses. Only two types of business losses identified in Table 23.1 are not mentioned in the bottom row of Table 23.2. These are the losses resulting from poor management decisions (#3) and the financial losses resulting from theft of money or goods (#5). Problems with information integrity, for example, can certainly cause such losses. Hence, there appears to be large areas where the risk analyst has little support from systematic analysis methods. It seems reasonable to conclude, that our methods to analyse events and consequences in the user organisations when computer systems fail are limited.

The use of business loss analysis results

As any organisational analysis, also the analysis of potential losses caused by IS risk requires time, skills and resources. Hence, also the analysis of business losses has to be justified. Because such analyses are not frequently conducted, the analyst should also know the purposes for which such analyses should be made and to whom the results should be reported.

The need for systematic analyses of IS risks depends on organisational context and the needs of the decision makers. When the overall cost of computer reliability and security is relatively small and potential business impact is limited, decisions regarding IT reliability and security can be taken by IS and security professionals. Companies can treat risk management as an overhead and allocate a defined amount of money to be spent. Then the question is reduced to 'what is the most I can get for $X' (Cavusoglu *et al.*, 2004). They can also compare their own systems management solutions with those employed by its peers (Stewart, 2004). Fear, uncertainty and doubt has also been used for years to justify investments to security (Cavusoglu *et al.*, 2004; Stewart, 2004).

In organisations, where IS risk is high, the analysts should consider employing several methods in order to provide different summaries of risk to different groups (Table 23.3). Traditional risk analyses serve the IS professionals and auditors in identifying information risks and in evaluating whether their organisation has developed sufficient protection against such risks. The way how the results of these analyses should be used is fairly well established.

Systematic analyses of potential losses in the user organisation can complement the overall image that IS managers and auditors have about IS risk. IS and security organisation often have little visibility to business processes in the user departments (Stewart, 2004). It is easier to estimate direct costs within the IS function than to create an understanding of

Table 23.3 Comparison of information systems risk analysis methods (shaded area represents the focus of this study)

Nature of risk	Systems risk	Systems security risk	Information risk	Business risk	Shareholder risk
Key questions	What are the main threats and their probabilities?	Should we invest on additional security?	Can critical information be affected?	How can our business operations be affected?	How can the company's share price be affected?
Methods employed	Checklists, probability analysis techniques, decision tree techniques	IT security analysis, codes of practice, ROSI	Information asset value analysis	Labour cost analysis, Lost sales analysis, Business process analysis	Stock market reaction analysis
Key users of reports	Technical specialists, IT managers	Security professionals, IT auditors	Chief information officers, business managers, auditors	Business managers, senior managers, auditors	Board of shareholders, senior managers, auditors
Mechanism to reduce risk and/or loss	Directing attention to most significant risks	Design of technical and administrative controls	Design of information security policies	Design of business processes; use of insurance and penalty clauses to reduce losses	Informing and influencing senior management and the board of shareholders

the variety of potential losses that can emerge in the business functions where IS are being used. In large companies with information infrastructures that serve thousands of users, IS professionals can hardly be aware of all the business impacts and consequences that a realised IS risks can have in the user organisation. In this respect, traditional analyses and business loss-oriented analyses are complementary.

Reports that document potential business losses in the user departments should, however, be delivered also to new stakeholder groups such as shareholders, senior management and business managers.

Board of shareholders is the highest level where decisions about IT are or should be made (Nolan and McFarlan, 2005). Because IS security professionals have found it difficult to get business managers committed to planning IS security and reliability efforts, reporting to the board of shareholders may seem even more challenging. And still, Sarbanes-Oxley Act requires organisations to analyse their financial reporting processes and systems in order to ensure integrity of financial reports (Damianides, 2005). In the credit and financial sectors, Basel Committee documents pay attention to the integrity of the bank's IS and, for example, to the risks related to centralised or outsourced IT departments (Ciborra, 2004; Basel Committee, 2006). If computers are causing a risk to shareholder value, it seems reasonable that they should get reports about the potential loss they can suffer.

Business managers constitute another user group for reports. Evidence of potential or realised business losses has been used as a lever to move executive management on the issues of computer security (Ott, 2003; Garg *et al.*, 2003a). Public reports on security incidents and losses are one of the means to seek for business management attention and commitment (Ott, 2003). Still, selling corporate management on shouldering the cost of IS security can often be a greater challenge than surmounting the technical problems involved (Toigo, 1989; Straub and Welke, 1998; Palmer *et al.*, 2001).

Business managers have also many concrete tasks and responsibilities that affect both the likelihood of risks and the amount of eventual losses. The overall design of organisational structures, processes, policies and values creates a context that either increases or reduces potential business consequences and losses (Dhillon, 2004). In addition, business managers are also responsible for insurances that can cover part of the business losses. Correct valuation of business losses is also necessary when reporting security incidents to law enforcement authorities and/or insurance companies (Stevenson-Smith, 2004). Systematic reports of potential losses should assist them in performing these tasks.

The need for business managers to be cognisant about potential losses becomes even more explicit in an IS outsourcing relationship. In such relationship, the IS service provider takes the responsibility for reducing the likelihood of risk, but the business losses caused by a realised risk are still carried by the client (Sherwood, 1997; Alner, 2001; Endorf, 2004; Khalfan, 2004). The management of systems risk becomes a joint effort, where the client and the service provider agree on appropriate service levels, penalty clauses and processes for controlling them (Fink, 1994; Sherwood, 1997). In the absence of analysis of potential losses for the client, negotiations about security and reliability measures are dictated by technical considerations that are typically far better mastered by the service provider. The practical significance of systems risks in an IS outsourcing relationship is evident in surveys, where managers both in private and public sector organisations have ranked corporate security and data confidentiality issues as the most significant IS outsourcing risk factor (Collins and Millen, 1995; Khalfan, 2004).

Hence, systematic analyses of potential losses in the user organisation would be useful for many stakeholder groups both in the IS and user organisations. Analysing all the operative, managerial, legal, and competitive impacts and losses that can result from computer problems is a complex and analytically challenging task. Because the task is practically significant and analytically challenging, it should provide an eligible target for research.

Study design

Action research was the investigative methodology in this study. It 'aims to contribute both to the practical concerns of people in an immediate problematic situation and to the goals of social science by joint collaboration within a mutually acceptable ethical framework' (Rapoport, 1970, p. 499). This twofold view of the objectives of action research – to solve a problem for a client and to advance science – is, perhaps, the most fundamental feature of action research (Clark, 1972; Susman and Evered, 1978; Argyris, 1982; Checkland, 1991; Jönsson, 1991; Baskerville, 1999; Baskerville and Myers, 2004).

Action research was selected because of the in-depth and first hand understanding that the researcher can obtain from organisational analysis practices by using it (Benbasat *et al.*, 1987). Furthermore, action research provides an opportunity to learn about practice and alternative ways of carrying it out (Argyris *et al.*, 1987). Hence, action research has been used in developing IS planning and implementation approaches such as ETHICS (Mumford and Weir, 1979), Soft Systems Methodology (Checkland, 1991), Multiview (Wood-Harper, 1985) and Evolutionary Model for IS Strategy (Reponen, 1993).

Thus, the author participated as an external advisor in two IS projects. He did so in conjunction with his position at a Finnish business school. He began working on one project, analysis of potential losses in a paper mill, in 1998. His work on the other similar project in a credit card department of a Nordic bank commenced in 2000. In both projects, the researcher had the two main, action research objectives: (1) to assist in solving a planning problem for the client and (2) to contribute to the ongoing study of the analysis of potential business losses caused by IS risk.

Because action research is a qualitative research method with a small sample size, it is vulnerable to positivist critics (Checkland, 1991). Because it attempts to contribute to practical concerns, it is sometimes confused with applied research or consulting (Jönsson, 1991). However, action research can follow rigorous guidelines.

One action research guideline suggests that action research should follow five phases: diagnosing, action planning, action taking, evaluating and specifying learning (Susman and Evered, 1978; Baskerville, 1999; Baskerville and Myers, 2004). Action researchers are also advised to seek for collaboration, which is based on equal power of the researcher and client (Clark, 1972; Argyris, 1982; Baskerville and Myers, 2004). In the two action research projects, the researcher and the client personnel shared the authority over the process in all five stages (Table 23.4).

The problem diagnosis phases in the two cases involved three companies (Table 23.5). In addition to the actual client organisation, a large IS service provider company was involved in both cases. The IS service provider's interest was to develop methods for the analysis of losses on the client side. The first company, paper mill, was selected because the IS service company was negotiating with the paper company about a possibility to outsource its IS services. Increased reliability was a selling argument, but neither the service provider nor the paper company had a clear understanding about the potential losses that the paper company could save through increased reliability. In the second case, the service provider was negotiating with the credit card department about the renewal of existing IS outsourcing contract. The client wanted to include penalty clauses to the new contract, but setting the amount was made difficult by the fact that neither party knew about the magnitude of potential losses for the client.

Since action researchers are active participants in the organisation, ethical issues need special attention. Researchers should be aware that

Table 23.4 Collaboration with the client in the five action research phases

	Paper mill	Credit card department
Diagnosing	Initial discussions first with the IS service provider and later with the IT manager of the paper mill. Both saw lack of methods to analyse potential business losses as a problem.	A joint meeting that involved representatives of both the credit card department, its IS service provider and the author. Lack of methods to analyse potential business losses for the client was seen as a problem by all parties.
Action planning	Two initial meetings, to define how to analyse losses. Analysis of core process (order to delivery process) was selected as a method to analyse losses.	Two meetings were organised to define the approach for analysis. Analysis of business losses as part of business process analysis.
Action taking	A series of seven interviews in different departments were organised to cover the whole order to delivery process.	A series of five workshops were organised, each workshop had a definite objective and participants from both organisations.
Evaluating	Continuous evaluation of the method. Three feedback meetings, two of them for the paper mill and one for the IS service provider.	Continuous evaluation of the method. One feedback meeting where participants from both organisations were present.
Specifying learning	First loop learning related to understanding of the nature of potential losses in paper mill operations. Second loop learning related to the analysis method used.	First loop learning related to understanding of the nature of potential losses in credit card department operations. Second loop learning related to the analysis method used.

Table 23.5 Presentation of client companies and the IS service provider

Company	Personnel[a]	Annual turnover[a]	Department(s) involved in the analysis
Nordic IS service provider	10.000	1.100 M€	First case: Forest sector in the IT services department Second case: Finance Sector in the IT Services Department and Business Process Competence Centre
Global paper company	19.500	5.900 M€	A paper mill specialised in the production of cardboard
Nordic Bank concern	33.000	5.900 M€	The credit card department of the bank

[a]Figures represent the situation in the year 2000.

in certain circumstances they could align themselves with particular groups who are at odds with other groups (Galliers, 1991; Jönsson, 1991). Perhaps the most significant ethical issue was related to the fact that in both cases, the IS service provider was negotiating with the client and thus both parties had a business interest on the immediate results of the analysis. The more fundamental problem recognised by both parties was, however, that neither party knew, how to analyse potential business losses that could result from systems reliability and availability problems. Development of methods to analyse potential losses in the client organisations was agreed as the primary target for the project. The author was part in this joint development effort, but the contract negotiations were considered as confidential and the author was not expected to be involved in those.

After initial meetings, the projects proceeded to action planning. The choice of business process analysis as the means to analyse losses in the user organisation was a joint decision between the researcher and the participating organisations. Both the IS service provider and the client organisations needed a detailed view of events that result from computer availability problems. Business process analysis appeared to provide a theory-based approach for conducting an analysis in the organisational setting.

One of the principal guidelines for conducting action research is that researchers should make their reasoning explicit and organise it in such a way that it is testable (Argyris, 1982; Checkland, 1991). Action research cases described here used an explicit business process analysis methodology aimed at identifying potential losses caused by IS risk. It prescribes how to analyse organisational environment using structured interviews or collaborative workshops with different stakeholder groups with an objective to deliver a profile of potential business losses that the systems availability risks can cause in the company's core business processes. The analysis method comprised the following stages:

1. The risk assessment began by identifying core business processes of the organisation.
2. A process chart was drawn to identify the main phases in the business process.
3. The potential losses resulting from information availability risks were analysed by asking users in different business process phases to describe the consequences of IS availability problems.
4. The consequences identified in each phase were then summarised in an overall description of potential business losses.
5. The potential losses were evaluated in terms of their likelihood and significance.
6. A risk report was written to describe the most critical negative business consequences that can take place in the analysed business processes.

Hence by using such a methodology, the researcher's reasoning was explicit and organised it in a testable way.

In the action taking phase, the role of the author was to interview users and managers, participate in workshops and assist in the planning and implementation of the business loss analysis project. Personal involvement in the planning process allowed data collection through direct observations, interviews and the review of company documents. The interviews in the first case were tape-recorded. Because the interviews were made in consecutive phases of the order-to-delivery process, the overall image of events and losses was built upon the image received in several interviews. In the latter case, data collection took place in workshops. The results of each workshop were documented and these documents were reviewed in the beginning of next workshop. The feedback seminars and other discussions also revealed some misinterpretations. The client participants also read and commented the case descriptions and this led to some corrections. In both cases, the whole process from initiation to reporting of results took approximately 6 months.

Evaluation comprises an important element in action research. Action researchers are advised to recognise that their theories and prescriptions for action are themselves the product of previously taken action and, therefore, are subject to re-examination and reformulation upon entering every new research situation (Susman and Evered, 1978). To follow this guideline, the loss analysis methods were continuously evaluated and improved during the two cases and improvements were made as needed. In the feedback sessions at the end of the cases, the representatives were asked to suggest improvements to the analysis. In this article, improvements to the method are suggested partly on the basis of previous IS literature and partly on the basis of the experiences in the projects.

According to Jönsson (1991) all action research reports should document the researchers' learning process. Participant learning, on the other hand, should be considered as an important outcome of an action research (Clark, 1972; Argyris, 1982). Because the objective was to develop a new type of analysis method, both the author and the client companies were experimenting something new. The comments from practicing managers were highly valuable for the researcher in evaluating and improving the analysis methods. For managers, first loop learning was related to the nature of business losses resulting from systems availability problems. The second loop of learning for both the researcher and the managers was related to the method itself – how to evaluate potential business losses.

Thus, the author sincerely believes that this paper provides accurate descriptions of the events in the projects and that it adheres to accepted action research guidelines. By meticulously following the guidelines, the contributions of the research are meaningful and useful.

Case 1: Paper mill

The first case organisation was a paper mill in Finland. It produces different types of board for global markets. While the mill is part of a large enterprise with several mills and sales units, it is fairly independent in terms of its operations and IS. Only the sales operating system used for transferring orders from sales units to mills is centralised. Other systems are largely local. The mill has a small IT department that is responsible for all typical IS services, including systems management services.

Problem diagnosis

The agreement to evaluate potential business losses resulting from IS availability risks was made between corporate level IS management of the paper company and the IS service provider with whom the company had been negotiating about a possibility of outsourcing its systems management services. The IS service provider (who financed the study) saw this project as a means to better understand the business benefits of its systems management services in general, and in paper products industry in particular.

For the paper company, the investigation aimed at clarifying the business benefits that could be achieved if the systems management services were to be outsourced. With advanced monitoring tools, the IT service company could monitor the status of different hardware devices, databases and software in a number of mills and other sites. The management team was, however, puzzled about the business benefits that their company would receive from such outsourcing. The corporate CIO expressed the need for the study as follows:

> we'd like to know how we actually benefit if we buy services to monitor those boxes (e.g. multiplexers in local area networks) 24 h a day, 7 days a week?

In broader terms, the managers wanted to know how incidents in IS could influence the core order-to-delivery process in paper mills. It was known, that a failure to identify and remove problems in the mill's technical infrastructure would affect most of the business applications and hence also practically all business processes in the mill. The analysis of all potential adverse consequences was, however, known to be challenging. For this purpose, an independent evaluation was ordered from an IS science department in a business school. The paper company also appointed one of its paper mills to the project.

Action planning

The action planning phase comprised two meetings with the IT manager and IT specialist of the paper mill. The first meeting focused on identifying basic steps in the process, which resulted in drawing of a process diagram about the order-to-delivery process. The diagram described the main phases of the process in chronological order and the organisational units that were responsible for each phase. The second meeting focused on the interview form and to the selection of interviewees and a series of 11 interviews were arranged. The interviews followed the chronological order in order-to-delivery process. Both the IT manager and the IT specialist had made long careers in the paper mill and possessed thorough knowledge about mill operations.

Action taking

The first interview was held with sales management and the last one in the mill warehouse, where the paper is stored before transportation to the harbour. Each interview started with a discussion of the use of computer equipment and applications that were needed to perform the tasks in the phase. Interviewees were also asked to describe how they behave in situations when the systems are not working. To analyse losses in such situations, they were first asked to recall past incidents and their consequences and then to discuss potential consequences in terms of process metrics (e.g. delays, cost, quality and customer satisfaction). In the interviews it turned out that past incidents (systems availability problems) were rare. Because of the nature of the physical papermaking, interrupts to production quite often disturb the whole order to delivery process. Hence, the respondents often referred to these situations when discussing the events that would take place if IS become unavailable.

A core deliverable of the analysis was a table that summarised the risks with reference to steps in the order-to-delivery process. The table reported the applications used in each step, behaviour in application malfunction situations, associated business risk and an assessment of risk in terms of probability and severity of impact. This document appeared to be useful for business managers, because it summarised the risks within a framework that they were accustomed to. Table 23.6 illustrates the document by showing the three first phases of the order-to-delivery process (presenting the full table was prohibited by the client).

In addition to the table, a written report discussed the losses. The report identified the shutdown of the papermaking machine as a major business risk. The fixed cost of this risk was estimated to be over 10,000 euros with an additional cost of approximately 10,000 euros for each hour. Three different systems that could lead to papermaking shutdown were identified. Even if numerous smaller problems were detected, it was actually quite surprising how moderate the business effects were. For instance, problems in the office functions such as receiving orders, scheduling production, writing delivery documents, invoicing, etc. caused only minor difficulties.

The business consequences of systems risks appeared to be conditional: the severity of business consequences depended not only on the length of the system breakdown, but also on the contextual situation in the business process. The system used in paper cutting could cause shutdown of the papermaking machine, but only if the malfunction lasts more than 6 h. In a 'normal situation', office functions such as order handling and deliveries could easily wait for few hours so that the computers are working again. But in the event that sales had promised

Table 23.6 Table used for reporting potential business risks

Process phase	Application used	Procedure if the application is not available	Business risk/loss	Significance	Likelihood of risk	Total
Definition of sales quotas for customer	Sales operating system (SOS)	Wait until the system works again	Overselling the quota (in situations when the demand for cardboard is exceptionally high)	3	1	3
Transmission of orders from sales offices to the mill.	Sales operating system	Wait until the system works again (for urgent orders, sales offices fax orders that are then keyed into the flow application)	Manual processing of urgent orders. If the SOS is not available for a longer time, a manually entered order cannot be shipped as SOS is needed for producing shipping documents.	1	2	2
Grouping of orders to different production slots	Flow	Wait until the system works again	Urgent orders cannot be added to daily production plan	2	2	4
Reserving transportation	Sales operating system, trafe	Wait until the system works again. For urgent orders, transportation is reserved by calling.	If the SOS is not available for a longer time, urgent orders cannot be shipped due to lack of export documents	3	1	3
Confirming the order	Flow	Confirm orders via e-mail or phone for the customers who need it	Customer does not receive order confirmation	2	2	4
...	...	...	...	...	...	...

Risk significance: 0 = User can delay the task without negative impacts; 1 = Disturbance increases manual work in performing the task; 2 = Disturbance causes significant additional costs or customer inconvenience; 3 = Disturbance reduces the quality of customer information; 4 = Disturbance can have serious long-term business consequences.

Likelihood of risk: 1 = Impact takes place only in exceptional situations; 2 = Impact takes place depending on the timing of the disturbance; 3 = Impacts take place always, in all business situations.

an exceptionally fast delivery of an order, this promise could not be kept, which led to problems both for the mill and for the customer. A short problem in the warehouse IS could be visible to domestic customers, but not to foreign customers, as international deliveries are always transported to harbour well before shipping.

The report also contained an analysis of business losses from the perspective of individual applications. Because a single application was used in many process phases, business losses typically emerged in several phases simultaneously. To make things even more complex, server and network problems could affect several applications simultaneously. Business process analysis appeared to provide at least some basis for analysing the overall effects to the core business processes even in these situations.

Evaluation

The analysis focused on the potential business losses that IS availability problems can cause in various phases of the order-to-delivery process. For this purpose, the analysis appeared to be sufficient. The IT manager in the paper mill was satisfied with the report. Nothing extraordinary or surprising had come up, but 'the report provides a good overview and helps us to set priorities for improving IS security and reliability'. Also the corporate CIO seemed to appreciate the business process approach adopted:

I like the report because it is easy to read. One can easily follow what happens in the mill operations when computer problems occur and thus understand how and why the risks are associated with extra costs in business operations. In this respect, the report is better than the one we received from an earlier investigation.

The corporate CIO commented, however, on the narrow approach to systems availability risk. His comment on the analysis was that:

Based on my experience on this [paper] industry, one of the most significant IT risks is that an order message gets somehow scrambled during the processing and we notice it only when the delivery is already in the middle of Atlantic Ocean. Then it costs.

Certainly, questions related to information integrity problems, that is, to the possibility that the content of information is changed would have raised new types of incidents. The original objective was, however, limited to availability risks.

There was also discussion about whether the consequences would be the same in other mills. The CIO and some other specialists were not sure about whether the rules for shutting down a paper machine would differ between the mills – for instance, in situations when the automatic quality control system of the paper machine becomes unavailable. The eventual losses resulting from systems availability risks appear to be organisation or even site specific.

Specifying learning

The first loop learning in this case is related to the nature of business losses that can emerge in the operations of a paper mill. The image of potential losses did not bring large surprises to the personnel in the paper mill. Perhaps the main observation, both for the practitioners and the researcher, was that the relationship between a realised systems availability risk and the resulting business loss appears to be contingent upon many situational factors.

The second loop learning is related to the analysis method itself. The overall impression about the use of business process analysis as a method to investigate potential losses was positive. Within a relatively short period of time and with a reasonable effort, the project group produced reports that illustrate major business risks that can emerge in the business mill's core business process. There was a sense of comprehensiveness, as the analysis produced a large number of potential losses in all stages of the process. Perhaps the main weakness, that was evident in the CIO's comment above, was that the analysis focused on the consequences of availability problems and ignored information integrity, confidentiality or authenticity problems.

Another limitation of the process was that the IS service provider commitment to the process remained very weak. The final report was also left with the IS service provider representatives, but their own personnel had not participated in the actual analysis. What the service provider was looking for was historical evidence of realised systems risks that would have caused significant business losses for the client. These would have provided arguments for selling advanced systems management services. Such incidents were, however, simply not found in the interviews. Overall, the benefits of the analysis for the service provider were modest.

Case 2: Credit card department

The second case organisation was a credit card department in a Nordic bank. The department is responsible for tasks typical to any credit card company, such as issuing new cards, setting and controlling credit limits, authorising purchases, paying the credit card purchases to merchants and collecting payments from card owners. In addition to issuing the bank's own credit cards, the department also manages credit cards issued by retail stores and other companies. The operations are typical bank operations in the sense that the department borrows money from the main bank and then lends it to card holders. The department has a small internal IT function. The core systems are partly managed by the own IT department of the bank and partly by an external IT service provider.

Problem diagnosis

The motivation for assessing the business consequences of systems availability risk was associated with a renewal of the outsourcing contract between the credit card department and its IS service provider. The IS service provider offered a large package of systems management services, for example, monitoring the servers where most of the credit card departments on-line and batch processing applications had been installed. The previous outsourcing contract had no penalties for losses resulting from systems risks. If a systems risk occurred because of negligence from the part of the IT service provider, there was no mechanism for the bank to receive compensation for its losses. The bank's management wanted to include penalty clauses in the new contract. While the overall business risk could not be transferred to IT service provider, a penalty would ensure some compensation and, perhaps more importantly, influence practices within the IT service company. The problem was that neither the service provider nor the bank had an understanding of the magnitude of potential business losses. Both parties recognised that they did not have methods to analyse such losses. This provided a good setting for the companies to collaborate in the development of a new method.

Action planning

For this purpose, a joint effort was initiated between the IT service provider and the credit card department to investigate risks and their consequences. The role of the author was to concentrate on the analysis of business risks. He was invited to the team partly because of his prior experience with the paper mill case. One of the senior managers from the IS service provider side expressed this by saying:

> Our professionals are good at technical analysis of threats and vulnerabilities and my fear is that the project will focus only on those issues – we need you to bring the business side to the analysis

The IT service provider had not made similar analyses of its customers' business processes before. However, it had for some time recognised a need to better understand customers' business processes. Hence, the assessment was considered as a pilot project. If the experiences were positive, the company would make similar studies with other customers.

In the project initiation meeting, the main business processes of the credit card department were identified. In addition, the business value of each process and the business risks associated with each process were discussed on a general level. After the initial meeting, the work continued in workshops that aimed at describing the most significant business processes.

The IT service company assigned two employees from its business process competence centre to manage and document the workshops: one with experience on managing workshops and the other one specialising in drawing process charts. In addition, the workshops involved technical specialists who provided information about work processes on the IS service provider side. The representatives from the credit card department were chosen so that they could describe the business processes in their side.

Action taking

For each business process, a process chart was drawn that identifies the main tasks within the process and also the computer applications used in completing the task. To detect errors, process charts developed in the previous workshop were discussed in the beginning of the workshop. Quite often the process charts had problems even in the second round, resulting to a third cycle of revision and review.

The potential business consequences of systems risk were discussed as the process charts were drawn. Questions such as 'how do you behave in this task when systems are not working?' were asked to identify business consequences. This led to a discussion about alternative actions and potential business consequences of systems risk. The actual task of describing and drawing the process charts turned out to be a challenging task. Hence, most of the time was spent in discussing how the credit card department actually works and what systems are being used. In addition, as the workshops involved representatives of the service provider and client, operational issues were addressed.

The IT infrastructure for the credit card department was fairly centralised. In effect, it meant that if one centralised server was down during normal service time, it influenced all on-line processes such as issuing new cards, setting and controlling credit limits, and authorising purchases. In addition, a server problem would affect customers using automatic teller machines or automatic phone services. A lengthy system break during night-time would delay batch processing jobs, such as paying the credit card purchases to merchants and sending out bills to collect payments from card owners.

The final report contained process charts of eight business processes. The process charts identified the main steps in each process, the organisational units responsible for the steps, as well as the IT applications used. For each business process a table was drawn that described potential losses in core business processes as well as IS risks that were related to them. Table 23.7 illustrates the tables by showing three identified potential business losses in one process, that is, credit application processing (presenting the full tables were prohibited by the client).

In addition to the tables, the potential business losses caused by IS risks were described in a 11 page narrative report. A characteristic feature in the business consequences was that the IT problems were immediately quite visible to large customer groups. They caused inconvenience both for the credit card owners, merchants and also for customer service personnel in bank offices. This, as such, had an indirect negative impact on future business. But there was also a more direct impact. The issuing of new cards requires merchants to make a phone call to the department's service centre. A visible IT problem immediately increases both the number of incoming calls and the average duration of a call, thus making it difficult for other merchants to get through. This causes direct losses for the credit card company.

Apart from losses in operating processes, it was acknowledged that systems risks could lead to negative media exposure and opportunities for international crime. The department had begun to offer credit applications via the internet with a promise to deliver a credit decision within a few minutes. This new service was expected to be publicised in the media with the side effect that any problems with this service would also be reported. Computer problems had also a connection to international crime. Situations when the card issuer's computer is not responding are closely monitored, because these situations open up possibilities for certain types of fraudulent transactions.

Evaluation

The analysis concentrated primarily on systems availability risks: what types of losses will emerge in the department's core business processes if critical applications are not available. For this purpose, the analysis appeared to work well. The business development manager commented

Table 23.7 Table used for reporting potential business losses

Process	Business process risk	Business loss	Significance H,M,S	Technical or functional risk	Likelihood H,M,S	Cause	Proposed action
Credit application processing	#1 All calls from merchants cannot be answered (rush hours Mon–Fri 10.30–13.30, 15–19; weekends 10:30–13.30)	Consumers or merchants lost to competitors → Lost revenues	H	Slow computer response time: phone calls for processing individual applications last longer than usual.		Slow network connection; server, operating system or application errors	Changes in reserve network connections, for example, UPS, automatic reconnection, etc.
	#2 All calls from bank offices cannot be answered (offices are open 9–19, rush hours as above)	Consumer customers are lost to own bank offices → increased credit cost, credit risk and concern expences	H				
	#3 Bank offices lack access to information required for making 'on-line' credit decisions	Offices call to call centre also in 'online' decisions → slow response time in call centre → risks #1 and #2 above	H	Bank offices lack access to credit card department's systems		In addition to above: problem in the bank client; lack of access to bank network	Automatic reconnecttion
...			...		...	...	...

H = High, M = Medium, S = Small.

the 11-page narrative description of risks for the bank operations as follows:

> I'll sure try to get all managers in our board of directors to read this. It will be difficult because they don't know much about this area (systems management) and they haven't really been very interested about it. Perhaps this report will help them see the business significance of this issue.

The analysis of business risks appeared to be beneficial also for the IS service company. A bit surprisingly, awareness of the business risks for the client appeared to influence the attitudes of the technical staff as well. A consultant from the IS service provider company commented this as follows:

> Our internal meetings are often quite relaxed and there is a lot of joking and informal discussion. In our previous meeting I noticed that when we started discussing the credit card company's affairs, the technicians became much more serious and the whole climate changed. I believe this is because they are now better aware of the significance of the actual business risks that can result if the systems don't work.

Hence, the assessment appeared to have a positive influence on the knowledge and attitudes within the IT service company. Overall, both the credit card department and the IS service provider were satisfied with the results achieved in this pilot case. The IS service provider has continued to conduct similar assessment studies with its other key customers.

Specifying learning

First loop learning in this case was related to the potential consequences of systems availability risks for the credit card department. The overall image of losses as being contingent upon many situational factors and being very idiographic to the department was evident also in this case. The range of potential consequences was broader than in the paper mill case. In addition to the operative losses and lost sales, also potential for image losses and theft of money were reported.

Second loop learning was related to analysis method itself. Again, the overall impression of the method and its results was positive. With a limited effort, the analysis produced a report of potential losses that was deemed as useful. The main difference to the previous case was that the data collection was organised within workshops (rather than as interviews) and that the IS service personnel was actively involved in all stages of the analysis. This was a clear improvement to the analysis process. However, rather than representing the learning curve of the author, the change can be attributed to the much higher initial interest that the IS service provider had in second case.

Wide involvement of both IS personnel and user representative in the analysis process appeared to have positive impact on the dissemination of loss analysis results. Based on the experiences in this case, wide participation of both users and IS service personnel can be highly recommended. The use of workshops created, however, also challenges, as business losses were only one of the issues addressed. The participants in workshops were more accustomed to discuss various technical and operational issues. It was, indeed, the researcher's role to make sure that also the issues related to potential losses received sufficient attention.

The wider commitment and involvement of the IS service provider in the second case also led to changes in the table format where the results of the loss analysis were presented. In the action-planning phase, the tables that had been produced in the paper mill case were closely reviewed. The table that was produced in the action taking phase (Table 23.7) was, however, slightly different. The contents of columns to the left, which identify potential business losses, were the responsibility of the author. The columns to the right, indicating technical risks and causes, was filled in by the representatives of the IS service provider. The table was filled from left to right – starting from potential losses in the core business processes and then proceeding to the identification of associated technical risks for each combination of process and loss.

The idea that the loss analysis reports could be further elaborated by analysing technical risks that could cause losses was present already in the reports produced in the first case. There was, however, no party that saw it as necessary. IS personnel in the paper mill was relative well acquainted with technical problems that could take place. In the second case, the wide involvement of the IS service provider meant, that the analysis was possible to make.

Overall, the second case also followed the principles of action research in the sense that the development of methods was a genuinely joint effort between the researcher and the participating organisations. From the research perspective, the slight differences in the method were positive as they enable comparisons to be made between the two cases.

Contributions for research

Prior research on IS risks has produced a detailed view of vulnerabilities and threats that a company is exposed to as a result of increased use of IS in business operations. Also the security measures to prevent risks from occurring are well documented. The methods that can be used to provide a systematic view of potential losses in the user organisation have, however, received only limited attention.

The first contribution of this paper is based on the review of five different loss analysis methods presented in prior literature. The paper compared the basic assumptions behind each method in terms of the type of information risks tackled, the type of analysis method employed and the nature of losses that the method is most likely to detect. By doing so the paper presented the methods in an overall framework and thus also illustrated lack of methods to analyse certain types of information risks and losses.

The contribution of empirical studies is related to the analysis method and to the experiences gained by applying it to the two action research cases. Following the principles of action research, the development of the method was organised as a joint effort with the participating organisations. The research applied a theory-based method (business process analysis) to a problematic situation of the clients. Naturally, the novelty of any organisational analysis method can always be questioned. All three organisations involved in this study are, however, large publicly listed companies. Even if their representatives were aware of the traditional auditing and security analysis methods, they perceived the methods developed in the current study as different.

The use of traditional risk analysis methods in the two cases would have been difficult, because the number of potential IS risks was known to be high and each individual risk, for example, a technical problem in the infrastructure, could affect several business applications and business processes in the user organisation. Analysing technical risks first and then projecting the consequences of each risk in the user organisation simply was not considered as a feasible approach. Therefore, the analysis focused first on the core business processes, where most severe business consequences were likely to take place. Also the notion of risk was limited to information availability problems. While these restrictions increased the risk that the analysis could omit some potential adverse consequences, they also provided a clear scope for the analysis of adverse consequences in the user organisation.

Other business loss analysis methods, such as labour cost analysis or lost sales analysis could also have been used to provide estimates of potential losses. Business process analysis was, however, expected to provide a more detailed description of events that lead from systems availability risks to business losses. Information asset value analysis and stock market reaction analysis could have been used, in particular if the objective had been to estimate the losses in situations where mistakes by the IS service provider would lead to information confidentiality risks. The analyses were, however, limited to losses resulting from systems availability problems.

Based on the experiences in the two projects it can be concluded that the potential business consequences are diverse and thus challenging to analyse. However, business process analysis succeeded in creating an overall image of potential losses. Immediate feedback from the managers suggests that reports focusing on potential losses at the enterprise level appear to be useful, in particular for the business managers. The experiences suggest, however, that also the analysis process itself can be used to raise awareness of potential losses among those who participate in it. This appeared to be of particular importance in the IS outsourcing context, where the technical personnel in the service provider side did not know about potential losses that the client can suffer. Similar situations can, however, also emerge in internal centralised IT departments that provide services to large number of business units.

Overall, the paper suggests that the analysis of losses in the user organisation requires organisational analysis skills, as opposed to the technical and mathematical analyses that are needed in the traditional analyses of systems risks. This study used methods that are typical in organisational studies (action research and business process analysis) in its investigation. They appeared to provide a good basis for the organisational analysis required. Hence, IS science could complement the more technical image that traditional risk analysis research has created about the relationship between IS risks and potential losses.

Contributions for practice

IS managers have often mentioned lack of managerial commitment to IS security and reliability as a severe problem. This research invites them to critically think how well the potential business consequences and risks are known in their own company. If the potential losses are not widely known, one means to increase managerial commitment is to comprehensively demonstrate the business risks that the company's core business processes are exposed to.

Increasing penetration of computers to business operations means that business managers also need to be cognisant about potential business losses. Auditing process comprises a transaction walkthrough that has similarities to the analysis described here. Auditing reports have, however, various purposes. Usually they place a lot of emphasis on detecting potential for errors (including systems security risks, systems risks and information risks) in processing transactions. Hence, they are often directed to reporting existing vulnerabilities, required corrective actions and losses if such actions are not taken.

This study suggests that IS and business managers should consider a separate analysis that concentrates solely on reporting potential business losses. When carrying out such analysis, they can employ methods that were described in the beginning of this article to identify, for example, the form the loss or damage will take. Alternatively, they can conduct a similar business process analysis as was carried out in the two cases.

Managers in IS service companies might also consider using similar business process analysis methods in cooperation with their key customers. The credit card department case provides an example of such cooperation. The analysis of customer's key business processes seemed to increase awareness of potential business losses and thus benefited both parties. The process descriptions also assisted the IS service provider to connect improvements in IS service to avoidance of concrete losses in client's business. The positive feedback from the client and from the company's own employees participating in the project motivated the management of the IS service company to continue conducting similar studies with other key customers.

Limitations and further research

This was, however, only one study conducted in two organisations. The methods were largely developed during the research process. They reflect the needs of the client organisations and the immediate situation that these companies faced. According to the principles of action research, the analysis methods used need to be critically re-evaluated and improved. Thus the paper leaves room for further development of the proposed method as well as further research about other methods.

Despite the positive immediate feedback, future research is needed in analysing the organisational impact of the assessment. The focus in this study was primarily on the development of the analysis method. The researcher did not have access to the commercial negotiations that provided the first initiative for the analysis of potential losses in the two cases. Future studies are needed to investigate the use of business process analysis results as part of a IS security education, planning, investment planning, and systems security analysis and design efforts. Future studies could also investigate a combined use of methods in order to provide a more comprehensive view of the potential losses in all categories. In the two cases, the scope of analysis was limited to operative processes and the questions were stated from the perspective of what if systems are not working (information availability risks). By investigating different types of business processes, for example, product development, and by adding more questions about different types of computer hazards (e.g. integrity and confidentiality risks), the results might reflect a broader view of business losses.

The main strength of business process analysis is in detecting potential for additional costs or lost sales due to problems in operative processes (categories #1 and #2 in Table 23.2). Even if the analysis in the second case identified possibilities for theft of corporate resources and negative media exposure, the possibility that IS risks could lead to poor managerial decisions, theft of corporate resources, negative media exposure, shareholder losses, legal processes or punishments, or unexpected IT costs (categories #3–#9 in Table 23.2) can easily be left behind by the method. In this respect, the business process analysis needs to be complemented with other loss evaluation methods.

Summary

Improved methods for documenting potential business losses resulting from IS risk benefit both IS managers and researchers. For years, such managers and researchers have been aware of the significant negative effect that computer problems can have on business operations. Still, this effect has often been considered as complex and difficult to analyse. The findings herein – that business process analysis can be used to systematically assess the nature and significance of such effects – should stimulate the imaginations of IS security managers and researchers alike. Perhaps most importantly, this study concludes that more research on the methods that assist in identification of business losses is needed.

References

Alner, M. (2001). The Effects of Outsourcing on Information Security, *Information Systems Security* 10(2): 35–43.

Argyris, C. (1982). *Reasoning, Learning and Action, Individual and Organizational*, San Francisco, CA: Jossey-Bass Publishers.

Argyris, C., Putnam, R. and McLain Smith, D. (1987). *Action Science*, 2nd edn, San Francisco, CA: Jossey-Bass Publishers.

Barki, H., Rivard, S. and Talbot, J. (1993). Toward an Assessment of Software Development Risk, *Journal of Management Information Systems* 10(2): 203–225.

Basel Committee (2006). International Convergence of Capital Measurement and Capital Standards: A Revised Framework, Comprehensive Version. Switzerland: Bank for International Settlements.

Baskerville, R.L. (1999). Investigating Information Systems with Action Research, *Communications of the Association for Information Systems* 2(19): 2–31.

Baskerville, R.L. and Myers, M.D. (2004). Special Issue on Action Research in Information Systems: Making IS research relevant to practice – foreword, *MIS Quarterly* 28(3): 329–335.

Baskerville, R.L. and Portougal, V. (2003). A Possibility Theory Framework for Security Evaluation in National Infrastructure Protection, *Journal of Database Management* 14(2): 1–13.

Benbasat, I., Goldstein, D.K. and Mead, M. (1987). The Case Research Strategy in Studies of Information Systems, *MIS Quarterly* 11(3): 369–386.

British Standard Institution (1993). BS7799 *Code of Practice for Information Security Management*. London, UK: British Standard Institution.

Cavusoglu, H., Mishra, B. and Raghunathan, S. (2004). A Model for Evaluating IT Security Investments, *Communications of the ACM* 47(7): 87–92.

Checkland, P. (1991). From Framework Through Experience to Learning: The essential nature of action research, in H.-E. Nissen and H.K. Klein (eds.) *Information Systems Research: Contemporary approaches & emergent traditions*, Amsterdam: North-Holland.

Ciborra, C. (2004). Digital Technologies and the Duality of Risk, Centre for Analysis of Risk and Regulation at the London School of Economics and Political Science, Discussion paper No: 27, 1–20.

Clark, P.A. (1972). *Action Research & Organizational Change*, New York: Harper & Row Publishers.

Collins, B.S. and Mathews, S. (1993). Securing your Business Process, *Computers & Security* 12(7): 629–634.

Collins, J.S. and Millen, R.A. (1995). Information Systems Outsourcing by Large American Industrial Firms: Choices and impacts, *Information Resources Management Journal* 8(1): 5–13.

Damianides, M. (2005). Sarbanes–Oxley and IT Governance: New guidance on IT control and compliance, *Information Systems Management* 22(1): 77–85.

DeMaio, H.B. (1995). Information Protection and Business Process Reengineering, *Information Systems Security* 3(4): 5–10.

Department of Trade and Industry (2007). Business Continuity Management, Impact Analysis [www document]http://www.dti.gov.uk/sectors/infosec/infosecadvice/continuitymanagement/impactanalysis/page33399.html (accessed 3 April, 2007).

Dhillon, G. (2004). Realizing Benefits of an Information Security Program, *Business Process Management* 10(3): 260–261.

Eloff, M.M. and von Solms, S.H. (2000). Information Security Management: An approach to combine process certification and product evaluation, *Computers & Security* 19(8): 698–709.

Endorf, C. (2004). Outsourcing Security: The need, the risks, the providers, and the process, *Information Security Management* 12(6): 17–23.

Fink, D. (1994). A Security Framework for Information Systems Outsourcing, *Information Management & Computer Security* 2(4): 3–8.

Fitzgerald, K.J. (1995). Information Security Baselines, *Information Management & Computer Security* 3(2): 8–14.

Galliers, R.D. (1991). Choosing Appropriate Information Systems Research Approaches, in H.-E. Nissen and H.K. Klein (eds.) *Information Systems Research: Contemporary approaches & emergent traditions*, Amsterdam: North-Holland.

Garg, A., Curtis, J. and Halper, H. (2003a). The Finaincial Impact of IT Security Breaches: What do investors think, *Information Systems Security* 12(1): 22–33.

Garg, A., Curtis, J. and Halper, H. (2003b). Quantifying the Financial Impact of IT Security Breaches, *Information Management & Computer Security* 11(2): 74–83.

Gordon, L.A. and Loeb, M.P. (2002). Return on Information Security Investments, Myths vs Realities, *Strategic Finance* 84(5): 26–31.

Hovav, A. and D'Arcy, J. (2004). The Impact of Virus Attack Announcements on the Market Value of Firms, *Information Systems Security* 13(2): 32–40.

Im, G.P. and Baskerville, R.L. (2005). A Longitudinal Study of Information Systems Threat Categories: The enduring problem of human error, *The DATA BASE for Advances in Information Systems* 36(4): 68–79.

Jönsson, S. (1991). Action Research, In: H.-E. Nissen and H.K. Klein (eds.) *Information Systems Research: Contemporary approaches & emergent traditions*, Amsterdam: North-Holland.

Kettinger, W.J., Teng, J. and Guha, S. (1997). Business Process Change: A study of methodologies, techniques and tools, *MIS Quarterly* 21(1): 55–80.

Khalfan, A.M. (2004). Information Security Considerations in IS/IT Outsourcing Projects: A descriptive case study of two sectors, *International Journal of Information Management* 24(1): 29–42.

Kokolakis, S.A., Demopoulos, A.J. and Kiountouzis, E.A. (2000). The Use of Business Process Modelling in Systems Security Analysis and Design, *Information Management & Computer Security* 8(3): 107.

Lederman, R. (2004). Adverse Events in Hospitals: The contribution of poor information systems, in European Conference on Information Systems, (Turku, Finland, 2004).

Lederman, R. (2005). Managing Hospital Databases: Can large hospitals really protect patient data? *Health Informatics* 11(3): 201–210.

Leopoldi, R. (2002). IT Services Management Service Brief: Business impact analysis, A White Paper Report Published by RL Consulting.

Loch, K.D., Carr, H.H. and Warkentin, M.E. (1992). Threats to Information Systems: Today's reality, yesterday's understanding, *MIS Quarterly* 16(2): 173–186.

Macfarlane, I. and Rudd, C. (2005). *IT Service Management*, Reading, UK: itSMF Ltd.

Mooney, J., Gurbaxani, V. and Kraemer, K. (1996). A Process Oriented Framework for Assessing the Business Value of Information Technology, *The DATABASE for Advances in Information Systems* 27(2): 68–81.

Moulton, R.T. and Moulton, M.E. (1996). Electronic Communications Risk Management: A checklist for business managers, *Computers & Security* 15(5): 377–386.

Mumford, E. and Weir, M. (1979). *Computer Systems Work Design: The ETHICS method*, London: Associated Business Press.

Nearon, B.H. (2000). Information Technology Security Engagements – An Evolving Speciality, *The CPA Journal* 70(7): 29–33.

Neumann, P.G. (1995). *Computer Related Risks,* New York: ACM Press.

Nolan, R. and McFarlan, W. (2005). Information Technology and the Board of Directors, *Harvard Business Review* 83(10): 96–106.

Olson, E.G. (2005). Strategically Managing Risk in the Information Age: A holistic approach, *Journal of Business Strategy* 26(6): 45–54.

Ott, J.L. (2003). The Real Cost of Computer Crime, *Information Systems Security* 12(1): 2–4.

Palmer, M.E., Robinson, C., Patilla, J.C. and Moser, E.P. (2001). Information Security Policy Framework: Best practices for security policy in the E-commerce age, *Information Systems Security* 10(2): 13–27.

Pate-Cornell, M.E. (1996). Uncertainties in Risk Analysis: Six levels of treatment, *Reliability Engineering and System Safety* 54: 95–111.

Rapoport, R.N. (1970). Three Dilemmas in Action Research, *Human Relations* 23(6): 499–513.

Renn, O. (1998). Three Decades of Risk Research: Accomplishments and new challenges, *Journal of Risk Research* 1(1): 49–71.

Reponen, T. (1993). Information Management Strategy – An Evolutionary Process, *Scandinavian Journal of Management* 9(9): 189–209.

Royal Canadian Mounted Police (1981). Security in the EDP environment, in *Security Information Publication.* Canada: Royal Canadian Mounted Police.

Sherwood, J. (1997). Managing Security for Outsourcing Contracts, *Computers & Security* 16(7): 603–609.

Smith, E. and Eloff, J.H.P. (2002). A Prototype for Assessing Information Technology Risks in Health Care, *Computers & Security* 21(2): 266–284.

Stewart, A. (2004). On Risk: Perception and direction, *Computers & Security* 23(5): 362–370.

Stevenson-Smith, G. (2004). Recognizing and Preparing Loss Estimates from Cyber-Attacks, *Information Systems Security* 12(6): 46–58.

Straub, D.W. and Welke, R.J. (1998). Coping with Systems Risk: Security planning models for management decision making, *MIS Quarterly* 22(4): 441–469.

Susman, G.I. and Evered, R.D. (1978). An Assessment of the Scientific Merits of Action Research, *Administrative Science Quarterly* 23(4): 582–603.

Toigo, J.W. (1989). *Disaster Recovery Planning: Managing Risk & Catastrophe in Information Systems,* Englewood Cliffs, NJ: Yourdon Press.

Tryfonas, T., Kiountouzis, E. and Poulymenakou, A. (2001). Embedding Security Practices in Contemporary Information Systems Development Approaches, *Information Management & Computer Security* 9(4): 183–197.

Vermeulen, C. and von Solms, R. (2002). The Information Security Management Toolbox – Taking the Pain Out of Security Management, *Information Management & Computer Security* 10(3): 119–125.

Whitman, M.E. (2003). Enemy at the Gate: Threats to information security, *Communications of the ACM* 46(8): 91–95.

Wood-Harper, T. (1985). Research Methods in Information Systems: Using action research, in E. Mumford, R. Hirschheim, G. Fitzgerald and T. Wood-Harper (eds.) *Research Methods in Information Systems,* Amsterdam: North-Holland, pp. 169–191.

Section VII
Alternative Approaches

24

A Semiotic Information Quality Framework: Development and Comparative Analysis

Rosanne Price and Graeme Shanks
Faculty of Information Technology, Monash University, Australia

Introduction

Quality information and information quality management in an organization is essential for effective operations and decision-making. The proliferation of data warehouses to support decision-making further highlights an organization's vulnerability with respect to poor data quality, especially given the widely disparate data sources, contexts, users, and data uses characterizing data warehouses and the much less predictable data usage involved in decision-making as compared to business operations.

Regardless of whether conventional databases or data warehouses are used to support decision-making, it is clear that management of information quality is critical to the effectiveness of the decision support systems employed. However, management of information quality pre-supposes a clear understanding of and consensus with respect to the meaning of the term 'information quality'. In fact, fundamental questions still remain as to how quality should be defined and the specific criteria that should be used to evaluate information quality. Addressing these research questions is an important step in establishing a basis both for developing information quality assessment mechanisms and for discussing related issues such as quality improvement and management.

Competing views of quality from *product-* and *service-based* perspectives focus on *objective* and *subjective* views of quality, respectively.

Reprinted from "A semiotic information quality framework: development and comparative analysis," by R. Price and G. Shanks in *Journal of Information Technology*, 20, 2005, pp. 88–120. With kind permission from the Association for Information Technology Trust.

Objective measures of information quality can be based on evaluating data's conformance to initial requirements specifications and specified integrity rules or its correspondence to external (e.g. real-world) phenomena. However, such a view of quality overlooks aspects, critical to an organization's success, related to data delivery and presentation, actual data use, and information consumer perceptions, where an *information consumer* is defined as an internal or external *user* of organizational data.

Actual operational use of data may differ substantially from that considered during system development as a result of omitted, unanticipated, or changing business requirements. This may, for example, result in deficiencies in data model quality (a separate topic on its own, but not the focus of this paper) with respect to actual user requirements, leading to consumer perceptions of poor information quality. Furthermore, even if data meet basic requirements; data judged to be of good quality by objective means may be regarded as inferior by consumers either due to problems resulting from data delivery (e.g. deficient delivery mechanisms, processes, or interfaces) or due to customer expectations that exceed basic requirements.

To address these concerns, subjective measures of information quality can be used based on consumer feedback, acknowledging that consumers do not (and cannot) judge the quality of data in isolation but rather in combination with the delivery and use of that data. Thus, data delivery and use-based factors are integral to a service-based view and to consumer perceptions of quality. The obvious challenge of this approach compared to the objective approach is the difficulty in reliably measuring and quantifying such perceptions.

Note that objective versus subjective views of quality reflect commonly discussed IS distinctions between the terms *data* and *information,* distinguishing between what is stored (i.e. stored data values) and what is retrieved from data collections (i.e. received data values). In this paper, the term *data* is used specifically to refer to stored database or data warehouse content; whereas the term *information* is used in a broader sense to include not only stored data but also 'received' data that have been delivered to, presented to, and interpreted by the user. Thus the term *information quality* refers to both objective views of stored data quality and subjective views of received data quality. Information quality research can then be characterized based on the view(s) of quality considered.

Information quality research is further characterized by the range of research approaches employed, that is, empirical, intuitive (i.e. *ad hoc),* theoretical, and/or literature-based. Although some authors, for example, Eppler (2001), have used the term *theoretical* to describe approaches based on review and analysis of existing quality literature; we distinguish explicitly between theory-based and literature-based approaches. The intuitive or *ad hoc* approach can be based on industrial experience, common sense, and/or intuitive understanding. A number of frameworks have been proposed in recent years for information quality (Redman, 1996; Wand and Wang, 1996; Wang and Strong, 1996; Kahn *et al.*, 1997, 2002; English, 1999; Lee *et al.*, 2002) based on these different approaches. A detailed comparison of these frameworks (and the research approach adopted by each) with the one proposed in this paper is given in the penultimate section. Here we highlight the steps involved in developing such a framework, the research approaches used, and their limitations – thus providing a motivation for the research reported in this paper.

An information quality framework typically consists of a set of quality criteria and their definitions grouped into general categories that have been separately defined. Even in the case of restricted frameworks that consider criteria from only one category (Wand and Wang, 1996), the different quality categories are initially delineated and defined before restricting the scope. In general, the steps, implicit or explicit, required in developing an information quality framework can be described as follows:

- derivation and definition of quality categories,
- selection of the derivation approach to use for deriving criteria,
- derivation and definition of quality criteria, and
- classification of criteria into categories.

Most notably, what all of the frameworks proposed to date have in common is a non-theoretical basis for these steps. Because the development of the frameworks thus depends (either directly or indirectly) on information consumer feedback or *ad hoc* observations and experiences rather than on a systematic theory, the resulting frameworks are likely to have some inconsistencies, redundancy, and/or omissions and thus are subject to criticism regarding the degree of rigor. This is particularly true of the definitions of quality categories and the subsequent classification of criteria based on these categories. Such inconsistencies have in fact been noted previously by Eppler (2001) and Gendron and Shanks (2003) among others. In general, the only exception to these observations is the theoretical and thus rigorous basis provided by

Wand and Wang (1996) for selecting a derivation approach for objective criteria and for deriving and defining those criteria. However, not only is their scope limited to the objective view of information quality (and thus does not consider subjective quality criteria) but also their initial delineation of categories is intuitive rather than theoretical.

These observations motivate the search for a different approach to developing an information quality framework – one that maintains rigor, especially with respect to the definition of quality categories and classification of criteria into categories, without sacrificing scope, that is, which incorporates both product and service quality perspectives in one coherent framework. This paper reports on an information quality framework, *InfoQual*, developed with these goals in mind. Previously published papers (Price and Shanks, 2004, 2005) have reported in detail on specific aspects of or developmental stages in the research. Here, we present the essential elements of the developmental process as a whole – both theoretical and empirical phases – in the context of a detailed comparison to other information quality frameworks with respect to the developmental approach adopted and consequent implications for consistency and scope.

The development of the framework can be described in terms of five steps:

1. defining quality categories, covering both objective product and subjective service quality views,
2. determining the derivation method to use for criteria in each category based directly on the definition of that category, which effectively provides an automatic and natural classification of criteria into categories,
3. deriving the criteria for the objective product quality component(s) of the framework,
4. deriving the criteria for the subjective service quality component(s) of the framework, and
5. empirically refining the criteria, especially subjective criteria, using focus groups. Note that this step does not involve any re-classification of criteria, since a sound basis for criteria classification is established based on category definitions as described in step 2.

To ensure rigor, a theoretical approach was used wherever possible, that is, in the first three steps. The first two steps were based on semiotics; whereas the third step employs database integrity theory and mapping cardinalities (based on an ontological view of an IS). This raises the question of scope. To be comprehensive, an information quality framework must include subjective component(s) that depend on information consumer judgments both with respect to establishing the relevant set of quality criteria to consider and with respect to assessing quality based on these criteria. Such components are obviously not amenable to a purely theoretical approach. Therefore, the set of subjective service quality criteria were initially derived using a literature-based approach and then – to ensure relevance – empirically refined and validated.

The rest of the paper is structured as follows: The following section reviews semiotic theory and its application in an Information Systems (IS) context. The next section then describes how semiotic theory is used to derive and define quality categories and to determine (and thus justify) the research approach employed for deriving quality criteria. The initial derivation of specific criteria for each category is explained in the subsequent section and their refinement, based on empirical feedback from focus groups, is reported in the section thereafter. The revised framework is presented in the penultimate section with a detailed comparison to previously proposed frameworks. The final section describes conclusions and future work.

Semiotics

Although semiotics has many different branches, the one most relevant in the current context is that proposed by Charles Pierce (1931–1935) and later developed by Charles Morris (1938). In particular, Morris describes the study of signs in terms of its logical components (Barnouw, 1989). These are the sign's actual *representation;* its *referent* or intended meaning (i.e. the phenomenon being represented); and its *interpretation* or received meaning (i.e. the effect of the representation on an interpreter's actions, that is, the actual use of the representation). Informally, these three components can be described as the form, meaning, and use of a sign. Relations between these three aspects of a sign were further described by Morris as *syntactic* (between sign representations), *semantic* (between a representation and its referent), and *pragmatic* (between the representation and the interpretation) semiotic levels. Again, informally, these three levels can be said to pertain to the form, meaning, and use of a sign respectively.

The process of interpretation, called *semiosis*, at the pragmatic level necessarily results from and depends on the use of the sign by the interpreter. The actual interpretation of the sign depends both on the interpreter's general sociolinguistic context (e.g. societal and linguistic norms) and on their individual circumstances (e.g. personal experience or knowledge). With this background, the correspondence between semiotics and information quality can be clarified and the applicability of semiotics to the formal definition of information quality justified.

A datum is maintained in a database or data warehouse precisely because it is representative of some external[1] (e.g. real-world) phenomenon relevant to the organization, that is, useful for business activities. However, the representational function of the datum is realized only when it is retrieved and used by some entity, either human or machine. Data use necessarily entails a process of interpretation that potentially influences the resulting action taken by the interpreter. For example, a clerk may issue a query and retrieve a stored integer number from a database that they then interpret as the current age of a particular employee. As a result, the clerk then sends a letter to that employee with notification that the employee is approaching mandatory retirement age.

A clear correspondence between the semiotic concept of a *sign* and the IS concept of *datum* can be observed by noting that a datum has the same three components described earlier for a sign: a stored *representation,*a represented external phenomenon as the *referent,* and a human or machine *interpretation.* In fact, a datum serves as a sign in the IS context. As is true for any sign, the actual interpretation of the representation (and the degree to which that corresponds to the referent originally intended in sign generation) will depend on the interpreter's background (i.e. programming for a machine interpreter and societal and personal context for a human interpreter).

Precedents for the application of semiotic theory to IS include the application of semiotics to understanding IS and systems analysis (Stamper, 1991), to evaluating data model quality (Krogstie *et al.*, 1995; Krogstie, 2001), and to evaluating information quality (Shanks and Darke, 1998). Following Stamper's lead, these authors introduce additional semiotic levels not supported by semiotic theory that (1) introduce overlaps obscuring the clear distinction between levels (e.g. both the pragmatic level and the newly introduced social level address shared social context) and (2) do not preserve the original congruence between sign components and semiotic levels described above. Therefore, we choose instead to adhere to the original three semiotic levels defined by Morris.

Given the congruence between the original Piercian semiotics and the concept of information, the syntactic, semantic, and pragmatic semiotic levels can serve as a theoretical foundation for (1) defining information quality categories, (2) using those definitions to select and rationalize the research approach suitable for deriving each category's quality criteria, and (3) categorizing quality criteria. In fact, it is important to note that the last step follows implicitly (i.e. automatically) from the first two, ensuring consistent criteria classification. Since quality criteria are initially derived with reference to a specific quality category based on that category's definition, there is no need for the separate and manual classification of criteria into categories necessary when criteria and categories are derived independently. This clearly differentiates our work from other information quality approaches. Rather than an *ad hoc* and/or empirical derivation of quality categories and classification of quality criteria, the use of semiotics provides a sound theoretical basis for both steps.

A semiotic view of quality categories

In this section, we describe the basic structure of the information quality framework InfoQual in terms of quality categories derived from the three semiotic levels. The intention throughout is to give an informal description sufficient to serve as a basis for understanding the rationale for and structure of the framework. A detailed description of the theoretical development with formal definitions of all the terms is found in Price and Shanks (2004).

We begin by presenting the relevant IS terminology used and its equivalents in semiotic terms. Essentially, *data* and *metadata* together comprise the contents of a database or data warehouse. They both serve as signs in the IS context representing respectively external phenomena relevant to an application and external rules or documentation relevant to an application or data model. For example, metadata include business integrity rules constraining the combinations of data values that are legally allowed in the database or data warehouse (i.e. based on *application* rules describing possible external states, e.g. employee age must be less than 65 years) and general integrity rules constraining the data organization in the IS (i.e. based on the underlying *data model* employed by the IS, e.g. the referential integrity rule that an employee department must exist). In other words, metadata include the set of definitions (and documentation) relating to either the business application domain or to the underlying data model that together form the IS design.

Having established the congruence between IS and semiotic constructs, the definition of information quality categories based on semiotic levels follows naturally. The *syntactic* and *semantic quality categories* have a direct correspondence to the definition of their respective semiotic levels. For example, since data and metadata are both signs in the IS context; the conformance of stored data (e.g. employee John's stored age of 55 years) to stored metadata (e.g. the stored rule that employee age must be less than 65 years) describes a relation between sign representations. Similarly, the correspondence of stored data (e.g. John's stored age) to represented external phenomena (i.e. John's actual age) describes relations between sign representations and their referents. In defining the *pragmatic quality category,* we focus on one aspect of the interpretation as described in the previous section, that is, the use of the representation. Thus the relation between stored data and its use describes relations between sign representations and the aspect of interpretation related to their use. In the context of information quality, *use* is further described in terms of a specific activity, its context, and user characteristics; since any judgement regarding the suitability and worth of a data set are dependent on these aspects of use. Note further that references to *stored data* assume a single abstract IS representation of the hierarchically structured logical and physical representations (e.g. files, records, fields, bytes, bits) of IS internals, which can be considered an example of nested signs. Given these explanations, the quality categories can then be defined with respect to a given data set as follows.

Definition 1. The *syntactic quality category* describes the degree to which stored data conform to stored metadata. This category addresses the issue of quality of IS data relative to IS design (as represented by metadata) and is assessed through integrity checking.

Definition 2. The *semantic quality category* describes the degree to which stored data correspond to (i.e. map to) represented external phenomena, that is, the set of external phenomena relevant to the purposes for which data are stored (i.e. the intended use of the data). This category addresses the issue of the quality of IS data relative to represented external phenomena and is assessed through random sampling.

Definition 3. The *pragmatic quality category* describes the degree to which stored data are suitable and worthwhile for a given use, where the given use is specified by describing three components: an activity, its context (i.e. geographic or organizational), and the information consumer characteristics (i.e. experience, knowledge, and organizational role). This category addresses the issue of the quality of IS data relative to actual data use, as perceived by users, and is assessed through the use of a questionnaire or survey.

To summarize, the three semiotic levels – *syntactic, semantic,* and *pragmatic* – describing respectively (1) form, (2) meaning, and (3) application (i.e. use or interpretation) of a sign can be used to define corresponding

Table 24.1 Application of semiotics to IS: semiotic theory and IS equivalent

Theory: semiotic level	Application: IS equivalent
Syntactic level (sign form) sign ← → sign	Data in database conform to integrity rules? For example, *emp.salary* > 0 or *emp.dept#* = *dept.dept#*
Semantic level (sign meaning) sign ← → referent	Data in database match external phenomena? For example, *emp* attribute values match real-world employee details
Pragmatic level (sign use) sign ← → use	Data in database useful for tasks? For example, include details needed for payroll

quality categories based respectively on (1) conformance to database rules, (2) correspondence to external phenomena, and (3) suitability for use. This is illustrated in Table 24.1 using the example of an employee database.

Essentially, the syntactic and semantic categories relate to the objective product-based and the pragmatic category to the subjective service-based quality views described in the first section. The advantages of having a single framework incorporating both views of quality is that it (1) provides a comprehensive description of quality and (2) facilitates comparison between different quality perspectives. In the context of quality assessment, such comparisons can be used to check for discrepancies between objective and subjective assessment methods that are likely to signify a quality problem and may facilitate analysis into the source of the quality problem.

Next, we consider the derivation of quality criteria for each category. As stated earlier, the goal is a general understanding of the approach adopted for each category.

Deriving quality criteria for each category

Regardless of the approach used to derive quality criteria, there are several requirements and goals that were formulated prior to and considered throughout the derivation process to ensure a systematic and rigorous evaluation of potential quality criteria. The requirements are as follows:

- criteria must be general, that is, applicable across application domains and data types, and
- criteria must be expressed as adjectives (or adjectival phrases) to ensure consistency.

The goals are as follows:

- the names of quality criteria should be intuitive, that is, corresponding as closely as possible to common usage,
- criteria must clearly defined,
- inter-dependencies between criteria should be minimized as far as possible and, where unavoidable, should be fully documented and justified, and
- the set of criteria should be comprehensive.

These are listed as goals rather than requirements since we cannot prove that these goals are satisfied – they can only be subjectively assessed over time through peer review and empirical feedback.

Theoretical techniques are used to derive quality criteria for both syntactic and semantic categories, as described in the following two consecutive subsections, respectively. The initial list of pragmatic criteria is derived based on an analysis of current information quality literature, as described in the 'Pragmatic criteria' section. The summarized list of initial criteria for each category is given in the subsequent subsection.

Syntactic criterion

The syntactic criterion of *conforming to metadata* (i.e. *data integrity rules)* is derived directly from the definition of the syntactic quality category based on integrity theory. Note that although in the most general theoretical sense metadata comprises definitions, documentation, and rules (i.e. the data schema); we operationalize the definition in terms of conformance to specified integrity rules to serve as a practical basis for syntactic quality assessment. In the context of relational databases, this would comprise general integrity rules relating to the relational data model (e.g. domain, entity, and referential integrity) and those integrity rules specific to a given business or application.

Semantic criteria

The derivation of semantic quality criteria is based on the work of Wand and Wang (1996) because it is unique in the quality literature for its theoretical and rigorous approach to the definition of quality criteria. As acknowledged by the authors, the scope of their paper is limited to the objective view of quality based on the stored data's fidelity to the represented external world (i.e. not on data use). However, this corresponds to our definition of the semantic quality category; so their work can serve as a basis for deriving semantic quality criteria.

The derivation of quality criteria in Wand and Wang is based on an analysis of possible data deficiencies arising during the transformation of real-world states to IS representations, assuming an ontological view that the IS represents the real-world application domain. Using the example of an employee database, a *good* representation of the real-world by an IS requires that the IS data be *complete* (i.e. not missing anything, e.g. all employees are represented), *unambiguous* (i.e. maps uniquely to the real-world, e.g. a given stored employee ID does not map to two different employees), *meaningful* (i.e. no spurious or unmapped data, i.e. no extra invalid stored employee IDs), and *correct* (i.e. corresponds, e.g. stored employee ID and details match that of the actual employee to be represented). These criteria and their definitions were amended as described in Price and Shanks (2004) to account for differences in goals and to remedy observed inconsistencies in the original analysis. Here we discuss only the two amendments that are directly relevant to the discussion of focus group results and resulting revision of framework criteria (including semantic criteria) in the section on 'Practitioner, academic, and end-user focus groups' and the penultimate section, respectively.

Wand and Wang's original definitions are expressed in terms of database and real-world states; however, that is not practical for information quality assessment. Instead, the definitions must be operationalized in terms of identifiable *IS data units* (consisting of one or more data items, e.g. relational records with fields) and *external phenomena* (e.g. represented real-world objects) whose states can be sampled individually. As discussed in Wand and Wang, these two perspectives are interchangeable when analysing data deficiencies, except in the special case of *decomposition deficiencies*. In this case, the overall IS state may not correspond to the real-world even though individual components do, as a result of differently timed update of individual components. In practice, in addition to sampling individual IS and real-world components, some degree of aggregation may be required to detect decomposition deficiencies.

Finally, Wand and Wang classify only *meaningless* but not *redundant* IS states as a mapping deficiency. This is despite the acknowledgement that either case has a significant potential to lead to data deficiencies. We felt that these two cases should be treated consistently. Specifically, we concluded that *meaningful* and *nonredundant* should both be considered information quality criteria, while acknowledging that they differ from other semantic criteria in that they represent a danger rather than a definite deficiency. This issue is revisited in the 'Criteria definition' section as a result of focus group feedback.

Pragmatic criteria

Having reviewed the derivation of quality criteria for the syntactic and semantic quality categories, we next consider the derivation of quality criteria for the pragmatic quality category. Theoretical derivation techniques were suitable for the first two quality categories. However, as described in the introductory section, a combination of literature-based (described in this section) and empirical (described in the next section) techniques are required for the pragmatic category because it relates to consumer use of data and thus is subject to information consumer judgement. The initial set of pragmatic level criteria, described next, were thus derived based on an analytic review of literature guided by the goals and requirements for quality criteria described in the beginning of this section.

Pragmatic criteria pertain either to the delivery or to the importance of the retrieved data. They address the ease of retrieving information *(accessibility)*, the degree to which the presentation of retrieved information is appropriate for its use *(presentation suitability)*, the comprehensibility of presented information *(understandability)*, the ease of modifying the presentation to suit different purposes *(presentation flexibility)*, the degree of information protection *(security)*, the importance and sufficiency of information for consumer's tasks *(value)*, and the relevance of information to consumers' tasks *(relevance)*. The last criterion, *relevance*, relates specifically to the types of information available (i.e. *data intent)* rather than to the quantity of information available (i.e. *data extent)*, since the latter is already covered by the semantic quality criterion *complete*. *Value* (i.e. the criterion *valuable)was* included despite acknowledged inter-dependencies with other criteria, because it was considered necessary to act as a generic placeholder for those aspects of quality specific to a given application domain. This is discussed further in the section on 'Inter-dependencies between criteria'.

The pragmatic category includes additional criteria addressing consumer *perceptions* of the syntactic and semantic criteria described earlier. These are included because an information consumer's subjective and use-based judgement may differ considerably from objective and relatively use-independent measurement of the same quality criterion.

Table 24.2 Quality criteria by category

Syntactic criteria (based on rule conformance)
Conforming to metadata, i.e. data integrity rules
Semantic criteria (based on external correspondence)
Complete, unambiguous, correct, non-redundant, meaningful
Pragmatic criteria (use-based consumer perspective)
Accessible (easy, quick), suitably presented (timely; suitably formatted, precise, and measured in units), flexibly presented (easily aggregated; easily converted in terms of format, precision, and unit measurement), understandable, secure, relevant, valuable
Perceptions of syntactic and semantic criteria

An example is that the *completeness* of a given data set may be rated as quite good based on an objective, sampling-based semantic-level assessment but may be considered unacceptably poor by those consumers whose particular use of the data impose unusually stringent requirements.

Summarized list of criteria

Table 24.2 presents the initial list of quality criteria derived for each level as described in this section, with any sub-criteria listed in parentheses.

In the next section, we describe the empirical research method used to refine the framework, particularly with respect to the pragmatic criteria.

Practitioner, academic, and end-user focus groups

The primary motivation for conducting focus groups was to refine the initial list of pragmatic criteria derived through an analytic and literature-based approach. The necessity of using such a combined approach was explained in the Introduction, that is, empirical techniques are required to solicit consumer input as to the appropriate set of pragmatic quality criteria since by definition they relate to the subjective consumer perspective. The choice of empirical technique adopted was based on the highly interactive nature of focus groups (Krueger, 1994), allowing for a full exploration of relevant (and possibly contentious) issues based on a direct exchange of views between participants. Such consumer input implicitly provides some indirect evaluation of syntactic and semantic criteria and the framework as a whole, since some of the pragmatic criteria are based on perceptions of syntactic and semantic criteria.

Three focus groups were conducted to solicit feedback from IT practitioners, IT academics, and end-users respectively. The practitioner focus group had eight participants including both data management/ quality consultants and in-house IT professionals at varying levels of seniority (i.e. from application developers to senior managers). The academic focus group consisted of seven academics whose research was in the area of data management. The end-user focus group of six participants included administrative, managerial, and technical database users with non-IT backgrounds. Participants were asked to complete an individual opinion form evaluating the pragmatic criteria prior to their attendance at a focus group discussion of those criteria and of related quality issues.

During the focus group discussion, participants were passionate about their views and experiences of quality issues and the challenges of ensuring quality. The wideranging discussion that ensued addressed topics such as defining, assessing, improving, and managing quality in organizations. Since the framework was presented as intended to serve as a basis for development of quality assessment techniques and tools, the relevance of the framework to quality assessment was a major focus of the discussion – especially for practitioners and academics. In this paper, we report those focus group results (based on both individual opinion forms and the group discussion) most directly impacting the InfoQual framework revision. Relevant focus group outcomes can be categorized as related either to missing criteria or sub-criteria, interdependencies between criteria, criteria definition, or framework context and are discussed in the following four subsections, respectively.

Missing criteria or sub-criteria

Participants suggested a number of potential additions to the list of quality criteria. Some were determined to be outside the scope of the framework. For example, the proposed criteria *data model quality* (i.e. metadata quality) is a distinct topic requiring separate analysis and treatment, as discussed in the Introduction. Although poor metadata quality can negatively impact information quality (i.e. be a source of poor information quality), the two terms are not synonymous. Other proposed additions were already covered by the original set of quality criteria. For example, privacy issues related to unauthorized access, use, or distribution of data can be addressed through a minor amendment to the definition of the existing quality criteria *secure*, as discussed in the section 'Criteria definition'.

Only one proposed addition was both within the framework scope and not currently addressed, *allowing access to relevant metadata*. As it is clearly use-related, this criterion is added to the pragmatic category. In fact, the suggestion to include this quality criterion arose more than once in feedback from separate focus groups and was motivated by the requirements of different application contexts, including the following:

- for documentation on version and update lag time of replicate data,
- for currency, lineage, granularity, transformation, and source documentation of spatial data,
- for documentation on data collection purposes to comply with privacy legislation, and,
- for documentation of context for data originating from disparate or unfamiliar sources, for example, as in a data warehouse or data collection external to the organization accessing the data.

A data set that does not provide access to relevant metadata may result in the data being unintelligible, misinterpreted, or unintentionally misused. This clearly impacts the perceived quality of the retrieved information. It further implies inter-dependencies that should be acknowledged between this new quality criterion and the criteria *understandable* and *secure*.

In terms of sub-criteria, concerns were raised by endusers regarding the level of detail considered by the *correct* criterion. They regarded it as extremely important to differentiate between the specific types of errors that could result in a violation of this quality criterion, that is, a mismatch between a database value (i.e. attribute field value) and the external property that it was supposed to represent. For example, recording that the errors were due to missing values could allow explicit evaluation of the percentage of missing values for a given type of attribute (i.e. field). Possible types of errors include a missing value (i.e. empty field), an inappropriate value (i.e. of the wrong type or an invalid type, e.g. an address or numeric value in the employee name field), or an appropriate but incorrect value (i.e. of the correct type but not matching the external property, e.g. an address value in the address field but not that of the relevant employee). These three types of errors can be re-phrased in positive terms as sub-criteria of the *correct* criterion as: *present* (i.e. field has a value), *appropriate* (i.e. field value is of the correct type), and *matching* (i.e. field value matches that of the external property represented) respectively. Note that these sub-criteria are not independent since *matching* implies *appropriate* which in turn implies *present*. Note also that the presence of NULLs in the database could potentially obscure such judgements unless their meaning is clearly defined. Of the four possible interpretations of NULL described by Redman (1996), *not applicable* and *none* would not violate the *correct* criterion, *applicable but unknown* would violate the sub-criterion *present,* and *applicability unknown* cannot be evaluated (i.e. might be an example of any of the other three cases). These sub-criteria are discussed further in the next section.

Inter-dependencies between criteria

In this section, we discuss inter-dependencies between criteria in the original framework. Inter-dependencies resulting from the addition of criteria or sub-criteria to the framework were discussed in the above section. Whenever possible without limiting framework scope, the framework was modified to eliminate identified inter-dependencies. Where such action would compromise the comprehensive coverage of the framework, the inter-dependencies were acknowledged rather than removed.

Syntactic and Semantic Criteria

Inter-dependencies were identified (a) within the set of semantic criteria and (b) between semantic and syntactic criteria. As discussed in the 'Semantic criteria' section, the original semantic definitions, expressed in terms of states, were operationalized in terms of identifiable IS and external (e.g. real-world) phenomena. As a result, *correct* was initially defined as having attribute values match property values for each represented external (e.g. real-world) instance. However, this resulted in inter-dependencies with other semantic criteria since a mismatch in key (i.e. identifying) attribute values could further lead to *ambiguous* (i.e. one identifiable IS data unit maps to multiple different external phenomena), *meaningless* (i.e. one identifiable IS data unit does not map to any external phenomena), or *redundant* mappings (i.e. multiple different identifiable IS data units map to the same external phenomenon) that violate the *unambiguous, meaningful,* or *non-redundant* semantic criteria, respectively.

The solution is to define two separate semantic correctness criteria, *phenomenon-correct* and *property-correct*. The first correctness criterion *phenomenon-correct* relates to the correctness of mapping identifiable IS data units to external phenomena. A violation would involve an unambiguous, meaningful, non-redundant mapping (based on key attributes) of an identifiable data unit to the *wrong* external phenomenon.

The second correctness criterion *property-correct* involves an identifiable data unit that maps correctly to the represented external phenomenon but has an incorrect representation of one or more non-identifier external properties by non-key attributes (i.e. un-matched values). To illustrate, an example of phenomenon-level correctness is when the ID field for a given employee record correctly maps to the real-world employee with that ID; whereas property-level correctness is when the recorded salary value matches the employee's actual salary.

It should be noted that although inter-dependencies are reduced and criteria definitions clarified by this framework revision, inter-dependencies between semantic criteria are not completely eliminated, since *property-correct* implies *phenomenon-correct*, which, in turn, implies a *meaningful* mapping. In fact, this inter-dependency originates directly from Wand and Wang's (1996) initial set of criteria where a *correct* mapping implies further that the mapping is *meaningful*. However, we consider the distinctions between these different cases significant (e.g. for error source analysis) and thus acknowledge rather than remove the inter-dependencies. A further concern is the apparent inter-dependency between the newly introduced semantic criterion *property-correct* and the syntactic criterion *conforming to integrity rules*. Incorrect property representation can result from either an illegal or a legal but invalid (i.e. incorrect, unmatched) attribute value. As currently defined, the former case seems to violate both the above-mentioned criteria; whereas the latter case seems to violate only the semantic criterion. However, it is possible that an IS attribute value may violate a syntactic formatting rule but still be able to be matched correctly to the relevant external (e.g. real-world) property value. We therefore clarify that *property-correct* is with respect to fidelity to external property values, but not necessarily to all specified integrity rules.

Based on this revision to the original semantic criterion *correct*, we then re-visit the issue raised in 'Missing criteria or sub-criteria' of possible sub-criteria. The discussion and examples given in that section apply without amendment to the addition of the *present, appropriate,* and *matching* sub-criteria to the new criterion *property-correct*. However, these sub-criteria do not apply to the new criterion *phenomenon-correct*, since we have said that any violation of this criterion is, by definition, an unambiguous, meaningful, and non-redundant mapping (therefore necessarily involving a *present* and *appropriate* but *non-matching* key value) or it would violate one of these other three semantic criteria instead. In other words, the key value successfully identifies exactly one external phenomenon (implying that the key value exists and is of the correct type) but it is the *wrong* phenomenon (implying that the key value does not match the identifier for the represented external phenomenon). So the data unit actually represents a different external phenomenon than that identified by the data unit's key values. We therefore conclude that the three new sub-criteria should be added to the *property-correct* but not the *phenomenon-correct* criterion.

Pragmatic criteria

Inter-dependencies were identified between pragmatic criteria relating to data delivery, in that information must first be *accessible* to judge whether it is *understandable* (and other presentation aspects) and must be *understandable* before judging whether it is *suitably* and *flexibly presented*. Conversely, information presentation affects perceived understandability and accessibility. In this case, we judged that, although inter-dependent, these criteria each represented essential and distinct quality aspects whose removal would result in a less comprehensive coverage of information quality. However, the sub-dimension *timely* was removed from *suitably presented* and made a separate delivery-related criterion. This restricts the criterion *suitably presented* to presentation style aspects (i.e. layout, precision, units), thus simplifying and clarifying its semantics. Further, it serves to acknowledge the critical importance of timeliness as a quality aspect in its own right, an issue raised in both academic and practitioner focus groups.

Further inter-dependencies between *understandable* and many other criteria (beyond those relating to data delivery) were identified. Essentially, information must be understood before its relevance, value, and perceived syntactic and semantic quality aspects can be judged. After consideration, the best response was judged to be explicit acknowledgement of the inter-dependency.

Finally, we consider the inter-dependencies between the pragmatic criteria *valuable* and most other criteria (insofar that satisfying other quality criteria implies high value), and especially with the pragmatic criteria *relevant*. Although these inter-dependencies were explicitly acknowledged; *valuable* was initially retained as a placeholder for domain-specific quality criteria that might not have been covered elsewhere in the framework. Focus group discussion failed to elicit any examples of such domain-specific criteria that did not fit into the framework (assuming the framework is revised as discussed in the section on 'Missing criteria or sub-criteria'), even though representatives of both general business and specialized technical applications (i.e. geographic information systems) were included in the focus groups. Furthermore, the evident confusion introduced as a result of these acknowledged inter-dependencies became clear during the course of the focus groups. The feedback clearly indicated that participants felt that the concept of *valuable* was too general and abstract to ensure consistent interpretation (i.e. rather it was likely to be understood quite differently by different people) or to convey any meaningful information. It was therefore judged not to be useful as a specific quality criterion and removed from the framework.

In a related issue, focus group feedback highlighted the fact that the *sufficiency* aspect of the original criterion *valuable* should instead be considered in the criterion *relevant* with respect to the types of information available. This aspect of quality is not considered elsewhere in the framework. Therefore, the criterion *relevant* can be replaced with the more comprehensive criterion *type-sufficient*, defined as the degree to which the given data set includes all of the types of information (i.e. *data intent*) useful for the intended information use. This is discussed further in the next section.

Criteria definition

In this section, we discuss focus group feedback relating to identified ambiguities in criteria semantics or wording not caused by dependencies between criteria (discussed in the above section). With respect to criteria semantics, it was evident from all of the focus groups that participants regarded the presence of redundancy in a data collection as quite common and not necessarily an indication of poor quality. In fact, they referred to replication, a synonym for redundancy with positive rather than negative connotations, as an integral part of effective organizational data management.

The argument presented in the 'Semantic criteria' section was that both *meaningless* and *redundant* data represented a potential rather than a definite quality problem and therefore should be treated similarly. However, as a result of the focus group feedback, the two cases could be clearly differentiated in that only the latter might be deliberately introduced because of associated benefits (e.g. with respect to improved access time for geographically dispersed consumers). The response to this observation is to redefine the quality criterion *non-redundant* as *consistent*, that is, not having duplicates or having acceptably consistent duplicates. Acceptable consistency is defined as either having consistent replicates (i.e. with matched attribute values) or inconsistency that is resolved within a time frame acceptable in the context of replicate use.

Considerations related to the impact of privacy laws on information quality led to the elaboration of the original definition of the pragmatic criterion *security* as 'appropriately protected from damage or abuse (including unauthorized access)' to include unauthorized use or distribution.

Another source of confusion raised by end-users was their difficulty in distinguishing between *suitably presented* and *relevant* (or the substituted *type-sufficient*), End-users' understanding of the type of information (i.e. attribute or field types) available is commonly based on what is displayed or made available through the presentation interface. Therefore, they tended to view this issue as just another sub-criterion relating to presentation rather than a separate and independent criterion. After further consideration, neither the original criterion *relevant* nor the newly proposed criterion *type-sufficient* are included in the revised framework. Instead, the sub-criteria *includes suitable field types* and *the selection of displayed field types easily changed* are added to the existing sub-criteria of *suitably presented* and *flexibly presented* respectively.

Other identified ambiguities in criteria definition are related to wording. For example, the term *meaningful* was often misinterpreted as important or significant rather than as defined in terms of a mapping cardinality constraint. Thus the implicit connotations of the English word took precedence over the definition given. Therefore the names of all the semantic criteria were amended to include explicit references to mapping, for example, *mapped meaningfully, mapped completely,* etc.

Framework context

Discussions relating to framework context helped to further clarify the scope and boundaries of the research.

Specialized data types

Focus group participants raised questions regarding whether specialized application domains, such as scientific data, were addressed by the framework, with spatial applications such as geographic information systems given as a specific example. This was discussed in the section on 'Interdependencies between criteria' in the context of the criterion *valuable*, which was deleted from the framework following the failure to identify any domain-specific criteria not covered at least generally by other framework criteria and the acknowledged confusion caused by the criterion's inherent inter-dependencies and ambiguity. It was additionally observed that although the framework did encompass spatial quality criteria, it was at a level that might potentially be too general to be useful in the context of specialized spatial applications. Therefore, the decision was made to explicitly acknowledge that the framework targeted (i.e. was specifically developed for) general business applications, although it might provide useful guidelines (i.e. a starting point) for conceptualizing quality even in specialized application domains. That is, if any domain-specific criteria exist in specialized application areas; it was judged more effective that individual organizations add them explicitly to create variants of the basic framework.

Unit of analysis

Questions were raised regarding the framework's intended unit of analysis, specifically whether it targeted data sets or individual data attributes (i.e. columns in the relational context). In the context of common organizational quality assessment requirements and the framework's potential for supporting those requirements, some practitioners felt that it was important to be able to assess not only entire data sets (e.g. the customer information relation) but also individual relational columns (e.g. the address column from that relation). On reflection, we realized that this represented one example of a more general issue. The general issue is that of quality assessment for data sets that do not include identifiers (e.g. any set of non-key columns in the relational context). In such a case, the individual data units (e.g. non-key field values from a record in the relational context) comprising the data set cannot be mapped to specific external phenomena. Two questions arise consequently: can the current framework support this type of assessment and how important is it to support this type of assessment?

It is immediately evident that because semantic category criteria are based on IS/real-world mappings, their evaluation requires identifiable data units in order to establish the necessary correspondence between data and external phenomena. Therefore, although parts of the framework are still relevant; the framework as a whole cannot support such quality assessments.

On first glance, it appears that such assessments are critically important to answer questions such as: *how reliable is stored customer address information?* However, closer examination reveals that this question is directed against the customer address attribute with respect to the customer identifier attribute(s), that is, *when we retrieve the address for any given customer, is it reliable?* If an address retrieved for a given customer is *reliable*, that means it is the correct address for that particular customer. Thus, such questions still involve data sets with identifiers, that is, identifiable data units that can each be mapped to individual external phenomena. In fact, the only type of quality assessment that is directed against an individual non-key attribute or attributes in isolation would be in the context of aggregation tasks, for example, *If we calculate the average or total employee salary, is it reliable?* In this case, there is no need to map salaries to employees. However, it is relatively rare that individual attributes are assessed for quality *only* with respect to aggregation tasks.

Objective versus subjective quality contexts

Several questions raised during focus group discussions highlighted contextual differences between the objective and subjective components of the framework in terms of the types of data and metadata that can be considered in practice (e.g. in quality assessments based on the criteria defined in the framework).

Although the syntactic criterion can be defined theoretically as *conformance to metadata (i.e. data integrity rules)*, in practice, actual conformance assessments at the syntactic level would be objectively judged against existing database integrity rules as they are the only integrity rules explicitly specified and practically accessible. However, information consumers generally do not know which integrity rules have been specified; therefore, subjective consumer judgments of perceived conformance at the pragmatic level would be in the context of their own understanding of the applicable integrity constraints.

Similarly, objective quality criteria can be practically assessed only with respect to derived data that are stored; whereas assessment of subjective quality criteria necessarily includes both derived data that are stored and that which are calculated, since consumers would not normally be able to distinguish between the two cases.

In fact, as long as such differences between objective and subjective quality perspectives are explicitly acknowledged and understood in using the framework, they represent one of the potential strengths of the framework, as discussed in the third section. To reiterate, comparisons between objective and subjective quality assessments can be used to check for discrepancies that are likely to signify a quality problem (and that may not be immediately obvious from only one type of assessment) and may facilitate analysis into the source of the quality problem. For example, differences between syntactic and perceived syntactic quality assessments may be due to significant omissions in the integrity rules specified in the initial schema (i.e. data model problems).

Revised framework and comparison

As a result of focus group feedback, the scope of the semiotic information quality framework discussed in this paper can be clarified as follows. The framework is specifically intended for general business applications with structured data and for use with data sets that include identifiers (i.e. key attributes) allowing data units to be mapped to external (e.g. real-world) phenomena and vice versa.

Focus group feedback was also used as a basis for refining the original quality criteria, especially for the pragmatic category. The revised set of quality criteria and their definitions for each quality category is shown in Table 24.3, with any sub-criteria listed in parenthesis after the criterion name. Note that the terms *external phenomenon* and *phenomena* refer to external (e.g. real-world) instances.

Table 24.3   Revised quality criteria by category

Syntactic Criteria (based on rule conformance)
   Conforming to metadata, i.e. data integrity rules: Data follows specified data integrity rules

Semantic Criteria (based on external correspondence)
   Mapped completely: Every external phenomenon is represented
   Mapped unambiguously: Each identifiable data unit represents at most one specific external phenomenon
   Phenomena mapped correctly: Each identifiable data unit maps to the correct external phenomenon
   Properties mapped correctly (present, appropriate, matching): Non-identifying (i.e. non-key) attribute values in an identifiable data unit match the property values for the represented external phenomenon
   Mapped consistently: Each external phenomenon is either represented by at most one identifiable data unit or by multiple but consistent identifiable units or by multiple identifiable units whose inconsistencies are resolved within an acceptable time frame
   Mapped meaningfully: Each identifiable data unit represents at least one specific external phenomenon

Pragmatic criteria (use-based consumer perspective)
   Accessible (easy, quick): Data are easy and quick to retrieve
   Suitably presented (suitably formatted, precise, and measured in units; includes suitable field types): Data are presented in a manner appropriate for their use, with respect to format, precision, units, and the type of information displayed
   Flexibly presented (easily aggregated; format, precision, and units easily converted; the selection of displayed field types easily changed): Data can be easily manipulated and the presentation customized as needed, with respect to aggregating data and changing the data format, precision, units, or type of information displayed
   Timely: The currency (age) of data is appropriate to their use
   Understandable: Data are presented in an intelligible manner
   Secure: Data are appropriately protected from damage or abuse (including unauthorized access, use, or distribution)
   Allowing access to relevant metadata: Appropriate metadata are available to define, constrain, and document data
   Perceptions of the syntactic and semantic criteria defined earlier

---

The revised quality criteria in Table 24.3 can be compared with the initial list of quality criteria in Table 24.2 to identify criteria whose definition or use in the framework were most affected by the empirical refinement process, as illustrated in Table 24.4. Other revisions relate to terminology or to framework context and thus are not shown in Table 24.4.

The revised semiotic information quality framework can then be compared to other information quality frameworks proposed previously. There have been a number of proposals that focus on a specific application domain (e.g. web quality from Barnes and Vidgen, 2002) or that consider information quality indirectly as one factor in a broader IS perspective (e.g. in the context of measuring IS success in DeLone and McLean, 2003 or modeling IS systems in Ballou *et al.*, 1998). Although these proposals are subject to some of the same criticisms relating to rigor and consistency discussed in the introductory section we restrict our comparison here to those information quality frameworks that are generic (i.e. not focused on a specific domain), applicable to general business applications (i.e. suitable for structured data in business databases or data warehouses), and frequently mentioned in recent information quality literature (i.e. from the last decade). Frameworks can be compared based on a number of different considerations. For example, Eppler's (2001) survey evaluates the clarity, positioning, consistency, conciseness, and practicality (in terms of examples and tools) of information quality frameworks. Our comparison in Table 24.5 focuses

Table 24.4 Summary of major revisions of quality criteria by category

Quality category	Initial quality criterion affected	Revision
Syntactic	None	
Semantic	*Correct*	Sub-divided into *property-* and *phenomenon-correctness* with further sub-criteria *present, appropriate, matching* added to the former
	Non-redundant	Re-defined in terms of consistency
Prágmatic	*Suitably presented*	Sub-criterion *timely* promoted to separate criterion
	Valuable	Eliminated
	Relevant	Definition changed to type-sufficient and demoted to sub-criteria of *suitably / flexibly presented*
	Secure	Definition amended to include use and distribution issues
		Addition of new criterion, *including access to metadata*

Table 24.5 Comparison of frameworks

Consideration	English (1999)	Wang and Strong (1996), Kahn et al. (1997), Kahn et al. (2002), Lee et al. (2002)	Wand and Wang (1996)	Redman (1996)	InfoQual
Derivation and definition of categories	*Ad hoc*	Empirical (original paper), Ad-hoc (follow-up papers, PSP/IQ model)	*Ad hoc*	Logical	Theoretical (semiotics)
Selection of criteria derivation method	Not discussed explicitly for framework	Based on stated assumption that empirical method best represents consumer perceptions	Theoretical (ontological view of IS)	Not discussed	Theoretical (semiotics)
Derivation and definition of criteria	*Ad hoc*	Empirical	Theoretical (mapping cardinality)	*Ad hoc*	Objective criteria: theoretical (integrity theory/mapping cardinality) Subjective criteria: literature-based (initial) and empirical (refined)
Classification of criteria into categories	*Ad hoc*	*Ad hoc* (initial) and empirical (refined)	Not applicable	*Ad hoc*	Theoretical (automatic consequence of selecting criteria derivation method)
Inter-dependencies considered?	No	No	No	Yes	Yes

(continued)

Table 24.5 Continued

Consideration	English (1999)	Wang and Strong (1996), Kahn et al. (1997), Kahn et al. (2002), Lee et al. (2002)	Wand and Wang (1996)	Redman (1996)	InfoQual
Criteria coverage (compared to InfoQual)	*Missing:* details regarding reliability, security criterion, *access to metadata criterion,* and *pragmatic* criteria based on perceptions of *syntactic and semantic* criteria.	*Missing: syntactic* criterion, details regarding reliability, *access to metadata* criterion, *pragmatic* criteria based on perceptions of *syntactic and semantic* criteria	*Missing:* does not consider *syntactic* and *pragmatic* categories of criteria.	*Missing:* details regarding reliability, *security* criterion, and *pragmatic* criteria based on perceptions of *syntactic and semantic* criteria. *Additional:* some consideration of data model and data storage quality	
Category and classification consistency	Inconsistency in classification of criteria into categories	Inconsistency in category names, definitions, and use in criteria classification	No classification done, categories consistent	Some inconsistency in classification	Theoretical foundation for these steps ensures consistency

on differences in framework development – in terms of the research approach(s) adopted and consideration of inter-dependencies – and the resultant implications for framework scope (i.e. specific criteria coverage) and consistency.

The most obvious difference between the frameworks highlighted by the table is the difference in research approach adopted. Only InfoQual provides a consistent theoretical basis for all of the development steps – with the single exception of the derivation of subjective quality criteria which is intrinsically dependent on information consumer judgements and thus requires empirical feedback (or industrial experience) to ensure relevance. Wand and Wang (1996) provide a rigorous basis for deriving and defining objective criteria using a theoretical approach, but are limited in scope and still rely on an *ad hoc* derivation of quality categories. Redman's derivation and definition of categories is termed *logical* rather than *theoretical* because although it is a result of logical reasoning and clearly stated objectives, it is not based on a systematic theory. Finally, neither English (1996) nor the frameworks based on the same set of empirically derived criteria (Wang and Strong, 1996; Kahn *et al.*, 1997, 2002; Lee *et al.*, 2002) provide any theoretical basis for their frameworks. For convenience, we will refer to the latter set of frameworks as *Wang's frameworks*.

The consequence of the lack of theoretical basis is clearly demonstrated when framework consistency is evaluated, especially with respect to the classification of criteria in categories. With the exception of InfoQual, all of the multi-category frameworks exhibit inconsistency in criteria classification and Wang's frameworks further show inconsistency (and ambiguity) in category definition.

Although the quality categories were empirically derived in Wang and Strong's (1996) original paper, the subsequent papers defined a new set of *ad hoc* quality categories (termed the *PSP/IQ* model) and re-classified criteria based on these new categories. The limited semantic basis for the selection of quality categories and their use in classifying the quality criteria in these frameworks is clear from both (1) the substantial changes evident in category names, definitions, and member criteria in successive papers (Wang and Strong, 1996; Kahn *et al.*, 1997, 2002) and (2) naming and definition ambiguities in categories and criteria, resulting in the lack of clear semantic differentiation between different categories or between a category and its criteria. Examples of the latter case include the *dependable* and *sound* categories in Kahn *et al.* (2002) and Lee *et al.* (2002); the *useful* and *effective* categories in Kahn *et al.* (1997), or the *access* category and its *accessible* criterion in Wang and

Strong (1996). Classification inconsistencies include the inclusion of the *believable* and *reputation* criteria in the *usable* rather than the *sound* or *dependable* categories, where intuitively it would be expected that these criteria are more directly related to reliability than usability.

Classification inconsistencies can also be clearly observed in English (1999) based on the specified category and criteria definitions. For example, although *precision* and *accessibility* are explicitly defined as being dependent on data use, they are classified as being *inherent* – a quality category explicitly defined by English as use-independent.

Redman's (1996) classification of criteria also shows inconsistencies. The scope of his framework includes data model quality (i.e. relating to the quality of *metadata* such as conceptual views) and data storage quality (i.e. relating to the quality of data *representation*) as well as information quality (i.e. relating to the quality of data *values* – both stored and received); with some ambiguity introduced as to the classification of criteria between these categories. For instance, schematic *conceptual view quality* is considered a separate category. It includes not only criteria relating to data model quality such as the *naturalness* and *clarity* of the entities and attributes defined but also criteria relating to information quality such as *accessibility* of data values. Similarly, the definitions of *format suitability* and *format flexibility* criteria in Redman's *data representation* category include both storage aspects (e.g. suitability/flexibility for specific/different physical media) and presentation aspects (e.g. suitability/flexibility for specific/different users), where the latter clearly relate to subjective views of information quality rather than to data storage or representation quality.

With respect to consideration of inter-dependencies between proposed criteria, Eppler (2001) notes that it is rarely considered in information quality frameworks proposed to date despite its importance for understanding the semantics and practical implications of an information quality framework. To illustrate the potential significance of such inter-dependencies, consider their acknowledged impact on the choice of appropriate analytic methods to be used, for example, in the application of such a framework to instrument development (see Straub *et al.*, 2004) for subjective information quality assessment.

Of the frameworks considered, only Redman's (1996) and InfoQual include any consideration of inter-dependencies between proposed criteria. Examples of significant inter-dependencies in Wang's frameworks that are not explicitly acknowledged or justified include those between *believability* and *reputation* criteria and between *ease-of-understanding* and *interpretability* criteria. Similarly, in English (1999), most of the criteria included in his *inherent* quality category (defined as use-independent) contribute to the criterion of *rightness* from his *pragmatic* quality category (defined as use-dependent). As discussed earlier in the section on 'Inter-dependencies between criteria', even Wand and Wang's (1996) restricted and theoretically-derived framework has an unacknowledged inter-dependency between the *correct* and *meaningful* criteria, where the former implies the latter.

When comparing the coverage (i.e. scope) of the different frameworks, we consider only significant omissions or additions with respect to the quality criteria defined by InfoQual.[2] Only InfoQual clearly differentiates between objective criteria and subjective perceptions of those criteria. Only Wand and Wang (1996) and InfoQual use mapping errors as the basis for deriving quality criteria relating to reliability (also called *accuracy, correctness,* etc.) and thus consider details of *reliability* in terms of the specific mapping cardinalities (*unambiguous, meaningful,* etc.). Coverage of InfoQual's syntactic category criterion, *security* criterion, and *access to metadata* criterion are inconsistent across the frameworks. As discussed earlier, Wand and Wang do not consider syntactic or pragmatic category criteria at all.

Notably, only Redman's framework contains criteria not considered by InfoQual, although these relate to data model or data storage quality rather than information quality. Data model quality has been more comprehensively treated by other authors (Krogstie *et al.*, 1995; Wand and Weber, 1995; Krogstie, 2001); however, data storage quality has not received the same attention in the literature. For instance, Redman describes criteria relating to the storage format's appropriateness or portability for different recording media (in effect, for different physical instances of the data). Such considerations can be important for an organization with enterprise information systems that may include multiple copies of data stored on different types of physical media. In the semiotic context, such criteria relate to the syntactic level as both *stored data format* and *stored data physical instances* (on physical media) can be considered signs (i.e. nested signs for the hierarchically structured levels of IS internal storage representation as described in the third section). Thus, a possible new adaptation or extension of InfoQual to include data storage quality considerations such as storage format quality is compatible with and naturally supported by the framework's existing theoretical foundation in semiotic theory.

Finally, we note that Redman considers both inter-record (i.e. replication) and intra-record sources of redundancy, where the latter case is the result of record fields with overlapping semantics. An example is a record containing both postal or zip code and state, where state information is redundantly determined by the code. Correctness of fields within a record (regardless of whether they overlap) is described by the *properties mapped correctly* criteria in InfoQual. However, in this case, no update lag should be allowed – the fields must be updated together to ensure consistency and thus correctness.

Conclusion

In summary, the comparative analysis from the previous section clearly shows that all of the frameworks except InfoQual suffer from limitations with respect to consistency and/or coverage. InfoQual addresses these problems by providing a consistent theoretical foundation for (1) the derivation and definition of quality categories, (2) the selection of derivation methods for quality criteria and consequent automatic classification of criteria into categories, (3) the derivation of objective quality criteria, and (4) the integration of objective, theoretically-based and subjective, non-theoretically based views of information quality. The use of empirical feedback to refine the framework ensures its relevance, especially with respect to the subjective quality view. The utility and power of using semiotic theory as the underlying theoretical foundation for the framework is further demonstrated by its relevance to unanticipated and new applications, for example, for data storage quality.

Since quality information is required for effective decision-making in an organization; continuous information quality management – including information quality assessment, problem identification and source analysis, and improvement strategies – is an essential element of decision support. A framework such as InfoQual that clearly and consistently defines the quality categories and criteria to be considered is an important pre-requisite for such a management program.

The explicit intention of the research reported here was to provide an information quality framework that could serve as a basis for further work in information quality in general and in information quality assessment in particular. Therefore, future work following on from this would include the development of assessment tools and techniques based on this framework. Additional areas of potential work include the evaluation of the utility and potential application of this framework to other aspects of information quality such as improvement and management and to specialized application contexts involving, for example, spatial or scientific data. Another possible direction would be to explore the application of InfoQual to data storage quality to include, for example, consideration of criteria related to storage format as outlined above.

Notes

1. We prefer the more inclusive term *external* to the frequently-used term *real-world* (e.g. in Wand and Wang, 1996), because of the latter's connotations that only concrete physical and not socially constructed phenomena (e.g. quotas) are considered.
2. Other apparent differences are shown not to be significant after a careful analysis of such factors as criteria overlap (i.e. what is the actual semantic coverage of additional criteria?) and validity (e.g. are the proposed criteria generic – applicable across application domains and data types?).

References

Ballou, D., Wang, R.Y., Pazer, H. and Tayi, G.K. (1998). Modeling Information Manufacturing Systems to Determine Information Product Quality, *Journal of Management Science* 44(4): 462–484.

Barnes, S.J. and Vidgen, R.T. (2002). An Integrative Approach to the Assessment of e-Commerce Quality, *Journal of Electronic Commerce Research* 3(3): 114–127.

Barnouw, E. (ed.) (1989). *International Encyclopedia of Communications*, Oxford: Oxford University Press.

DeLone, W.H. and McLean, E.R. (2003). The DeLone and McLean Model of Information System Success: A ten-year update, *Journal of Management Information Systems* 19(4): 9–30.

English, L. (1999). *Improving Data Warehouse and Business Information Quality*, New York: John Wiley & Sons, Inc.

Eppler, M.J. (2001). The Concept of Information Quality: An interdisciplinary evaluation of recent information quality frameworks, *Studies in Communication Sciences* 1: 167–182.

Gendron, M. and Shanks, G. (2003). The Categorical Information Quality Framework (CIQF): A critical assessment and replication study, *in Proceedings of the Pacific-Asia Conference on Information Systems*, (Adelaide, Australia, 2003), Adelaide, South Australia: University of South Australia, 1–13.

Kahn, B.K., Strong, D.M. and Wang, R.Y. (1997). A Model for Delivering Quality Information as Product and Service, *in Proceedings of Conference on Information Quality*, (Massachusetts Institute of Technology, Cambridge, MA, USA, 1997), Cambridge, MA, USA: Massachussets Institute of Technology, 80–94.

Kahn, B.K., Strong, D.M. and Wang, R.Y. (2002). Information Quality Benchmarks: Product and service performance, *Communications of the ACM* 45(4): 184–192.

Krogstie, J. (2001). A Semiotic Approach to Quality in Requirements Specifications, in: *Proceedings of IFIP 8.1 Working Conference on Organizational Semiotics*, (Montreal, Canada 2001), London: Chapman and Hall, 231–249.

Krogstie, J., Lindland, O.I. and Sindre, G. (1995). Defining Quality Aspects for Conceptual Models, in *Proceedings of IFIP8.1 working conference on Information Systems Concepts (ISCO3): Towards a consolidation of views*, (Marburg, Germany, 1995), Berlin: Springer, 216–231.

Krueger, R.A. (1994). *Focus Groups: A practical guide for research,* Thousand Oaks, CA: Sage.

Lee, Y.W., Strong, D.M., Kahn, B.K. and Wang, R.Y. (2002). AIMQ: A methodology for information quality assessment, *Information and Management* 40: 133–146.

Morris, C. (1938). Foundations of the Theory of Signs, in *International Encyclopedia of Unified Science,* Vol. 1, London: University of Chicago Press.

Pierce, C.S. (1931–1935). *Collected Papers,* Cambridge, MA: Harvard University Press.

Price, R. and Shanks, G. (2004). A Semiotic Information Quality Framework, in *Proceedings of the IFIP International Conference on Decision Support Systems (DSS2004),* (Prato, Italy, 2004), Melbourne, Victoria, Australia: Monash University, 658–672.

Price, R. and Shanks, G. (2005). Empirical Refinement of a Semiotic Information Quality Framework, in *Proceedings of Hawaii International Conference on System Sciences (HICSS38),* (Big Island, Hawaii, USA, 2005); Silver Spring, MD: IEEE Computer Society Press, 1–10.

Redman, T.C. (1996). *Data Quality for the Information Age,* Boston, MA: Artech House.

Shanks, G. and Darke, P. (1998). Understanding Data Quality in Data Warehousing: A semiotic approach, in *Proceedings of the MIT Conference on Information Quality,* (Boston, MA, USA, 1998), Cambridge, MA, USA: Massachusetts Institute of Technology, 247–264.

Straub, D., Boudreau, M.C. and Gefen, D. (2004). Validation Guidelines of IS Positivist Research, *Communications of the Association for Information Systems* 13: 380–426.

Stamper, R. (1991). The Semiotic Framework for Information Systems Research, in: Nissen H, Klein H and Hirschheim R (eds.) *Information Systems Research: Contemporary Approaches and Emergent Traditions,* Amsterdam: North-Holland.

Wand, Y. and Wang, R.Y. (1996). Anchoring Data Quality Dimensions in Ontological Foundations, *Communications of the ACM* 39(11): 86–95.

Wand, Y. and Weber, R. (1995). On the Deep Structure of Information Systems, *Information Systems Journal* 5: 203–223.

Wang, R.Y. and Strong, D.M. (1996). Beyond Accuracy: What data quality means to data consumers, *Journal of Management Information Systems* 12(4): 5–34.

25

Complexity and Information Systems: The Emergent Domain

Yasmin Merali
Warwick Business School, The University of Warwick, UK

Introduction

This paper is concerned with the emergence of the information systems (IS) domain as a central feature of the management research landscape in the networked world. It shows that the emergence of the network economy and network society (Castells, 1996) necessitates a paradigm shift in the IS discipline, and that complexity science offers the apposite concepts and tools for effecting such a shift.

Lichtenstein and McKelvey (2006) point out that although complexity science has been heralded as the new paradigm in management, providing a powerful set of methods for explaining non-linear, emergent behaviour in organisations (Stacey, 1992; Brown and Eisenhardt, 1997; McKelvey, 1997; Anderson *et al.*, 1999), the emergence of a 'complexity science of organisations' is stalled because:

- there are conflicting views about the application of complexity concepts in the management domain and
- the egregious use of complexity metaphors has resulted in fundamental principles from complexity science being inappropriately applied to organisations.

To avoid confusion of fundamental complexity science concepts with the more colloquial uses of complexity terminology, this paper provides

Reprinted from "Complexity and information systems: the emergent domain," by Y. Merali in *Journal of Information Technology*, 21, 2006, pp. 216–228. With kind permission from the Association for Information Technology Trust. All rights reserved.

an introduction to concepts from complexity science for those in the IS field who are unacquainted with complexity theory. It then proceeds to explore the utility of these concepts for developing IS theory and practice for the emergent networked world.

The paper is organised in the following way. The following section provides an overview of the networked world, highlighting the features that have led to the current interest in complexity science across the management field. The next section defines the information and systems characteristics of the networked world. It shows how the network phenomenology and the network form of organising have the potential for creating *and* absorbing high levels of complexity, raising a number of issues that pose challenges for the 'traditional' IS paradigm. The subsequent sections introduce concepts from complexity science that are useful in addressing the complexity of the networked world, and provide an overview of the role that models play in exploring complex systems' behaviour. The penultimate section discusses the contribution that complexity science can make to the development of ontological and epistemological frameworks for IS in the networked world, and reflects on the positioning of the IS discipline in the management field. The paper concludes with a summary of the key implications for IS research.

The networked world

The advent of the internet and attendant emergent technologies has resulted in a step change in the level of complexity inherent in the effective world.[1,2] At the most fundamental level, the technological developments have the potential to increase:

- connectivity (between people, applications and devices),
- capacity for distributed storage and processing of data,
- reach and range of information transmission and
- rate (speed and volume) of information transmission.

The realisation of these affordances has given rise to the emergence of new network forms of organisation embodying complex, distributed network structures, with processes, information and expertise being shared across organisational and national boundaries. The increase in the number of components to be integrated across diverse technological platforms and business systems demands complex architectures. Greater connectivity and access to an increased variety and volume of information constitute greater informational complexity (Chaitin, 1990), creating the need for more powerful semantic, algorithmic and computational capabilities. Increased global connectivity and speed of communication effectively contract the spatiotemporal separation of events – informational changes (or information about changes) in one locality can very quickly be transmitted globally, influencing social, political and economic decisions in geographically remote places.

The network form of organising is thus a signature of the internet-enabled transformation of economics and society: the strategy and managerial discourse is shifting from focusing solely on the firm as a unit of organisation to networks of firms, from considerations of industry-specific value systems to considerations of networks of value systems and from the concept of discrete industry structures to the concept of ecologies.

The consequent emergence of the network economy and network society (Hamel and Prahalad, 1994; Castells, 1996; Shapiro and Varian, 1999) has catalysed the resurgence of academic and practitioner interest in issues of complexity. For organisations operating in the network economy, the strategy and management literature (Axelrod and Cohen, 1999; Eisenhardt and Galunic, 1999; Evans and Wurster, 2000; Stacey, 2001; Bonabeau and Meyer, 2001; Bonabeau, 2002) highlights as key concerns:

- increased dynamism, uncertainty and discontinuity in the competitive context,
- the escalation of pressures for fast decision making under conditions of greater informational uncertainty,
- the importance of (internal and external) intelligence and
- the importance of flexibility and adaptability (and learning) for survival.

To deal with the challenges posed by this set of concerns, scholars have turned to complexity theory in order to develop an understanding of

- the dynamics of the competitive landscapes,
- what constitutes organisational fitness (with respect to survival in changing landscapes) and
- the relationship between decisions and actions of individuals, collections and collectives of individuals (e.g. organisations, groups, clusters and networks of organisations) and the emergent networked world.

The vocabulary of chaos, co-evolution, emergence and self-organisation has been deployed to articulate the aspects of adaptation, discontinuous change and dynamism that are attributed to the network economy.

More specifically from the IS perspective, there is the realisation that the dynamics of the networked world are profoundly influenced by the generation, manipulation, communication and utilisation of information (Castells, 1996). There is an escalation of interest in the idea that information technology networks and social and economic networks self-organise into a constellation of networks of networks (Watts, 1999, 2003; Barabasi, 2002). This is analogous to conceptualising the networked world as a kind of global distributed IS (Merali, 2004b, 2005).

In the following section, we develop this conceptualisation by defining the information and systems characteristics of the networked world. This view through the information lens constitutes an effective level of abstraction for exposing the dynamic network capabilities that give rise to the complex phenomenology of the network economy and society and its challenges for the traditional IS paradigm.

Network dynamics: a view through the information lens

From the IS perspective, an interconnected world that is comprised of technologically mediated networks of networks can be conceptualised as:

- a complex multi-dimensional network which
- connects a diversity of agents (individuals, groups, institutions, nations, computers, software components, etc.) through
- multiple and diverse communication channels.

The socially defined and the socially defining nature of technology is well established in the IS literature (Leavitt and Whistler, 1958; Marcus, 1983; Zuboff, 1988; Davis, 1989; Jarvanpaa, 1989; Hiltz and Johnson, 1990; Orlikowski, 1992; Merali, 1997; Merali, 2004a). The system constituting the socially situated technology *in use* has properties that are distinctive (different in kind) from those of the nascent technology.

The *realised* internet-enabled information network (i.e. the *network-in-use*), comprises social, economic, political, legal, informational and technological dimensions. The information *network-in-use* can thus be viewed as an *informational representation* of the interactions of participating agents situated in their social, economic, political, informational and technological contexts. While the technological infrastructure provides the *possibility* of communication between interconnected nodes, the *actual* form and content of the active *network-in-use* at any given time is defined by *interaction* of social actors with the technological network in order to communicate with agents situated at other nodes in the network.

This section outlines the network characteristics that arise when the technological network capability is deployed by human agents, giving rise to the complex phenomena that draw us to the language and paradigms of the 'science of complexity' for their articulation.

Network connectivity: emergent topology

Networks consist of interconnected agents (nodes) that are able to communicate with each other. The connectivity of each node is defined by the nature and number of its links (relationships) with other nodes, and by its position in the network. Nodes send, receive, transform and transmit information throughout the network, and they can also be information repositories. The ways in which connections intersect create the distinctive traits and functions that characterise the behaviour of the network as a whole.

Each node may be connected to a number of different nodes at any given time. Depending on the task at hand, attendant constraints and proclivities, individual nodes activate particular connections in the network at particular times. Not all nodes are necessarily equally connected. The heterogeneity (with regard to strength and density of connections) of links in social networks has been studied extensively (Granovetter, 1973, 1985, 1995; Burt, 1992, 1997). Snapshots of internet-enabled social networks reveal denser clusters of networks with looser connections to other clusters of networks (Watts, 1999, 2003; Barabasi, 2002; Buchanan, 2002).

The patterns of connectivity can change over time: some connections may become stronger due to repeated transactions and the development of lasting relationships, new connections may appear as entities embark on innovative ventures, some connections may atrophy due to a lack of communication, while dying connections may be revived due to a renewed interest or necessity for collaboration. Over time we can expect to observe a dynamic network topology, with individual constellations in the network becoming activated selectively *as and when* needed for particular collaborative and transactional contingencies. If we were to plot the shape of the network over time, we would find changing patterns of connection that would redefine not only the intensity of existing connections between individual nodes in the network but also the edges of the network.

The contingent nature of the network dynamics highlights the emergent nature of the information *network-in-use*. Individual connections are established or activated in accordance with *here-and-now* requirements and dispositions of individual nodes. The global network form at any given moment is a manifestation of the collective pattern of interconnections. This view of network dynamics is in marked contrast with the treatment of networks in traditional social network theory (Wasserman and Faust, 1994), which takes a 'snapshot' approach to describe network evolution over time.

Information content: emergent diversity

Each node both constitutes *and* utilises the network. The nodes collectively give rise to both the *topology* (i.e. the network structure emerging from inter-node connections) and the *information content* of the *network-in-use*. The information that is transmitted in the network is defined by the transmitting nodes' selection and articulation of the informational content and the recipients' interpretation of the 'message' and its import. Different nodes receiving the 'same' message may propagate a variety of interpreted versions.

As discussed earlier, a node also has the possibility of amplifying or attenuating the message.

We thus have a highly complex system of networks of networks of communication. The potential informational complexity of the networks arises both from the *variable connectivity* over time and the *multiple versions of information* transmitted through the network. The *actual* state of the information *network-in-use* emerges from the negative and positive feedback cycles that are generated when the heterogeneous nodes interact.

Information and action: local acts, emergent global behaviour

The introduction of human agency, bounded rationality and free will adds to the complexity of the network. It is impossible for any one agent in the network to have complete knowledge of the state of the whole network at any given time. Agents must act on the basis of the limited information that they can glean from their network and immediate environment. The overall state of the network *emerges* from the local actions of the individual agents, none of whom have complete knowledge of the entire network, and all of whom are susceptible to conditioning by their diverse social and cultural environments and backgrounds, their personal experiences, and events and information about events from their immediate environment and their extended networks. The network thus embodies both a degree of path dependency (history matters) and a spontaneous departure from the past. Individual agents learn and they forget. Social groups have established rituals but also succumb to fads and fashions. Inventions may lead to sweeping innovations or they may die unnoticed. No overall design can predetermine exactly how the network will be at any future point in time: the observed properties of the 'whole' come about as a consequence of bottom-up interactions, the precise nature of which may not be predicted in advance.

The resultant scenario is one where a multiplicity of representational and interpretative frames co-exist and are engaged in information processing, generation and storage. From the IS perspective, this poses problems for technological implementations and for the individual and collective social agents who interact with them at three levels:

Technical level: Related to storing, reconciling and (selecting) choosing between alternative interpretive and representational frames.

Individual agent level: Related to the application of appropriate interpretative frames for received representations and the use of appropriate frames for creating representation for sending through a variety of transmission paths through the network.

Collective agent level: The legitimisation of representational and interpretive frames to be used by individual agents on behalf of the collective (group, organisation, community, etc.).

At the global level, if there is differential adoption of frames among diverse populations, we can expect to see the emergence of distinctive, parallel representations of 'the world'. This makes it necessary to move from considering issues of discontinuity in the world over a single time line to considerations of discontinuity of *contemporaneous parallel worlds* as distinctive (possibly competing) representations evolve.

Issues with the 'classical IS' paradigm

Consistent with the 'classical' definition of systems,[3] the *network-in-use* is composed of a large number of interacting elements. However, the dynamics of interaction between elements gives rise to a number of features that are difficult to reconcile with some of the tenets of the 'classical' IS paradigm and its methods for dealing with complexity (see, for more detail, Merali, 2004b).

The heterogeneity in node characteristics is an important source of complexity – we would expect nodes to vary in their connectivity, their faithfulness in transmitting the volume and content of incoming information, their interpretation of received information and the degree to which they process/modify incoming information before transmitting it.

Consequently, there will be some systems where there is relative stability in internal and external conditions, with nodes repeatedly behaving with predictable consistency over time. The focus of this paper, however, is on dynamic complex systems that are changing over time, and are able to persist in the face of external and internal perturbations – this is where the conceptualisation of systems as networks leads us to question the adequacy of the classical IS paradigm.

The classical IS approach of top-down design and modularisation is predicated on the definition of clear system and sub-system boundaries and interfaces. The associated methodological developments entail a top-down definition and representation of the system and its components, predicated on ontological assumptions of

- a *persistent* hierarchy of organisation embodied in
- a fixed set of relationships between components and
- regulation of processes by *stable* feedback loops that
- implement the defined *causal* relationships leading to the achievement (or maintenance) of a desired steady state.

On the other hand, in the case of the more complex *network-in-use* we find that

- the emergent, 'bottom-up' network dynamics challenges the classical 'top-down' paradigm for understanding systems structures and behaviours;
- the complex connectivity and evolving information content of the network make it impossible to accurately predict the exact state of the network for a specific future point in time;
- the network structure is difficult to represent with the classical method of structural modularisation;
- it becomes difficult to use the concept of the boundary to demarcate the cleavage of the system from its environment;
- the classical device of using discrete state changes for the *separation of 'becoming' from 'being'* does not capture the mutually defining relationship between dynamics and structure. In the case of the dynamic network, the global topology is defined by the collective dynamics and the global dynamics emerges from locally responsive actions defined by structural coupling between local components.

It would appear then that the classical systems paradigm is limited in its capacity for representing and articulating the salient features of the structural dynamics and behaviour of the socially realised active information network. In the next section, we explore what complexity science offers as concepts and methods for addressing this gap.

Concepts from complexity science

The terms 'complexity theory' and 'complexity science' do not refer to a clear-cut scientific paradigm – they constitute the label for an emerging set of concepts and constructs that have surfaced during the quest for a paradigm capable of addressing those aspects of complex systems behaviour that are not accommodated by the deterministic and probabilistic conceptual frameworks of classical mechanics and thermodynamics. Thus, it is more realistic to see the developments in complexity science as an emergent paradigm shift in the Kuhnian sense (Kuhn, 1962), rather than the birth of a new science.

Complex systems are non-linear systems, composed of many (often heterogeneous) partially connected components that interact with each other through a diversity of feedback loops. Their complexity derives from the partially connected nature and the non-linear dynamics which make the behaviour of these systems difficult to predict (Casti, 1997). The non-linearity of these systems means that small changes in inputs can have dramatic and unexpected effects on outputs.

While the term 'chaos' has been popularised in the management literature, most relevant for articulating the dynamic characteristics of IS in the interconnected world are the concepts of *complex adaptive systems (CAS), emergence, self-organisation* and *co-evolution* (see Anderson (1999) and Maguire *et al.* (2006) for a review of the utilisation of complexity concepts in organisational theory literature, and Merali (2004b) for a review of complexity concepts and their relevance for IS). These concepts derive from results of computational modelling and computer simulations of complex systems – modelling is the principal methodological device deployed for exploring the definition and dynamics of complex systems. The next paragraphs outline what these concepts bring to our discourse on the structural dynamics and behaviour of the socially realised information *network-in-use.*

Chaos and complexity

The term chaos[4] has tended to dominate popular discourse on the relevance of complexity science in management. The concept of chaotic systems is often conflated with the concept of complex systems. It is therefore particularly important to recognise that in mathematical terms, chaotic systems have specific properties that are not universally shared by all complex systems.

Technically, a chaotic system is a *deterministic* system that is difficult to predict. As Bar-Yam (2000) points out, in practice, the concept of chaotic systems presents a paradox. By definition, a deterministic system is one whose state at one time completely determines its state for all future times, but in practice a chaotic system is difficult to predict because of its sensitivity to initial conditions:[5] what happens in its future is very sensitive to its current state. In practice, the degree of accuracy (of measurement of start conditions) needed in order to predict an outcome is likely to be impossible to obtain.

Chaotic systems share properties with complex systems, including their sensitivity to initial conditions. However, models of chaotic systems generally describe the dynamics of a few variables, and the models reveal some characteristic behaviours of these dynamics. Conversely, complex systems generally have many degrees of freedom, as illustrated by our description of the information network: they are composed of many elements that are partially but not completely independent, with ambiguous system–environment relationships. Our discussion of the information network and the IS paradigms and practice is concerned with the wider class of complex systems.

Complex adaptive systems

The concept of CAS serves very well to characterise the phenomenology of organisation in the interconnected world. CAS are characterised as open, non-linear dynamical systems that adapt and evolve in the process of interacting with their environments – they have the potential (capacity) for adaptation *and* transformation. Adaptation at the macro-level (the 'whole' system) is characterised by emergence and self-organisation (see below) based on the local adaptive behaviour of the system's constituents. The emergent global systems behaviour is very sensitive to initial local conditions.

The relationship between the system and the environment is a reflexive one: changes in the system both shape and are shaped by changes in the environment. If a number of systems cohabit in a particular environment, the environment is itself an emergent manifestation of its multiple interactions with the systems it 'hosts'.

While in classical representations of systems, the environment is viewed as the source of a discrete set of inputs and a sink for a discrete set of outputs, the CAS paradigm imposes the need to consider the dynamics and *mutually* defining consequences of the relationship between the system and its environment, taking us from issues of simple adaptation to issues of *co-adaptation* and *co-evolution* in dynamic contexts.

Emergence

Emergence refers to the phenomenon whereby the macroscopic properties of the system arise from the microscopic properties (interactions, relationships, structures and behaviours) and heterogeneity of its constituents. The emergent macroscopic 'whole' displays a set of properties that is distinct from those displayed by any subset of its individual constituents and their interactions. For example, the temperature and pressure of a gas can be viewed as emerging from the collisions between a large number of gas molecules: temperature and pressure are properties that can be ascribed to the mass of gas, but they do not exist as properties of isolated individual molecules. In other words, the whole *is more than* (and certainly *different in kind* to) the sum of its parts.

At the microscopic level, the behaviour of an individual constituent at a given instant in time and place is contingent on the precise state of that constituent and conditions in its local environment *at that instant*. For constituents on the boundary of the system, the local environment will constitute 'internal' and 'external' components. The collective behaviour of the individual constituents at the microscopic level will manifest itself as the behaviour of the 'whole system' visible at the macroscopic level.

The existence and persistence of the system is thus a relational phenomenon, predicated on the relationship of the constituents of the system to each other and to constituents of the environment in continuous time. Local, contingent, neighbourhood interactions and adjustments at the micro-level are at the same time detectable as a coherent pattern of properties constituting the 'whole' system.

This is consistent with our earlier observation that the classical separation of 'becoming' from 'being' does not advance our understanding of complex systems. In order to identify how emergent properties are produced we need to be able to access descriptions of the system at multiple scales from the micro to the macro *at the same time*. This presents us with a problem of representation in the classical mode of top-down refinement. Typically, complex systems representations are either developed as mathematical models or as computer simulations.

At the micro-level, system and environment components interact in a contiguous space and, depending on the nature of particular relationships, can to a lesser or greater degree be considered to be mutually effective. Thus, the dynamic definition of a system is contingent on the dynamic definition of its environment, and system constituents are an integral part of the landscape in which they exist. The concepts of systems adaptation and evolution are thus extended to the dynamics of the ecosystem within which systems are situated.

These characteristics require us to redefine the way that boundaries are conceptualised: from the classical view of boundaries as defining the bounds of a system, towards a more dynamic view of boundaries as relative and relational phenomena, linking system and environmental elements through differential coupling.

The emergence of the macro-level phenomenology from micro-level interactions and the mutually defining relationship between the system and its environment are defining characteristics of our information network dynamics. The question of how to deal with boundaries in this context remains a non-trivial one.

Self-organisation

Self-organisation is the ability of complex systems to spontaneously generate new internal structures and forms of behaviour. This *generative* aspect takes the complex systems concept of self-organisation beyond the early cybernetics concept of self-organisation, which focused on the self-regulatory and control aspects of organisation. The generative process of self-organisation in complex systems highlights that they are open systems, with continuous flow of energy and resources passing through them enabling them to maintain an existence far from equilibrium. In the self-organisation process, the components *spontaneously* re-orientate and restructure their relationships with neighbouring components giving rise to the emergence of structures that embody an increased level of internal complexity.

Self-organisation is not the result of *a priori* design, it surfaces from the interaction of system and environment, and local interactions between the system components. This capacity for the spontaneous *creation* of order through *intrinsically* generated structures is captured in Stuart Kauffman's (1993) expression 'order for free', in the notion of Prigogine's dissipative structures[6] (Prigogine, 1967), and in Maturana and Varela's theory of autopoiesis[7] (Maturana and Varela, 1973).

Co-adaptation and co-evolution: fitness landscapes and genetic algorithms

As highlighted above, the paradigm of CAS imposes the need to consider the dynamics and mutually defining consequences of the relationship between the system and its environment.

For example, consider an ecosystem cohabited by a diversity of species. The environment, each individual and each species will affect and be affected by the actions of the other individuals and species. The fitness or chances of survival for each species will be related to its ability to adapt to the environmental changes and, over time, selective pressures (resulting from the interaction of the habitat and surviving cohabiting species) will lead to the evolution of new traits in the various populations, changes in the habitat and the emergence of new species. Co-adaptation and co-evolution in dynamic environments can be viewed as important mechanisms for sustainability of the ecosystem. The capacity for adaptation is predicated on the capacity for self-organisation described above.

Fitness landscapes are often used to explore these dynamics. The fitness landscape is a simulation constructed from representations (in terms of the fitness function, which is a mathematical expression of the relative value of a population with reference to a particular criterion), of the relative fitness of all actors. The peaks and valleys in the landscape represent, respectively, the most and least fit. Each actor only has knowledge of the local environment and acts accordingly. The landscape undergoes distortions due to the actions of the actors, and to changes in the environmental conditions. The concept of fitness landscapes has been used extensively to develop simulations of competitive landscapes, notably deploying Kauffman's NK model (see, for examples, Kauffman, 1995).

John Holland's genetic algorithms (Holland, 1995, 1998) provide a very elegant means for exploring adaptive behaviour and fitness in dynamic landscapes. The concept derives from the notion that biological fitness (i.e. survival and reproduction) is based on successful adaptation, and that adaptation is effected by the heterogeneity of genetic endowment subject to processes of mutation, variation and selection. These processes have been abstracted into the design of adaptive algorithms (called genetic algorithms). We can think of the string of instructions that each agent is endowed with as the 'genotype' of that agent. As agents interact with each other, we have the opportunity of introducing variation and innovation into the available gene pool. The process of mutation (random flipping of some part of the rule specification) and 'genetic' cross-over (when two different agents' rule sets exchange part of their complement of instructions resulting in the birth of two new 'hybrid' gene complements) give rise to the generation of new 'gene' combinations. This injection of innovative combinations into the 'gene' pool of the population is associated with the possibility for emergence of innovative behaviour traits in the agent population. If the new combinations are robust enough to survive the selective pressures exerted by the environment, we observe the emergence of new strategies and the phenomenon of adaptation or learning in agent populations over time.

Network connectivity and state changes

The pattern of interactions that underpins the dynamics of CAS is explained in terms of the network of interconnections. A CAS comprises multiple, interconnected components ('agents'). The resulting network connectivity allows for the generation of feedback loops.

CAS embody the potential for simultaneous existence of *both* negative *and* positive feedback loops. Hence, a diversity of feedback cycles may be interlinked in a variety of ways, with different consequences.

Order creation

The emergence of self-organising structures is due to the complex patterns of interactions between heterogeneous[8] components. The pattern of interactions is explained in terms of the network of interconnections. Network connectivity allows for the generation of self-regulating feedback loops. A diversity of feedback cycles may be interlinked in a variety of ways, with different consequences. The interlinked cycles may maintain a homeostatic condition or they may spontaneously generate new, more complex forms of organisation under certain critical conditions (Prigogine, 1967; Langton, 1991; Kuaffman, 1993; Sigmund, 1993). The experimental foundations for this understanding come from artificial life simulations using cellular automata[9] (Berlekamp *et al.*, 1982; Langton, 1991) and Boolean networks[10] (Kauffman, 1993).

Langton and Kauffman both showed that the patterns of behaviour of their emergent structures fell into a regular sequence (or cycle) of three distinctive states: an ordered regime (comprised of rigid structures that do not change, or of periodic oscillations), a highly disordered regime (which is too unstable for the emergence of order) and a transition regime (ordered enough to afford stability, but capable of transformation into new structures).

Kauffman (1993) found that the degree of connectivity (that is the number of connections that each component has with other components) is a critical factor in the emergence of self-organised structures: if the connections are too few, the network becomes 'frozen' into the same state cycle, and if they are too many, the system becomes excessively unstable and highly disordered. At what Kauffman called combinatorial optimisation (i.e. between the frozen and the unstable states), there occurred the spontaneous emergence of self-sustaining webs. The critical transition takes place at the tipping point where quantitative change (observable simply at the micro-level as the increase in the number of links per node) suddenly leads to qualitative change (observable at the macro-level as a change in the whole system's state). The argument is that in the ordered regime, the connectivity is too low for changes to be propagated through the system, and in the highly disordered regime, the system would be too sensitive to perturbations for persistent structures to develop.[11]

The importance of heterogeneity of connectivity for conferring scalability, stability, robustness and flexibility of network organisation is underlined by more recent work on small world and scale-free networks.

Power-law dynamics

Watts and Strogatz's models (Watts and Strogatz, 1998) demonstrate how a network of tight clusters interconnected by a few random links has the property that any node can reach any other in an average of only a few steps (hence the 'small world' label).

Subsequent work by Barabasi and his colleagues (Albert and Barabassi, 2000; Albert *et al.*, 2000) has shown that the World Wide Web and other complex systems networks have a power-law distribution of connections, that is, the probability of any single node having k links (P_k) is inversely proportional to k raised to some power. The power-law distribution (showing that most nodes will have relatively few connections, but that a small but significant number of 'hubs' will emerge with very dense connections) suggests that these large networks (like the World Wide Web) are robust against random attacks (as these would most be most likely to knock out one of the numerous sparsely connected nodes), but vulnerable in the face of attacks targeted on hubs.

However, as Watts (2003) highlights, Barabassi *et al.* assume 'cost-free' connectivity and free flow of information, but in socially situated systems there are search and connection costs, as well as social dynamics that will constrain connection patterns. Consequently, not all networks can be thought of as small-world or scale-free networks.

Nonetheless, the recognition of power-law dynamics provides useful insights for IS activities at all levels, ranging from low-level software and component design through to the strategic deployment of IS. For example, the recognition that object-oriented programs evolve scale-free object networks on execution makes it possible to develop designs for more efficient garbage collection and de-bugging by focusing on the highly connected 'hubs' (Potanin *et al.*, 2005). At the other end of the spectrum, Benbya and McKelvey (this issue) show that scale free co-evolutionary dynamics across multiple organisational levels constitutes the mechanism for emergent IS alignment (or misalignment) with the business environment.

To summarise, the network form is integral to self-organisation: network connectivity is instrumental for both, sustaining stability *and* for propagating transformational state changes. It is the capacity for self-organisation and adaptation that confers robustness upon organisational forms in dynamic environments. This resonates with Ashby's law of requisite variety. In the account of networks presented in this paper, the system has the *generative capacity* to respond to contingencies in the environment by realising its adaptive potential for transformation and co-evolution. The adaptive potential is conferred by

- the micro diversity of the components and
- the existence of the requisite degree of connectivity between nodes and
- the capacity for spontaneous re-configuration of the pattern of linkages.

The complexity concepts introduced in this section and the network explanation of CAS dynamics offer a powerful way of conceptualising the properties of IS and infrastructures required for supporting the diversity, volatility and extent of user requirements in an interconnected world.

The next section introduces the principal tools that have been developed for exploring the behaviour of complex systems in particular problem domains.

Tools for studying complex systems behaviour

There are two main ways in which complexity concepts have been deployed to study complex systems and their dynamics. The first is through the direct use of complexity concepts and language as sensemaking and explanatory devices for complex phenomena in diverse application domains. The second is through agent-based computational modelling to study the dynamics of complex systems interactions and to reveal emergent structures and patterns of behaviour.

The manner in which modelling is deployed in the 'classical' IS paradigm is *fundamentally* different from the way in which it is used in the science of complexity. In the former, models are developed from definitions of the system. In the latter, models *are* arguably the specification of the system that emerges from the interactions of its specified components.

The most popular simulation methods are based on agent-based models deploying the logic of Boolean networks, cellular automata and genetic algorithms.[12] We have already encountered examples of the first two in Langton and Kauffman's experiments with self-organising structures. Cellular automata and Boolean networks can be used to produce quite sophisticated patterns of organisation (see, for examples, Kauffman, 1993, 1995; Sigmund, 1993). However, the most significant enhancement to the power and versatility of models for studying emergent phenomena comes from John Holland's conception of genetic algorithms (Holland, 1995, 1998) for agent-based models in general.

Describing dynamics

To capture the 'unfolding' of the *emergent* dynamics, we need to have methods that can provide a view of the *dynamics* of the *changing* state in continuous time. The complex systems approach to doing this is by describing state cycles using mathematical models or by running simulations (see below) using the phase space technique.

The phase space

The dynamics of a system are traced by plotting the value of each of its variables at different points in time. The variables of the system are displayed in abstract mathematical space called the phase space. Each variable is allocated a dimension in phase space, and its value at any given time is represented by a coordinate in that dimension.[13] Multidimensional phase space can be used to develop quite complex descriptions.

Attractors

As the system changes step by step from one state to the next, the succession of states traces a trajectory in the phase space. The concept of attractors is used to classify the trajectories of different sequences of state changes. There are three basic types of attractors:

Point attractors: These describe the trajectories of systems reaching a stable equilibrium.

Periodic attractors: These describe systems that are executing periodic oscillations (such as a frictionless pendulum).

Strange attractors: These correspond to chaotic systems. In these cases, the system never repeats itself (i.e. it never covers the same trajectory in phase space more than once), but the set of trajectories conform to a distinctive pattern. Although it is not possible to predict exactly which point in phase space will be traversed by the trajectory at any given point in time, it is possible to identify the pattern that it will trace out in phase space: all trajectories starting out in a given region of the phase space will eventually lead to the same attractor. The region is called the basin of attraction.

As discussed earlier, in distributed networks, each actor only has knowledge of the local environment and tries to optimise its own performance (or utility function) while maximising its consistency with influences from the other nodes. Linear networks have a single attractor: a single configuration of states of nodes that the network converges toward no matter what the starting point, corresponding to the global optimum. Consequently, 'hill-climbing' (where each node always moves directly toward increased local utility) can be used as a strategy for optimising overall network performance. This is because local utility increases always move the network toward the global optimum. Nonlinear networks, by contrast, are characterised by having multiple attractors and multiple-optima utility functions. Consequently, for nonlinear networks, searching for the global optima cannot be performed successfully by pure hill-climbing algorithms because of the danger of getting stuck in local optima that are globally suboptimal.

Agent-based modelling

Agent-based computational modelling has characteristics that are particularly useful for studying socially embedded systems like the information *network-in-use*. An agent-based model is comprised of individual 'agents' commonly implemented as software objects (Holland, 1995, 1998; Casti, 1997). Agent objects have states and rules of behaviour. They can be endowed with requisite resources, traits, behaviours and rules for interacting with, and adapting to, each other. Running such a model entails instantiating an agent population, letting the agents interact, and monitoring what happens. Typically agent-based models deploy a diversity of agents to represent the constituents of the focal system. The modeller defines the environmental parameters that are of interest as the starting conditions for the particular study. Repeated runs of the model reveal collective states or patterns of behaviour as they emerge from the interactions of entities over time. Agent-based models are very well suited for revealing the dynamics of far-from equilibrium complex systems, and have been widely used to study the dynamics of a diversity of social and economic systems.[14]

As discussed earlier, CAS have many degrees of freedom, with many elements that are partially but not completely independent, with ambiguous system–environment relationships. There is a greater diversity of local behaviours than there is of global outcomes. To achieve an effective representation of the dynamics of the processes connecting the local (micro-level) and global (macro-level) characteristics, we need to develop a multi-scale description of complex systems. Agent-based modelling facilitates the inclusion of micro-diversity (e.g. the rationality of agents can be limited, agents can be made diverse so there is no need to appeal to representative agents, payoffs may be noisy and information can be local), allowing us to study the diversity of (local) behaviours at fine scales and to observe the emergence of the global characteristics at the large scale. Running the model furnishes us with an *entire* dynamical history of the process under study.

With the escalation of available computational power, it will be possible to build models with a million agents of reasonable complexity (Axtell, 2000). The mathematicians and the natural scientists have a powerful battery of technologies for studying dynamical systems. However, for social systems, the specification of the components (agents) for the construction of agent-based models is a challenging prospect. The challenge of creating entire mini-economies in silicon is not one of processing power, but one of learning how to build sufficiently realistic agents: agents who trade in markets, who form firms, who procreate, who engage in political activity and write constitutions and bribe other agents for votes while trying to pass term limits. The diversity of social relationships and the idiosyncrasy of individuals makes it difficult to develop models that are both, sophisticated enough to capture the essential features of the social interactions and characteristics, and simple enough to make visible the dynamics of the system. The difficulty lies in identifying what constitutes the requisite set of variables for defining social systems – and *this* is a matter that necessitates a discourse between the IS community and scholars of sociology, philosophy and psychology among others.

The next section summarises the contribution that complexity science may make towards the development of the IS paradigm for the future and reflects on the positioning of IS in a trans-disciplinary research arena.

Application of complexity concepts for IS in the networked world

This paper suggests that the increase in the informational and effective complexity of IS poses challenges and opportunities for the IS community that are *different in kind* from ones that we have addressed in the past. It shows that while traditional paradigms for IS development have been predicated on designing for *complexity reduction* (through prescriptive complete, top-down specification and design of modularised information content and processes), the contingencies of the network economy and its evolving information infrastructures demand designs for *complexity accommodation.*

It has been argued in this paper that the partially connected nature and the complex non-linear dynamics of the interconnected world means that the information *network-in-use* is constantly evolving and changing. We find that there are some characteristics of this world (particularly those concerned with dynamism) that cannot be adequately addressed by traditional systems approaches for handling complexity. This suggests the need for new concepts to articulate the issues of dynamics and structure in the theory and practice of IS. The phenomenology of the information *network-in-use* suggests that in order to engage effectively in the discourse of the network society, there are two shifts necessary in the in 'classical' conceptualisation of IS:

- a shift in the focus of 'systems thinking':
  o from focusing on discrete bounded systems to focusing on networks and
  o from focusing on the structural properties of systems to engaging with the *dynamics* of systems, and
- a shift in ontological assumptions about information: from focusing solely on discrete entities (individuals, organisations or applications) as loci for information creation and interpretation to incorporating the role of the network as a locus for these processes.

Turning to complexity science as a potential source of useful concepts, we find that the information *network-in-use* can be defined as a CAS (open, non-linear dynamical system that adapts and evolves in the process of interacting with its environment). Doing so highlights the importance of

- understanding the macro-level system as an *emergent* realisation of micro-level dynamics,
- the mutually defining relationship between network dynamics and structure (the concept of emergence transcends the classical separation of *being* from *becoming),*
- co-evolution of 'system' and environment,

- the need to attend to dynamics in continuous time (as opposed to working with snapshots of systems states at regular time intervals),
- the role of micro-diversity in determining the *potentiality* of the emergent system and its constituents and
- articulating the present and persistent with the possible and transient (given the non-deterministic, path-dependent and context-sensitive nature of CAS dynamics).

Below we consider the manner in which concepts from the science of complexity can be articulated in ontological and epistemological constructs for IS in the network society.

Ontological constructs from the science of complexity

With regard to the ontology of systems, the science of complexity offers us the following constructs for IS:

- *Definition of IS as CAS*: This definition of systems shifts the emphasis from the 'classical' characterisation of systems in terms of stability and structural hierarchy to one that is engaged directly with the dynamic properties of systems' existence in relation to the environment. Implicit in this definition is the existence of networks of networks of interactions and emergence. The network as an organising form serves to articulate the structural and dynamic properties.
- *Origins and existence of IS as emergent and contingent on a reflexive relationship with the environment:* The concept of emergence transcends the classical separation of being from becoming. The attribution of here-and-now dynamism and the open nature of systems results in a conceptual shift away from the 'classical' paradigm of top-down design to the bottom-up connectionist paradigm. This imposes the need to deal with histories of systems' dynamics in continuous time instead of working with statistically representational 'snapshots' in a series of time frames.
- *Presence of IS as cyber-socio entities in multi-dimensional phase space:* The information *network-in-use* is simultaneously informational (representational, perceived patterns, with many degrees of freedom in the informational dimensions) and experiential (embodied in specific behaviours and bounded by specific histories of experiences) in its manifestation and evolution. As we see later, the CAS framework provides a 'unifying frame' to articulate the technological and the social across multiple levels of organisation.

Epistemological constructs from the science of complexity

With regard to epistemological constructs to address the phenomenology and dynamics of IS, complexity science offers

- constructs for the explicit conceptualisation of emergent systems' behaviour,
- modelling in multi-dimensional phase space as a method for studying and defining the systems dynamics in continuous real time, allowing access to micro- and macro-level systems descriptions simultaneously and
- the theoretical basis (Pareto distributions, fractals, power laws and scale-free theory) for dealing with phenomena that are ill-suited to study via Gaussian statistics (Lichtenstein and McKelvey, 2006), and
- metaphors for articulating network concepts, making sense of observed behaviour patterns and developing phase-space definitions for models (Holland, 1998; Merali, 2000).[15]

The ontological constructs emphasise the dynamics of emergence and existence, while the epistemological constructs enable the exploration of these dynamics in continuous time, and the paradigm is principally one of sense-making and emergence.

Paradigm shift

The distinction between the 'classical' IS paradigm and that of 'complexity science' is broadly articulated in Kant's (1790) distinction between the *mechanical* and the *organic*. The *organic* is characterised by emergence, self-organisation and networks of relationships, while the *mechanical* is organised according to an externally defined design for articulating structural components. The phenomenology of CAS is an *organic* one.

As we have seen, while the classical IS paradigm is quite adequate for dealing with the *mechanical,* it does not cater for the emergent nature of the *organic*. The complexity science paradigm, on the other hand, is primarily concerned with emergence and the dynamics of chaotic and CAS, offering us

- language and concepts for describing and defining complex phenomena and
- concepts and modelling techniques for articulating the dynamics giving rise to those phenomena.

Arguably the adoption of complexity concepts constitutes a paradigm shift in IS theory and practice. It is possible that the shift is already emerging as writers on the innovative fringes of established management disciplines demonstrate the utility of ideas that can be traced to complexity science.

Incorporation of complexity concepts in the IS domain

Language and ideas

The value of metaphors as an exploratory device is well-established in the management literature (Morgan, 1986). Complexity concepts have been used in the management literature and ideas of emergence and self-organisation and improvisation in the IS literature (Orlikowski, 1996) have a strong resonance with CAS definitions. More concretely, recent literature shows evidence that complexity concepts (scale-free networks, co-evolution and fitness landscapes) are becoming incorporated into ways of conceptualising IS design (see Benbya and McKelvey, this issue; Vigden and Wang, this issue) for the interconnected world.

Modelling

The traditional use of models within the IS domain has tended to be rather conservative, and linked to the top-down modularisation paradigms of structured methodologies and operational research system dynamics models. The adoption of complexity science modelling approaches is central to advancing our understanding of complex systems behaviour and may represent a paradigm shift for the IS domain. With regard to the epistemological issues associated with the interconnected world, incompleteness of information necessitates a trial and error method, and patterns that emerge from running models may offer insights into problem situations and the possible solution space. Modelling serves as a device for exposing the emerging system specification and for exposing assumptions implicit in traditional conceptualisations of systems. Engagement with this use of modelling in the IS field is an emergent phenomenon as researchers become concerned with issues of responsiveness, robustness and flexibility in the interconnected world.

Systems development

The dynamics of the networked world demand designs for *complexity accommodation*. It is recognised that it is not possible to produce *a priori* systems design specifications that are complete, closed or correct (Allen and Varga, this issue). In other words, information infrastructures need to co-evolve with their context of use, and must embody the potential for requisite variety to service (possibly novel) demands as they emerge. Recent developments in IS design are predicated on multiple *possible* pathways for realisation through dynamic 'run-time' configuration of information content and processes to service contingent contextual requirements, with 'system' and 'context' boundaries being a function of dynamic relationships rather than of predetermined structure.

CAS as a unifying concept

The conceptualisation of IS as CAS provides a framework for accommodating complexity at multiple levels of aggregation of heterogeneous agents as nested CAS addressing:

- *Societal Complexity* – Incorporating social, cultural, political and economic dimensions.
- *Collective (Group) Complexity* – Incorporating issues of coherence, communication, co-ordination and legitimisation of representational and interpretive frames and relational constructs, for positioning in the dynamic landscape.
- *Individual Complexity* – Incorporating issues of selecting representational and interpretive frames and relational constructs, for positioning in the dynamic landscape.
- *Informational Complexity* – Incorporating issues of recognising, interpreting, organising and linking informational content from multiple diverse sources;
- *Technological Complexity* – Incorporating the issues of providing technological architectures and infrastructures to accommodate diversity, and deliver the requisite responsiveness, robustness and flexibility for the interconnected world.

The nested CAS construct enables the dynamic instantiation of the agent into different levels of organisation at the same time. This affords a powerful device for exploring the dynamics of emergence of complex individual and collective identities and ideologies in cyberspace.

It is this capacity for accessing multiple levels of description within a single representational construct that allows us to trace the dynamics of emergence. This is in contrast with the capabilities of existing theories in IS such as Actor Network Theory (ANT). While ANT has the capacity to develop very fine-grained models of micro-level networks and associated information processes, its capacity for linking micro-level dynamics with macro-level behaviours is limited, and ANT researchers are turning to complexity science for concepts to address this deficiency (Moser and Law, 2006).

Positioning IS in the management field

The exposition of the information *network-in-use* in this paper accentuates the existence of the information network as an integral, constitutive element of the network society and economy. The information network both serves and shapes the networked world.

As illustrated above, conceptualising the networked world as a CAS transcends the traditional boundaries between disciplines in the management field. This has two important implications for future IS research:

- The travail of IS in the interconnected world is a transdisciplinary one, and demands the active development of a discourse with the other disciplines. The adoption of complexity science concepts would speak for a discourse not only across the management field, but also across the natural and human sciences.
- The centrality of IS in the network economy and society places the IS domain at the heart of the management field, and we should, as a discipline, recognise our responsibilities for informing the discourse pertaining to information *networks-in-use* in other management disciplines.

Conclusion

To summarise, this paper has shown that the complexity and dynamics of systems are not readily treated with traditional research approaches that simplify the world with high-level generalisations predicated on macro-level observations of structural persistence and assumptions of Gaussian statistics. Complexity science furnishes us with the concepts and tools for building multi-level representations of the world and for making sense of the dynamics of emergence. The dynamics of emergence is predicated on micro-diversity, and fine-grained representations are essentially descriptive models of the detailed complexity of the world and its dynamics. However, to understand the dynamics of emergence, we need to access representations at different levels of granularity and abstraction simultaneously. Thus, it is through exploratory modelling that we discover how the complex world works, and how macro-level properties and behaviours of systems emerge from micro-level diversity and dynamics. Consequently, modelling is the principal research tool for complex systems, and sense-making is a legitimate research goal. This implies a significant shift in the established thinking about what constitutes knowledge and how it is best obtained. *This* is the challenge for traditional research and in particular for the hypothetico-deductive school.

Notes

1. The term 'effective world' is used to connote the world as perceived, experienced, understood or believed to exist by players, which serves as the context within which decisions are made, and actions taken, and consequences realised.

2. It should be noted that while this paper is concerned with complexity in the networked world, the internet and its attendant technologies also have the potential to *simplify* processes – for example, as evidenced by the rationalisation and disintermediation of value chains.

3. The term 'classical systems paradigm' is used to refer to the ontological and epistemological constructs that underpin established IS methodologies including structured methodologies, object-oriented approaches and the set of cybernetic methods including system dynamics, VSM, etc.

4. See Gleick (1987) for a very accessible discussion of chaos theory, and Guastello (1995) for examples in organizational studies and social evolution.

5. The 'butterfly effect' is a popular caricature of the sensitivity of chaotic systems – 'a butterfly flapping its wings over the Amazon leads to a hurricane on the other side of the world'. Technically, the sensitivity is the phenomenon created by the divergence of trajectories of the system. Over time, a system starting from one state becomes less and less similar (farther and farther away in state space) to a system which starts out in a similar, but not exactly the same, state (Lorenz, 1963).

6. Prigogine's explanation of the Bénard cell experiment furnishes us with a very elegant illustration of the non-linear dynamics of self-organisation in open systems that are far from equilibrium. The experiment is concerned with observing the changes in a very thin layer of liquid when it is heated from below. As the liquid was heated, when the temperature differential between the top and bottom surfaces of the liquid reaches a certain *critical value,* there emerges spontaneously, within the liquid mass, a honeycomb pattern of hexagonal cells (referred to as Bénard cells after Henri Bénard who first recorded this observation). Heating the liquid further resulted in a loss of the ordered state. Prigogine explained this phenomenon in terms of non-linear equations to describe the dynamics in the mass of liquid as an open system receiving energy from outside. In this explanation, changes in the internal structure (observed as instabilities and the jump to the new structural form) are the result of local fluctuations in the interactions between molecules amplified by positive feedback loops. Prigogine called the emergent, ordered structures 'dissipative structures'. As Capra (1996) points out, non-linear thermodynamics the 'runaway' positive feedback loops which had always been regarded as *destructive* in cybernetics appear as a source of new *order* and complexity in the theory of dissipative structures.

7. Maturana and Varela (1973) identified *autopoieis* (self production) as the defining characteristic of all living systems. The term is sometimes used in a more general sense to refer to self-organising systems with non-equilibrium dynamics capable of maintaining stability overlong periods of time.

8. Heterogeneity here refers both to the types of components and to their relative states.

9. Cellular automata comprise a grid of rectangular squares or cells. The state of each cell is defined by the values that the cell takes, and there are rules defining how many of its neighbouring cells are allowed to influence its value. The state of the cell changes in discrete steps that are determined by a set of transition rules that apply simultaneously to all cells. They are used extensively in experiments to identify the dynamics of self-organisation, and provide an alternative to the use of differential equations. The complexity literature highlights the importance of cellular automata in revealing the emergence of complex behaviour from simple rules.

10. Boolean networks are networks connecting sites that are only allowed to have one of two values (e.g. 'on' or 'off'). Using Boolean networks comprised of a number of inter-connected light bulbs, Kauffman (1993) demonstrated that starting out with a random collection of connected sites, there developed over time a network of spontaneously organised cycles of interactions between sites. Varying the number of cells and the number of connections per cell in the network, he found that the level of connectivity (i.e. the number of cells sites with which a given site interacts) was a crucial parameter.

11. Both Kauffman and Langton refer to the highly disordered regime as the 'chaotic' regime. Concurring with Langton, Kauffman suggests that living systems exist in the 'at the edge of chaos', in the transition regime, as this offers the differential potential for homeostasis *as well as* for adaptation, evolution and transformation. Following on from this, the expression 'life at the edge of chaos' has gained popularity in the management literature, which equates 'chaos' with disorder. In order to avoid confusing this usage of 'chaos' with the mathematical definition of deterministic chaos it is advisable to use Langdon's 'transition regime' or McKelvey's (McKelvey, forthcoming) 'region of emergent complexity' instead of 'the edge of chaos'.

12. Holland (1995, 1998) gives us a very lucid and accessible introduction to the development of agent-based models, while Casti (1997) affords a wider view of modelling concepts and their application. Gilbert and Troitzsch (1999) is a comprehensive text covering simulation in social science, and Prietula *et al.* (1998) and Ilgen and Hulin (2000) both provide collections of papers on computational modelling in organisation science. Tesfatsion and Judd (2006) and Abu-Mostafa *et al.* (1999) constitute authoritative reference bases for applications of computational modeling in economics and finance, respectively. Sigmund (1993) is a very accessible and comprehensive overview of artificial life simulations with cellular automata.

13. For example, for a pendulum the dynamics of the systems state can be defined in a two-dimensional phase space by its velocity and its angle of displacement.

14. Epstein and Axtell (1996) give a fairly comprehensive bibliography of agent-based models in the social sciences that were either in working paper form or published by 1996. Since then there has been a rapid expansion of

agent-based modeling efforts, and anything like a complete listing of this work would reference several hundred papers. Robert Axelrod's (1984) *The Evolution of Cooperation* demonstrates the potency of agent-based models for developing insights into the gamesmanship of social systems. Watts and Strogatz (1998) work on small-world networks is particularly relevant to our current interest in internet-enabled social networks. Arrow *et al.*'s *The economy as an evolving complex system* and Arthur *et al.*'s (1997) *The economy as an evolving complex system II* provide an extensive treatment of complexity science-inspired models in economics. Axelrod and Cohen's (1999) Harnessing Complexity provides a very lucid overview of the use of models in addressing complexity in the competitive context. For more contemporary examples of the use of agent-based models in financial markets supply chain management and e-business see the *Economist,* October 11th 2003 and Bonabeau, 2002; Bonabeau and Meyer, 2001.

15. It must be noted that issues related to the complexity of 'the social' pose questions about transferability of complexity science concepts in their entirety from the 'hard sciences' to the domain of information systems. Because human beings are endowed with free will, learn from experience and speculate about the future and associated risks, their position and role in the social system is defined by intent, purpose and utility. Consequently, these metaphors need to be treated with due caution.

References

Abu-Mostafa, Y.S., LeBaron, B., Lo, A.W. and Weigend, A.S. (eds.) (1999). *Computational Finance,* Cambridge, MA: MIT Press.

Albert, R. and Barabassi, A. (2000). Statistical Mechanics of Complex Networks, *Review of Modern Physics* **74**: 47–97.

Albert, R., Joeng, H. and Barabassi, A. (2000). Attack and Error Tolerance of Complex Networks, *Nature* **406**: 378–382.

Anderson, P. (1999). Complexity Theory and Organization Science, *Organization Studies* **10**(3): 216–232.

Anderson, P., Meyer, A., Eisenhardt, K., Carley, K. and Pettigrew, A. 1999. Introduction to the Special Issue: Applications of complexity theory to organization science, *Organization Science* **10**: 233–236.

Arthur, W., Lane, D. and Durlaff, S. (eds.) (1997). *The Economy as an Evolving Complex System II,* Reading, MA: Addison-Wesley.

Axelrod, R. (1984). *The Evolution of Cooperation,* New York: Basic Books.

Axelrod, R. and Cohen, M. (1999). *Harnessing Complexity: Organizational Implications of a Scientific Frontier,* New York: Free Press.

Axtell, R. (2000). Why Agents? On the Varied Motivations for Agent Computing in the Social Sciences, Center on Social and Economic Dynamics Working Paper No. 17, November 2000, Washington: The Brookings Institution.

Barabasi, A. (2002). *Linked: The New Science of Networks,* Massachusetts: Perseus Publishing.

Bar-Yam, Y. (2000). About Complex Systems, http://necsi.net/guide/

Berlekamp, J., Conway, J. and Guy, R. (1982). *Winning Ways for Your Mathematical Plays,* New York: Academic Press.

Bonabeau, E. (2002). Predicting the Unpredictable, *Harvard Business Review* 80(3): 109–116.

Bonabeau, E and Meyer, C (2001). Swarm Intelligence, *Harvard Business Review* 79(5): 106–114.

Brown, S.L. and Eisenhardt, K.M. (1997). The Art of Continuous Change: Linking complexity theory and time-based evolution in relentlessly shifting organizations, *Administrative Science Quarterly* 42: 1–34.

Buchanan, M. (2002). *Nexus*, New York, NY: Norton.

Burt, R.S. (1992). *Structural Holes: The Social Structure of Competition*, Cambridge, MA: Harvard University Press.

Burt, R.S. (1997). The Contingent Value of Social Capital, *Administrative Science Quaterly* 42(2): 339–365.

Capra, F. (1996). *The Web of Life*, London: HarperCollins.

Castells, M. (1996). *The Rise of the Network Society*, Oxford: Blackwell Publishers.

Casti, J. (1997). *Would-Be Worlds: How Simulation is Changing*, Wiley: New York.

Chaitin, G. (1990). *Information, Randomness, and Incompleteness*, Singapore: World Scientific Co.

Davis, F.D. (1989). Perceived Usefulness, Perceived Ease of Use, and User Acceptance of Information Technology, *MIS Quarterly* 13(3): 319–340.

Eisenhardt, K. and Galunic, C. (1999). Coevolving: At last, a way to make synergies work, *Harvard Business Review* 78(1): 91–99.

Epstein, J.M. and Axtell, R. (1996). *Growing Artificial Societies: Social Science from the Bottom Up*, Washington, DC and Cambridge, MA: Brookings Press and MIT Press.

Evans, P. and Wurster, T. (2000). *Blown to Bits: How The New Economics of Information Transforms Strategy*, Cambridge, MA: Harvard Business School Press.

Gilbert, N. and Troitzsch, K.G. (1999). *Simulation for the Social Scientist*, Philadelphia, PA: Open University Press.

Gleick, J. (1987). *Chaos: Making a New Science*, New York: Viking-Penguin.

Granovetter, M. (1973). The Strength of Weak Ties, *The American Journal of Sociology* 78/6: 1360–1380.

Granovetter, M. (1985). Economic Action and Social Structure: The problem of embeddedness, *American Journal of Sociology* 91: 481–510.

Granovetter, M (1995). Coase Revisited: Business groups in modern society, *Ind. Corp Change* 4: 93–131.

Guastello, S.J. (1995). *Chaos, Catastrophe and Human Affairs: Applications of Nonlinear Dynamics to Work, Organizations, and Social Evolution*, Mahwah, NJ: Lawrence Erlbaum Associates.

Hamel, G. and Prahalad, C. (1994). *Competing for the Future*, Boston, MA: Harvard Business School Press.

Hiltz, S.R. and Johnson, K. (1990). User Satisfaction with Computer-Mediated Systems, *Management Science* 36(6): 739–764.

Holland, J.H. (1995). *Hidden Order*, Reading, MA: Addison-Wesley.

Holland, J.H. (1998). *Emergence: From Chaos to Order*, Oxford: Oxford University Press.

Ilgen, D.R. and Hulin, C.L. (2000). *Computational Modeling of Behavior in Organizations: The Third Scientific Discipline.*, Washington, DC: American Psychological Association.

Jarvanpaa, S. (1989). Effects of Task Demand and Graphical Format on Information Processing Strategies, *Management Science* 35(3): 285–303.

Kant, I. (1790). *Critique of Judgement* (translated by J. Meredith). New York: Oxford University Press, 1973.

Kauffman, S. (1993). *The Origins of Order: Self-Organization and Selection in Evolution,* New York, NY: Oxford University Press.

Kauffman, S. (1995). *At Home in the Universe: The Search for Laws of Self-Organisation and Complexity,* New York, NY: Oxford University Press.

Kuhnb, T. (1962). *The Structure of Scientific Revolutions,* Chicago: Chicago University Press.

Langton, C.G. (1991). *Computation at the Edge of Chaos: Phase-Transitions and Emergent Computation,* Ph.D. dissertation, University of Michigan.

Leavitt, H. and Whistler, T. (1958). Management in the 1980s, *Harvard Business Review* 36: 41–48.

Lichtenstein, B.B. and McKelvey, B. (2006). Toward a Theory of Emergence by Stages: Complexity dynamics, self-organization, and power laws in firms. Working paper, Boston, MA: Management/Marketing Department, University of Massachusetts.

Lorenz, E. 1963. Deterministic Nonperiodic Flow, *Journal of the Atmospheric Sciences* 20: 130–141.

Maguire, S., Mckelvey, B., Mirabeau, L. and Öztas, N. (2006). Complexity Science and Organization Studies, in S.R. Clegg, C. Hardy and T. Lawrence (eds.) *The Sage Handbook of Organization Studies,* (2nd edn), Thousand Oaks, CA: Sage.

Marcus, L.M. (1983). Power, Politics and MIS Implementation, *Communication of the ACM* 26: 430–440.

Maturana, H. and Varela, F.J. (1973). Autopoiesis: The *Organization* of the living, in H.R. Maturana and F.J. Varela (eds.) *Autopoiesis and Cognition: The Realization of the Living,* Vol. 42, Boston Studies in the Philosophy of Science, Dordrecht, Holland: D. Reidel Publishing Company.

McKelvey, B. (1997). Quasi-Natural Organization Science, *Organization Science* 8: 351–381.

Merali, Y. (1997). Information, Systems and *Dasein,* in F. Stowell, I. McRobb, R. Landor, R. Ison and J. Holloway (eds.) *Systems for Sustainability: People Organisations and Environments,* New York: Plenum Press. 595–600.

Merali, Y. (2000). The Organic Metaphor in Knowledge Management, *Emergence, Special Issue on Organic Knowledge Management* 2(4): 14–22.

Merali, Y. (2004a). Ethics in an Inter-Connected World. Proceedings of International Conference on Corporate Social Responsibility, November 2004, Korea, pp. 45–65.

Merali, Y. (2004b). Complexity and Information Systems, in J. Mingers and L. Willcocks (eds.) *Social Theory and Philosophy of Information Systems,* London: Wiley. pp. 407–446.

Merali, Y. (2005). Complexity Science and Conceptualisation in the Internet Enabled World, 21st Colloquium of the European Group for Organisational Studies, July 2005, Berlin.

Morgan, G. (1986). *Images of Organization,* California: Sage.

Moser, I. and Law, J. (2006). Fluids or Flows? Information and Calculation in Medical Practice, *Information Technology & People* 19(1): 55–73.

Orlikowski, W. (1992). The Duality of Technology: Rethinking the concept of technology in organizations, *Organisation Science* 3(3): 398–427.

Orlikowski, W.J. (1996). Improvising Organizational Transformation Over Time: A situated change perspective, *Information Systems Research* 7(1): 63–92.

Potanin, A., Noble, J., Frean, M. and Biddle, R. (2005). Scale-Free Geometry in OO Programs, *Communications of the ACM* 48(5): 99–103.

Prietula, M.J., Carley, K.M. and Gasser, L. (eds.) (1998). *Simulating Organizations: Computational Models of Institutions and Groups*, Cambridge, MA: MIT Press.

Prigogine, I. (1967). Dissipative Structures in Chemical Systems, in S. Claessons (ed.) *Fast reactions and Primary Processes in Chemical Kinetics*, New York: Interscience.

Shapiro, C. and Varian, H. (1999). *Information Rules: A Strategic Guide to the Network Economy*, Cambridge, MA: Harvard Business School Press.

Sigmund, K. (1993). *Games of Life*, New York: University Press.

Stacey, R. (2001). *Complex responsive Processes in Organisations: Learning and Knowledge Creation*, London: Routledge.

Stacey, R.D. (1992). *Managing the Unknowable: Strategic Boundaries Between Order and Chaos in Organizations.*, San Francisco, CA: Jossey-Bass.

Tesfatsion, L. and Judd, K. (2006). *Handbook of Computational Economics* (2nd edn.), Amsterdam: North-Holland/Elsevier Science.

Wasserman, S. and Faust, K. (1994). *Social Network Analysis: Methods and Applications*, Cambridge, UK: Cambridge University Press.

Watts, D.J. (1999). *Small Worlds: The Dynamics of Networks between Order and Randomness*, Princeton, NJ: Princeton University Press.

Watts, D. (2003). *Six Degrees: Small Worlds and the Groundbreaking Science of Networks*, New York: Norton.

Watts, D.J. and Strogatz, S.H. (1998). Collective Dynamics of 'Small World' Networks, *Nature* 395: 440–442.

Zuboff, S. (1988). *In the Age of the Smart Machine – The Future of Work and Power*, New York: Basic Books Inc.

26
A Conceptual Framework for Studying Gender in Information Systems Research

Melanie Wilson
Manchester School of Management,
University of Manchester Institute of Science and Technology, UK

Introduction

Approaching the issue of Information Systems (IS) from an innovation perspective (Quintas, 1996), this paper seeks to enhance our understanding of IS process by introducing theoretical concepts and observations advanced in sociology and technology management disciplines under the heading of 'Social Studies of Technology' (SST).[1] Specifically, the proposal of the paper is that a focus on gender within this approach will mean an increased awareness of organisational and social concerns of both the IS development process and the consequences of IS deployment into organisations. In so doing, I am assuming, in line with significant feminist research elsewhere, that gender relations involve difference, inequality and power. This is deemed pertinent to access to, and control over, material and symbolic resources (Knights and Willmott, 1986).

I propose one potential means to theorise both the way user interaction with developed IS is gendered, and the way the technology itself comes to be gendered through the process of its design, development and diffusion into organisations and society as a whole. Although studies on gender differences in relation to computers, as well as on the under-representation of women in computing exist, within the IS literature, the role of gender and Information and Communication Technologies (ICTs) is largely under-theorised (Adam *et al.*, 2002; Wilson, 2002), restricting itself to the (laudable if limited) project of add-more-numbers (Adam *et al.*, 1994). This is partly because of the assumption that technology is gender neutral – 'a sure guarantee that it embraces all sorts of taken-for-granted assumptions' (Knights and Murray, 1994: 17).

In discussing gender and IS, my experience leads me to believe that the comparative novelty of such a project means one is required (to some extent, at least) to justify the endeavour in the first instance. On a fairly straightforward level, it would appear that if the social nature of IS is recognised, then surely it follows that user interaction is shaped by the context in which that interaction takes place. Given the existence of gendered spheres (see below) then user interaction will carry the hallmarks of this context. Further, the gendered division of labour in society as a whole also means that the same is true of the work processes incorporated in the IS. This gendering obviously varies in its degree of intensity, with traditionally masculine occupations such as engineering at one end, and traditionally female ones, such as nursing, at the other. And, if we look not just at impacts but also to the social context of the innovation process, then it becomes evident that the IS itself will be imbued with the gendered environment of its creation.

The thrust of the argument is that we as academics and practitioners cannot eschew the task of exploring neglected social and organisational concerns associated with IS, especially when this is likely to produce new insights, which in turn can guide our actions in practice – and hopefully improve the IS development record. A conceptual framework for carrying out this task is developed over the course of the paper. In order to achieve this, an interdisciplinary approach has been adopted.

In the following sections, the case for a gendered approach to IS in organisations is made, firstly, by reviewing the statistics indicating the under-representation and under-valuing of women and information and communication technologies (ICTs); and secondly, by highlighting the under-theorisation of gender and within IS research. The construction of the proposed conceptual framework to overcome these deficiencies is achieved in a two-key moves – both entailing interdisciplinary couplings. The first of these moves concerns the Critical Management Studies approach to organisations that incorporates insights from the feminist tradition concerning gendered spheres in the workplace. The second move is constituted by drawing on the strengths of the interpretivist tradition, established both in IS research and the SST approach to innovation, and outlining suggestions for overcoming potential weaknesses that this tradition entails. The framework is tabulated including proposals for future research areas. In addition, potential research questions are outlined and illustrated with examples from the field of nursing. Finally, remarks in conclusion are added.

Gender, IS and IS Research

Under-representation of women in ICTs

From an optimistic viewpoint, the move away from heavy industrial technology associated with the proliferation of ICTs in organisations could have inaugurated a period in which 'the gender stereotyping of technology would diminish' (Wajcman, 1991: 150). Indeed, computing could have been gender neutral or appropriated by women because its alliance with the typewriter and compatibility with the skilled of the secretary (Webster, 1990: 52). Nevertheless, computing is dominated by men. Some of the latest figures suggest that although IT jobs had grown at a rate of 50% over the previous 5 years (compared with a general job growth rate of 8%), only 22% of the people working in the IT sector are women (compared with around 50% of the general workforce) (Ward, 2001). Rubery and Fagan (1994) report that in Britain, the proportion of female entrants into computer science degrees has steadily dropped from an initial low level of 24% in 1978 to a mere 13% by 1989, while 1995 figures suggest women constitute only one-fifth of computer science undergraduates in the UK. Although records of GCSE attempted in 1995 show that 45% of computer studies and 35% of IS students were female, University and Colleges Admissions Service (UCAS) figures for computer science degree accepted applications that same year were less than 17%. The record of negative experiences of women with ICTs (Rasmussen and Hapnes, 1991; Adam, 1997) suggests that the relative exclusion of women from computing is likely to continue for some time. Further, it appears that women also continue to underestimate their skills and to equate technical competence and skill with masculinity and men (Henwood *et al.*, 2001).

Despite some differences in the interpretation of data on women's (under-) representation in ICTs, it is generally recognised that the gender inequality exits and constitutes a problem that should be overcome (Snizek and Neil, 1992; Baroudi and Truman, 1994; Baroudi and Igbaria, 1995; Adam, 2002) not just because there may be something unfair about all of this, but because women can be used to overcome the so-called IT skills shortage (Liu and Wilson, 2001; Maitland, 2001: Quicke, 2001). Indeed in the past, cases had been made for the inclusion of women due to their gender-specific skills: their mastery of language for programming; their propensity to screen out irrelevancies, realise tasks and problem solve in stressful conditions; their recognition that although possible, not all tasks are worth performing on a computer (Gerver, 1989). However, we should recognise that these arguments are in danger of reproducing precisely the kinds of essentialist[2] arguments that are used to justify women's unequal treatment in the IT industry. And indeed it is possible to recognise difference without ascribing this to 'nature' (see for example, Trauth, 2002).

Under-theorisation of gender and IS research

The relative paucity of treatment of gender issues in IS research has been recognised (Adam *et al.*, 2002). Further, since women are excluded from formal design one suggested strategy is to 'bring women in' by shifting focus to consumption of technology (Webster, 1996: 5) and the process of 'innofusion'[3] (Dutton *et al.*, 1995). The same conclusions have been drawn more recently by Wajcman (2000) who states that the absence of women from view is due in part to the concentration by SST on technology at the *design* stage, where male 'heroes' dominate. So, in order to include women we need to focus towards other areas of technology development and diffusion (Wilson, 2002).

> Women are the hidden cheap labour force that produces technologies, the secretaries, cleaners and cooks, they are part of the sales force, and the main users of domestic and reproductive technologies. The under-valuing of women's 'unskilled' and delegated work serves to make them invisible in mainstream technology studies. (Wajcman, 2000: 453)

Having argued for the need to deal with the issue of gender and IS, in the next section I suggest some theoretical approaches that can be drawn on and applied to IS research. The phenomenon of gender and IS is a subset of four broader phenomena: gender and ICTs, gender and society, gender and organisational arrangements and gender and technology, as summarised in Table 26.1. Consequently, in researching this phenomenon we will have recourse to other disciplines.

Incorporation of feminist research into critical management studies

Critical management

Writers in the gender and computer field have deliberated new research perspectives for some time (see, for example, Grint and Gill, 1995; Star, 1995; Lander and Adam, 1997: 1–59). In turning to social science

Table 26.1 Gender and IS research

Field of Study	Theoretical influence	Topic of study	Incorporated	Potential areas for application in IS research
Gender and computing	Feminism	Women and ICTs	Under-representation of women in ICTs Under-theorisation of gender in IS research	Statistical enquiry into IT profession
Gender and Society	Feminism Social constructivism	Existence of gendered spheres	Culture of dichotomies Socialisation and skills acquisition Symmetry of socialisation	Development of IT competence Comparison of male and female interactions
Gender and organizations	Critical management studies	Social division of labour	Conflict, contradiction and power Gendered spheres in workplace Gendered jobs	Context of systems development Modelling work by developers Interaction of users with IS
Gender and technology	Social shaping of technology	Gendered Culture of Technology	Interpretivist accounts of technology Social construction of gender and technology	Sexual and social division of labour Organization of work by management Allocation of skills attributes

to develop a conceptual framework for studying gender, I favour a social constructivist approach (For examples: Webster, 1990, 1996; Van Zoonen, 1992; Green *et al.*, 1993; Wagner, 1993; Adam *et al.*, 1994; Knights and Murray, 1994). In addition, a critical perspective[4] is needed to question precisely those areas of organisational relationships left in tact by non-political approaches (Howcroft and Wilson, 2003) and so critical management studies (CMS) have appeal. Now relatively well developed, one advantage of CMS is that conflict and contradiction become the focus of attention instead of something to be eliminated. Further, a critical perspective acknowledges that some actors are disadvantaged in terms of power and skills in relation to others, and accepts that the level of commitment is likely to be uneven, as all members cannot be considered equal stakeholders. A critical perspective framework has been summarised as: concerned with questioning assumptions; committed to emancipation; taking a social perspective as opposed to an individualised one; and, sensitised to power relations (Burgoyne and Reynold, 1997).

This contribution from CMS, I feel, will be productive for understanding the rubric of gender, IS and organisations. As well as making room for feminist insights into the world of work and beyond into society, it has the added advantage of being in keeping with the parallel intention – to bring together the work of SST with IS literature. The next section outlines some of the feminist insights to be incorporated into the framework for studying gender in IS.

Socialisation and the persistence of gendered spheres

In relation to the gender issues discussed in this paper, I am assuming that gender divisions are part of the structure of social life, concurring with Webster (1996) that a sexual division of labour exists prior to the introduction of IS in organisations. These gender divisions mean the existence of 'separate spheres' (Smith, 1997) or distinct 'cultural codes' (Davies, 1995) for men and women. In sum, we live in a society that tends to classify the world into opposites, a culture of dichotomies (see Figure 26.1).

[I]t is argued that technology, computer technology in particular, is anchored in values that most societies consider to be the preserve of men: objectivity, progress, rationality, productivity and competition. Care, emotionality, intuition and co-operation – features usually ascribed to women – are said to be at odds with the premises of technology. (Van Zoonen, 1992)

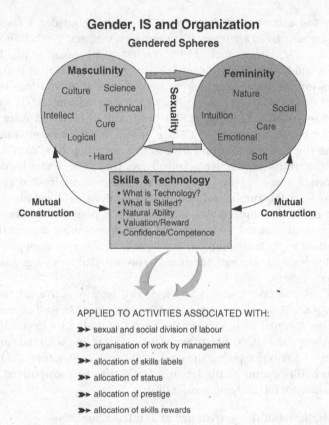

Figure 26.1   Applications to activities associated with: sexual and social division of labour, organisation of work by management, allocation of skills labels, allocation of status, allocation of prestige and allocation of skills rewards (adapted from Wilson, 2002: 149)

Let us note for now that, given the unequal sexual division of labour, it is generally agreed that these attributes will be differently estimated, giving rise to a tendency to undervalue that half of the dichotomy identified as feminine. In terms of organisations, this means that 'male jobs tend to be more valued and, in particular, better paid than female' (Alvesson and Billing, 1997: 18), and 'qualities associated with manliness are almost everywhere more highly regarded than those thought of as womanly' (Wajcman, 1991: 9). Thus, there is a tendency to associate certain types of skills and knowledge as typically male or female.

The totalising effects of these separate spheres means that despite the diversity of responses to their existence, no one escapes their influence since we are all classified (inappropriately or not) in relation to masculinity or femininity. Although the ideals and stereotypes we are expected to live up to are precisely that, society rarely accepts happily people who openly trespass over the conventional boundaries, and those who do face being labelled with terms that designate the abnormality, the going-against-nature of their behaviour, or what they are (Carlin, 1989).

Explanations of women's participation in IS that reject sexist, essentialist and deterministic arguments and explanations are based on the role of socialisation in creating gender difference – rather than rely on accounts of innate abilities and characteristics (Smith, 1997) (see note 1). Although the gendering process may be very strongly resisted, it nevertheless leaves its mark on us all, impinging on every aspect of our lives. However, the gendering process will be different according to cultural contexts and times. In our own society then, cultural ideas and social practices rather than genes account for the ratio of male/female occupations (Alvesson and Billing, 1997: 10). Another important observation is that the ongoing process of gender socialisation is a symmetrical one; the genders are defined in relation to one another, and give rise to the associated notions of the 'other' as well as a culture of dualism between masculinity and femininity.

Gendered spheres in the workplace

There are valuable theoretical developments derived from the synthesis of feminist analysis of organisation with IS literature. Firstly, what can we learn for our understanding of the social and organisational context of IS by focusing on gender in organisations? According to Alvesson and Billing (1997: 8):

A gender perspective will not only mean dealing with the way men and women are constructed as individuals...but will also include a broader view on organisations.

Although we should not totalise organisational life through seeing everything in terms of gender, still the existence of separate spheres at work is well documented (see, for examples Walby 1988; Ledwith and Colgan, 1996). Indeed, for Cockburn (1988: 29):

Occupational segregation by sex is one of the most marked and persistent patterns that characterize our world and its nature has by now been thoroughly rehearsed.

Cockburn goes on to describe the way in which we utilise different areas of the workplace and cluster in different echelons, different skills and different areas of service provision. While we are at work, we are not only producing goods but also producing culture and the study of gender makes visible gender relations that have been subsumed, providing 'a vivid illumination of the way that technology is inescapably a social and political phenomenon' (Knights and Murray, 1994: 18).

Following on from the idea that skills are assigned to people according to sex we find the notion of gendered jobs. A gendered job is one that is commonly considered to be a woman's job rather than a man's (or *vice versa*). Davies and Rosser (1986: 103) summarise the idea of 'a gendered job' as 'one which capitalised on the qualities and capabilities a woman had gained by virtue of having lived her life as a woman.' The corollary of this is that skills acquired in this way are not acknowledged as skills in the same way as learned knowledge and skills, nor are they financially rewarded. Cockburn (1986: 169) notes that occupations themselves have come to be gendered:

> [I]t is of course a two-way process. People have a gender and their gender rubs off on the jobs they mainly do. Jobs in turn have a gender character which rubs off on the people who do them.

While work deemed to be women's prerogative tends to be devalued as a matter of course, by the same token, it is a tautology to talk about a 'career man' even though men also have to work at getting a career. Evidence exists indicating that the skills involved in doing a particular job are ignored or undervalued merely because it is women who are generally employed in that field of work. Women's work tends to be regarded as semi-skilled merely *because it is women's work*. In 'high-technology' work, men dominate and have resisted the encroachment of women who are systematically excluded from managerial positions, yet over-represented in the lower echelons of computing in an organisational process that is itself profoundly masculinised (Knights and Murray, 1994; Webster, 1996). But even if IT work is an extreme case of the inequalities between men and women, it is not alone. Skilled work is not just defined by objective dexterity or training, but the very fact that men rather than women carry it out (Phillips and Taylor, 1980; Davies and Rosser, 1986). This has implications for the context of systems development, the modelling of work by systems developers, and the interaction of users with the developed IS.

In addition to the critical approach to organisational studies, incorporating feminists insights as described above, we can call on more critical traditions already established in the IS discipline to develop the framework. Of most significance is interpretivism as opposed to the positivism that had previously held sway in IS research. Interestingly, interpretivism is also very influential in the SST field.

Interpretivism in IS research and social studies of technology

The relevance and appropriateness of an Interpretivist approach in IS research (Walsham, 1993) has now achieved more mainstream acceptance. In contrast to the positivist approach, the interpretive tradition is occupied with understanding what meaning and significance the social world has for people who live within it, thus seeing the world as socially constructed. Interpreting IS in terms of social action suggests that the social world can only be tackled from within and by methods different from those suited to the natural sciences. However, taken to an extreme, Interpretivism can imply a thoroughgoing relativism – a point we shall return to below.

Meanwhile, within SST there are different strands or schools that reflect fundamental epistemological and ontological disagreements concerning the appropriateness of a relativist standpoint in dealing with technology (Williams and Edge, 1996). Thus, included in SST are those who subscribe(d) in some way to the validity of meta-narratives that seek to provide general, even universal explanations of the nature of human society, such as Marxism and Feminism (Noble, 1984; Shwartz Cowan, 1985; Wajcman, 1991; Webster, 1996) and those who have rejected such universalisations as inappropriate for social scientists. This scepticism of the so-called 'meta-narratives' has induced SST researchers to look for more local-oriented approaches. The social construction of technology (SCOT) (Pinch and Bijker, 1987) adopts a methodology that claims to open the black box of innovations to examine the patterning and shaping of particular 'selection environments'. Such an approach acknowledges social factors, but proceeds from the technology 'outwards' to the context shaping it (Williams and Edge, 1996). Here, Interpretivism appears in the form of 'interpretative flexibility', whereby technologies and technological problems are open to various interpretations. Similarly, in actor network theory (ANT) (Callon, 1986, Latour, 1987; Law, 1987) the notion of the script and inscription (Akrich, 1992) account for the way in which technologies are variously 'translated'. Together, interpretative flexibility and inscription have been useful to feminist research as they also allow for consumers and users being 'an integral part of the process of technological development' (Wajcman, 2000: 451).

This is not the place to rerun all the differences, similarities and debates that have taken place within SST. Rather, my aims are to highlight the strengths of Interpretivism as well as the weaknesses in the SST approaches with regard to their treatment of gender, to offer a means of overcoming those weaknesses, and thereby to indicate ways in which the various approaches may be used together to improve our descriptions and understanding of IS. In order to achieve these aims we begin by referring to Wajcman's (2000) critique of SCOT and ANT.

Deficiencies in the science and technology studies treatment of gender

The IS discipline is not alone in its paucity of systematic gender study. For even in SST,[5] despite the fact that the relationship between gender and technology has been theorised over the last 20 years or so, nevertheless, a clear imbalance in the incorporation of gender analysis and innovation persists (Wajcman, 2000). Wajcman asks why, if social studies look at the social, they have largely ignored gender issues – leaving this task to feminists. The problems begin with ANT and SCOT's methodology that has a flawed conceptualisation of power. This methodology focuses on observable conflicts among social groups and networks, but largely ignore what Lukes' (1974) radical analysis called the third dimension of power. This refers to the exercise of power beyond the observable but existent in the structural dimensions of power, where exclusion and absence of parties are evidence of hidden manipulations of situations. Hence, the need to look to structural arrangements to understand the systematic exclusion of women from certain areas of technological development. On this Wajcman (2000: 452) comments:

> While the effects of structural exclusion on technological development are not easy to analyse, they should not be overlooked. Feminists have stressed that women's absence from spheres of influence is a key feature of gender power relations.

So, focusing on relevant social groups (in SCOT) ignores the pre-excluded. Nor in ANT is the Foucauldian conceptualisation of power likely to assist a study of gender because it makes it awkward to address the obduracy of the link between men and technology. Further to this:

ANT does not always recognize that the stabilization and standardization of technological systems necessarily involve negating the experience of those who are not standard, "a destruction of the world of the non-enrolled". (Star, 1991, cited by Wajcman, 2000: 453).

One further problem with the fact that the masculinity of technology has not been made explicit is that this has meant that constructivist studies have then assumed gender to have little bearing on technological developments. But the point is that gender is an issue *even when women are absent*: gender should not just equate to women.

Overcoming deficiencies: the mutual construction of gender and technology

In contradiction to the general weakness of SST's treatment of gender, those studies that have focused on issues of gender can offer a starting point for understanding the organisational and broader societal context of IS development and implementation. Notable examples include Mackenzie and Wajcman (1985), Wajcman (1991), Cock-burn, (1983, 1986, 1988), Cockburn and Omerod (1993), and Webster (1996). As Webster (1996: 5) suggests, the theoretical and empirical focus of SST should be on those activities concerned with the sexual and social division of labour, the organisation of work by management, and the allocation of skill labels, skilled status, prestige and rewards (see Figure 26.1).

One further advantage of pursuing the SST approach to technology when studying gender is that it offers us a culturally inspired, rather than deterministic frame for our research. The case for a cultural approach – that is, one which sees both technology and gender as social constructions – has many advantages. Not least because it overcomes the weaknesses associated with the biological determinism and essentialism that constitute 'a type of rationalised pessimism' (Segal, 1994: 131). The latter may serve to replicate the arguments of those who would see women remain in a subordinate position in society.

In contrast, a rejection of both biological and technological determinism means that the differences and inequalities discussed in this paper are seen not as a matter of nature but of culture. A social constructivist approach to gender states that there is nothing inherently more 'natural' about one human activity than another – it depends on context (Carlin, 1989). Talk of 'natural' instincts, and so forth, is in many circumstances false or inappropriate. Human abilities and characteristics develop within the constraints of social relations:

> All social conventions come to appear natural when in reality there are no inflexible and unchanging patterns, rhythms or relationships in which human development occurs. What is most essentially human is precisely that our lives, women's and men's, are not just determined by biological necessity but crucially also by human action and vision (Segal, 1994: 10–11).

So, the term 'human nature' is often a generalisation from observations of current, local human behaviour, since there is always a tendency to read off from one's immediate reality, the natural state of the world. The result is that the current state of affairs is presented as unchangeable. Yet, the universality of our current model of gendered roles has been challenged by Marxists (Engels, 2001; Carlin, 1989), and rejected by anthropological research (Burke Leacock, 1981; Strathern, 1980). Hence, MacKinnon *et al.* (1993) argue that in a less sexist society women can excel at computer studies.

However, it is not the case that sexist culture and its discriminatory repercussions are merely imposed on women from the outside. Socialisation is all encompassing in two respects: firstly, it affects both men and women, differently but symmetrically (Davies, 1995: 21); and secondly, women internalise the views of society and (resistance aside) are shaped by it. Notions about the natural place of women in society are not only held by men.

One feature of the socialisation process is that girls are socialised into having an orientation towards activities related to home creation, child rearing and care of others as part of their preparation for womanhood. This includes not only what will be expected from them by others but also *what they will expect from themselves*. Hence, the possibility of women acting conservatively, even acting against their 'own interests' (Alvesson and Billing, 1997).

If we accept that the associated characteristics of gender are socially constructed, then this has repercussions for the inter-relationship of gender and IS. Gender is a significant issue in discussions of technology when we look at what is meant by technology as described in the SST tradition:

> Technology is more than a set of physical objects or artefacts. It also fundamentally embodies a culture or set of beliefs, desires and practices. (Wajcman, 1995: 149)

Hence, the word 'technology' has various layers of meaning: it is a form of knowledge; it refers to human activities and practices; it is defined as hardware – a set of physical objects (MacKenzie and Wajcman, 1985). If we accept that technology is more than the hardware, and includes human actions and thoughts, it follows that the gender training we receive is significant in this process. In addition, it would seem that machines and artefacts used predominantly by women do not have this elusive power of conferring high status on the user (Karpf, 1987). This is further witnessed by the arbitrary nature in which some artefacts commonly perceived as 'technology' (cars, video recorders, computers) and others are not (sewing machines, domestic appliances, typewriters). The very attribution of the word 'technology' to an artefact magically confers a higher status on it. Where skills become highly valued they tend to be redefined and appropriated by men (MacKinnon *et al.*, 1993).[6]

Social shaping then, can be appropriated as a tool for challenging the gendered nature of technology. There is an understanding that technology is made more explicable by analysing it as a *culture*, and therefore historically and materially contingent.

Technology as masculine culture

The discussion of skills above relates to views of technological ability. Cockburn and Omerod (1993) suggest that occupations involve sex segregation because the technological know-how required to carry them out is usually culturally denied women, in that the qualities required for entry to the professions and success in them are seen as masculine. Both women and men are implicated in the systematic under-valuation of women's rationality and expertise (Cockburn and Omerod, 1993; Knights and Murray, 1994) although this is evidently to women's disadvantage. Again, it is not just that women are excluded by a male-dominated culture (Rasmussen and Hapnes, 1991), they internalise the views of society and (resistance aside) are shaped by it. Consequently, many girls avoid obtaining skills that might undermine their femininity (Wajcman, 1991), including high levels of computer competence. By contrast, boys are encouraged in computer use, contributing to difference in usage and 'the absence of technical confidence or competence does indeed become part of feminine gender identity, as well as being a sexual stereotype' (Wajcman, 1991: 155). As a result, boys do not want to be seen as girlish. (Indeed since masculine attributes have higher status it is more acceptable for a girl to behave as a tomboy than it is for a boy to be 'girly'.) Crossing cultural boundaries into arenas demarcated for the other sex can be costly at the vulnerable time of puberty, which appears to be precisely the critical time for acquiring those skills that will provide confidence for the manipulation of 'mechanical' and 'technical' objects in later life (Wajcman, 1991).

In sum:

> Technology enters into our sexual identity: femininity is incompatible with technical competence; to feel technically competent is to feel manly. The gendering of men and women into 'masculine' and 'feminine' is a cultural process of immense power. People suffer for disregarding its dictates. (Cockburn, 1986: 12)

Women, it appears, are perhaps as susceptible to the belief in their own lack of technological ability as men are likely to delight in their own supposed superiority. As Smith (1997: 158) comments: 'it is hardly surprising if we sometimes confuse how we are treated – what we are told about ourselves – with what we know about our own natures and capacities.' This would suggest, then, that technology be seen as masculine culture – that technological competence has come to be identified with 'masculinity':

> Men's affinity with technology is...seen as integral to the constitution of male gender identity. (Wajcman, 1991: 38)

This does not necessarily derive from technology's inherent masculine character. Rather, competent use of the technology has been traditionally associated with men (Wajcman, 1991).

This ends the literature review that has sought to combine approaches and insights from a variety of sources, overcome their weaknesses and to show their compatibility within a framework for studying IS. This is summarised in Table 26.1, which will also serve to suggest the further areas of research as part of the case for the significance of the framework.

Significance of the conceptual framework for IS research

As stated previously, the framework is intended to contribute in a number of ways. Firstly, it may provide additional, deeper explanations for certain organisational phenomena – such as user rejection related to subjective assessments of incompatibility and so on. Secondly, by studying gender, using this framework we might deepen our understanding of the innovation process through increased awareness of social processes and structures that impinge on the development and usage of IS. Thirdly, the new insights produced by using the framework could well improve

IS practice and lead to more appropriate technology. One of the main contributions of the paper is to suggest future areas for IS research where the framework may be applied as well as to generate a number of research questions as a starting point for that endeavour.

As shown in Table 26.1, the framework incorporates elements from the multi-disciplinary literature review. Firstly, they include an acknowledgement of the under-representation of women in ICTs, as well as the under-theorisation of gender in IS research as described in the gender and computing literature. The area of potential future research implied concerns supplementary empirical and statistical enquiry into the make up and activities of the IT profession (and possible IT usage, even academic activity). Secondly, literature concerning gender and society as a whole has produced insights into the culture of dichotomies, the acquisition of skills through the gendered socialisation process and the way this process is of a symmetrical nature (men's and women's attributes being formed alongside each other). Such revelations give rise to research areas on the topic of the development of IT competence and connote comparative studies into male and female interactions with IS. Thirdly, from gender and organisational analysis, we are furnished with insights into the incorporation of the critical elements: conflict, contradiction and power. We also have the descriptions of the existence of gendered spheres in the workplace, especially the fact of gendered jobs. These findings will be useful for studying the context of systems development, modelling work by developers and interactions of users with the IS. Finally, from gender and technology observations we can integrate Interpretivist elements as well as the mutual construction of gender and technology. These will support examinations in the area of the sexual and social division of labour, the organisation of work by management and the allocation of skills attributes.

The implications and relevance of the framework for IS research are then further drawn out by the inclusion of recommended research questions and illustrations from a nursing environment. I have chosen to provide some instance from an in-depth case study that is well documented elsewhere (for example, Wilson 2002; Wilson and Howcroft, 2002). The details of the case study need not concern us here, as the illustrations as merely suggestions of how one may venture to answer the research questions in practice. Needless to say, the points made are not intended to be universally applicable, but rather act as a starting point for consideration of other areas of work. It is worth noting, however, that since the intensity of gendering of job varies, so the gendering of interaction surely varies. Hence, in more stereotypical jobs, such as nursing, a culture of dichotomies and thus gender will play a greater role in determining the relationship of users to the IS.

Breadth of study

In the second section of the paper, I stated that the relative absence of women from computing suggests that concentrating solely on the *development* of technologies (where women are excluded) then women will be invisible. Yet, as Webster (1996) argues, employees play a role in the shaping the development and application of technologies.

> It is clear in many spheres IT has been designed and developed with the view that primarily women will use it in their function as clerical, secretarial and administrative processing workers. (Knights and Murray, 1994: 18)

Thus, by broadening our scope to the *use* of technology as a change *process*, women as users play an important role. This is very much in keeping the perspective of innovation through implementation – 'innofusion' (Dutton *et al.*, 1995) especially in relation to software. Undoubtedly, if we accept the import of the socialisation process, all user interaction is shaped in some way by gender. Furthermore, by analysing women users of technological artefacts and systems as *shapers and/or resisters* of the technology, we can avoid an implicit 'victim' approach to the issue of gender and inequality. Consequently, it is suggested we can avoid technological determinism in IS research by not restricting the field of study to 'impacts'. Such a study would also entail an analysis of the ways gender spheres are replicated in IS process: the inclusion and exclusion of women. This broadening of the field of study is in addition to the examination of the way in which the technology itself comes to be gendered.

These points imply some basic *research questions*. The overarching question concerning gendered spheres in relation to IS is a double-headed one. In the first instance, we can apply it to the IT professionals: in what ways do the development and implementation activities of IT professionals replicate the attributes of gendered spheres found in wider society? However, the expansion in the breadth of study recommended above means a second question can be directed toward the domain organisation where the IS is being deployed. In the case of Nursing, similar questions would relate to the overall division of health work into the care work of nurses and the clinical work of doctors and how this division replicates the role of women and men in society as a whole.

Another question generated by the increased breadth of study is: where are women included and where excluded? Directing the question to Nursing Information Systems (NIS), we can state that, as is the case with IS in other areas, women are typically less included in the design stage of the NIS, and rarely figure in the management of the design process. Nevertheless, 'downstream' as it were, nurses are using the technology and we might ask: which functions and elements of the system are open to users? For example, auxiliary nurses do not have authority to access the IS. A third question we might construct from the framework is: in what ways has the IS been adapted in usage (by women)? In the case of time-pressed nurses' interaction with a 'long-winded' IS, they may find short-cuts through the procedures or even avoid usage by operating a manual system more than is prescribed.

Theoretical and empirical focus for study of IS in organisations

One important area of focus in IS research concerns the way in which men and women utilise different areas of the workplace and cluster in different echelons, different skills and different areas of service provision. Thus, in keeping with the territory covered in the construction of the conceptual framework, it is suggested that it is applied in IS research to: (a) those activities associated with IS and the sexual and social division of labour; (b) those activities associated with IS and the organisation of work by management; and (c) those activities associated with IS and the allocation of skill labels, status, prestige and rewards (see Figure 26.1). In the case of IT work, one might argue that even if the profession is seen as an extreme case of the inequalities between men and women, it is not alone. Skilled work is not just defined by objective dexterity or training, but the very fact that men rather than women carry it out (Phillips and Taylor, 1980; Davies and Rosser, 1986). This has implications for: the context of systems development; the modelling of work by systems developers; and the interaction of users with the developed IS, which is also dealt with above.

These points are suggest yet more *research questions* that will inform a study of IS in organisations. For example: how is work divided (vertically) among men and women? Interestingly, general nursing is predominantly female; psychiatric nursing predominantly male. Equally, we might ask: how is work divided (horizontally) among men and women? In the case of nursing, women are predominantly at the lower end of nursing (auxiliary upwards) and men predominate in nurse management positions. Another broad question that merits a significant amount of research is: how is work organised (and controlled) by management? Nursing is a very hierarchical profession, with uniforms to designate position. In addition, inclusion into the professional body requires the acquisition of certificates and includes adherence to ethical code of practice. There are several questions relating to the issue of skills. We can start by asking: how are skills requirements and execution assessed? Despite the acquisition of formal knowledge in nursing, nursing skills are deemed to be acquired largely through practice; and lack of practice means membership of the qualified nursing body will expire. Furthermore, a 'good' nurse has qualities associated with 'a good woman' – caring, altruism, patience, self-sacrifice, etc. As for the labelling of skills, we might pose the question: what terminology and classification are applied to different skills? For example, the nursing hierarchy is deemed to reflect the level of skills of the nurse: auxiliary (non-skilled), newly qualified nurse (semi-skilled) and so on. An associated research question concerns differences in how these are valued is: what status do the skills have relative to other skills? Any study in nursing has to take into account the fact that in health work, caring skills are valued less than those related to clinical intervention. In addition, despite the manipulation of complex machines on the wards, the technical skills of nurses are rarely acknowledged. Likewise we might ask: do some skills confer status on the owner? And it is broadly agreed that clinical skills are highly regarded in society, while nurses are valued for their self-sacrifice. Finally, how are different skills rewarded? Although doctors are often not well paid for their work, nurses are notoriously poorly paid.

Technology, organisations and division of labour

Further to the areas of study suggested, and in keeping with feminist, critical, Interpretivist and SST perspectives it is advised that the IS researcher in studying gender issues should be attentive to a number of points and their implications for IS:

- the social and organisational concerns of IS must be deemed to include gender issues;
- given that IS are imbued with gender hallmarks of the context of invention, gender may be built into developed IS;
- the fact that gendered spheres exist in the workplace will impinge on work and skill;
- the existence of gendered jobs impinges on views of 'compatibility' with IS;

- a social constructivist perspective on gender and technology suggest things open to change;
- technology and gender are mutually defining and therefore, what is deemed 'technical' can alter over time;
- technology is seen as a masculine culture and this will affect user interaction.

We can generate a number of *research questions* from these points in a fairly straightforward fashion. So, we might start by asking the very broad question: In what ways have assumptions about gender been built into the technology? This may include many innovation activities. One example is the human computer interface development and to what degree user competence and cognitive style have been assumed. A related question is: where it exists, how does the gendering of jobs impinge on views of compatibility with the IS? In nursing, generally, there is an emphasis on caring skills and this may lead to feelings of incompatibility with the IS. However, a shift in focus to the many technical skills possessed by nurses encourages a view of potential affinity with the computer system. In line with the commitment to emancipation, we might wish to emphasise the potential for change and therefore enquire: in relation to gender and IS, which things are changing and how? Nursing, in common with other areas of work, has experienced increasing familiarity with IS to the point where in many areas a cultural shift in attitude towards IS may be observed, marking a transition from outright hostility to a degree of acceptance, else resignation to the role of IS in nursing. Another question related to change is: which elements, objects and machines are deemed 'technical' and can this change? In nursing, what is considered technical may in some instances be deemed alien, given a level of assumed incompatibility. Hence computers for administration may be dubbed 'technical' (alien) whereas heart monitors for mediating care are not. Finally, another over-arching question to pose is: how does the masculine culture of technology affect user interaction – especially with regard to confidence and experience? Nurses' preference for the 'social' or human can suggest a lack of confidence, a perception of incompatibility with and even hostility toward computers.

The research questions and their illustration from the field of nursing are summarised in Table 26.2, which concludes this section of the paper.

Table 26.2 Questions for gender and IS research

	Suggested research questions	Illustrations from nursing
Breadth of study	1. In what ways do organisational activities replicate gendered spheres?	Overarching question relating to division in health work between doctors and nurses
	2. Which elements of the system are open to women (users)?	Restrictions on access according to professional rank
	3. In what ways has the IS been adapted in usage (by women)?	Nurses may find short cuts for procedures and avoid usage
Theoretical and empirical focus	4. How is work divided (vertically) among men and women?	General nursing is predominantly female; psychiatric nursing predominantly male
	5. How is work divided (horizontally) among men and women?	Women are predominantly at the lower end of nursing (auxiliary upwards) and men in nurse management positions
	6. How is work organised (and controlled) by management?	Nursing is very hierarchical with uniforms to designate position. Inclusion into professional body includes adherence to ethical code of practice
	7. How are skills requirements and execution assessed?	Nursing skills largely acquired through practice; a 'good' nurse has qualities associated with 'a good woman'
	8. What terminology and classification are applied to different skills?	Nursing hierarchy deemed to reflect level of skills (e.g. skilled, semi-skilled, non-skilled)
	9. What status do the skills have relative to other skills?	Caring skills are valued less than clinical intervention; technical skills of nurses less acknowledged
	10. Do some skills confer status on the owner?	Clinical skills highly regarded in society
	11. How are different skills rewarded?	Nurses notoriously poorly paid

Technology, organizations and division of labour

12. In what ways have assumptions about gender been built into the technology?	This may include a study of style of interface and assumptions about user competence
13. Where it exists, how does the gendering of jobs impinge on views of compatibility with the IS?	In nursing the emphasis on caring skills will suggest less compatibility with IS; focus on technical skills of nurses suggest more compatibility
14. In relation to gender and IS, which things are changing and how?	Increasing degrees of familiarity with IS; cultural shift in acceptance of role of IS in nursing
15. Which elements, objects and machines are deemed 'technical'?	Computers for administration may be dubbed 'technical' (alien) whereas heart monitors are not
16. How does the masculine culture of technology affect user interaction – especially with regard to confidence and experience?	Nurses' preference for the 'social' or human can suggest lack of confidence, incompatibility and even hostility toward computers

Conclusion

The imperative of the paper is for a focus on issues of gender that can offer a starting point for understanding the organisational and broader societal context of IS development and implementation. The argument is based on a number of assumptions commencing with the view that gender is vital social factor shaping organisational life, and thus it is inconceivable that the interaction of users with IS as well as their development is not shaped by gendered spheres we inhabit (Wilson, 2002). As stated at the beginning of the paper, I have assumed that gender relations involve difference, inequality and power which is important with regard to access to, and control over, material and symbolic resources.

The literature review concerning gender, work, organisation and technology provided the building blocks for the conceptual framework for research into gender and IS. I have made the case for a social shaping approach to the issue of women's apparent disadvantage in their relationship with what is considered to be 'technology'. This has been achieved by making a case for a social constructivist account of gender phenomena arguing that both technology and gender are socially constructed and mutually defining (see Figure 26.1). In attempting to provide a coherent theoretical approach to drawing together a number of different disciplines for the purpose of studying gender, a Critical Management approach that incorporates feminist insights into the world of work and integrates a structuralist understanding of social and organisational concerns has been proffered.

The resultant framework identified a number of insights from the multidisciplinary literature, which can be used in formulating new research. Areas for future investigation were proposed and fitting research questions outlined to assist in the construction of prospective research proposals. Of course, the suggestions are intended merely as spring boards rather than straight jackets for future investigations.

Having offered explanations as to the disadvantage suffered by women in their relation to technology, I hope to have played a part in reducing the power of 'common sense ideas' which typically involve underestimating women's technological ability and are partially a consequence of how technology is defined in society. The social construction approach is intended moreover to persuade that women's relationship with technology is not a fixed entity but rather due to social convention. One consequence of this is that the relationship is open to change – a non-incidental consideration given that 'gender research... is clearly a political project' (Alvesson and Billing, 1997: 11).

Notes

1. SS of Technology is a broad church, incorporating several approaches including systems thinking (Hughes, 1983 looking at infrastructures; the SCOT (Pinch and Bijker, 1987) emphasising interpretative flexibility and relevant actors; and, actor-network theory (ANT) (Callon, 1986; Latour, 1987; Akrich, 1992) dealing with networks, inscription, translation, and irreversibility.
2. In common with determinism, essentialist approaches ascribe differences between men and women to innate characteristics. In so doing, they are criticised for universalising the experience of women and for failing to attend to the contingency of gendered roles and characteristics. As Segal (1994: 142) explains: 'any theory which pays only lip service to the actual variations, complexities, dialectics and history of social relations inevitably becomes raw material for essentialist analysis and politics'. Equally, descriptions of males as 'naturally' oppressive contain strong essentialist overtones. With specific reference to the under-representation of women in computing, Grundy (1996: 108) criticises the fact that men are seen as logical, rational and intelligent and women as intuitive, non-rational and emotional. Further, Lloyd (1984) argues that these stereotypes relate to older ideas that connect women with the body and men with the mind.
3. 'Innofusion' refers to the local redevelopment of the software takes place (Dutton *et al.*, 1995: 28).
4. The term critical here does not necessarily refer to a Habermasian approach. Rather, I am making reference to the Labour Process tradition that originates from Braverman (1974) and his radical aims (see Spencer, 2000).
5. In her paper for Social Studies of Science, Wajcman refers to the broader discipline and audience of Science and Technology Studies (S&TS). Here, I apply her comments more narrowly to SST as this discipline is more familiar to IS audiences.
6. A radical challenge to the notion that women are not technically minded is to question the way in which technology is defined in terms of male activities. So, for example, women, as early horticulturists, are likely to have used tools and methods involved in this work (Faulkner and Arnold, 1985). Other technologies are not included in the technology equation: for example, the knowledge needed to prepare food, healing, making clothes and caring for children (Cockburn, 1986; Knights and Murray, 1994).

References

Adam, A. (1997). What Should We Do With Cyberfeminism?, in R. Lander and A. Adam (eds.) *Women in Computing*, Exeter: Intellect Books.

Adam, A. (2002). Exploring the Gender Question in Critical Information Systems, *Journal of Information Technology* 17(2): 59–67.

Adam, A, Emms, J, Green, E and Owen, J. (eds.) (1994). *Women, Work and Computerization: Breaking old boundaries – building new forms*, Amsterdam: North-Holland.

Adam, A, Howcroft, D and Richardson, H. (2002). Guest Editorial, *Information Technology and People* 15(2): 94–97.

Akrich, M. (1992). The De-scription of Technical Objects, in W. Bijker and J. Law (eds.) *Shaping Technology/Building Society*, Cambridge: MIT Press.

Alvesson, M and Billing, YD. (1997). *Understanding Gender and Organizations*, London: Sage.

Baroudi, J and Igbaria, M. (1995). The Impact of Job Performance Evaluations on Career Advancement Prospects: An examination of gender differences in the information systems workplace, *MIS Quarterly* **19**(1): 107–123.

Baroudi, J and Truman, G. (1994). Gender Differences in the Information Systems Management Ranks: An assessment of potential discriminatory practices, *MIS Quarterly* **18**(2): 129–141.

Braverman, H. (1974). *Labour and Monopoly Capital*, New York: Monthly Review Press.

Burgoyne, J and Reynolds, M. (1997). *Managing Learning, Integrating Perspectives in Theory and Practice*, London: Sage.

Burke Leacock, E. (1981). *Myths of Male Dominance*, New York: Monthly Review Press.

Callon, M. (1986). Some Elements of a Sociology of Translation: Domestication of the scallops and the fishermen of St Briuec Bay, in J. Law (ed.) *Power: Action and Belief*, London: Routledge and Kegan Paul.

Carlin, N. (1989). The roots of gay oppression, *International Socialist Journal* **2**: 42.

Cockburn, C. (1983). *Brothers, Male Dominance and Technological Change*, London: Pluto Press.

Cockburn, C. (1986). *Machinery of Dominance: Women, men and technical knowledge*, London: Pluto Press.

Cockburn, C. (1988). The Gendering of Jobs: Workplace relations and the reproduction of sex segregation, in S. Walby (ed.) *Gender Segregation at Work*, Milton Keynes: OUP.

Cockburn, C and Omerod, S. (1993). *Gender and Technology in the Making*, London: Sage.

Davies, C. (1995). *Gender and the Professional Predicament in Nursing*, Buckingham: Open University Press.

Davies, C and Rosser, J. (1986). Gendered Jobs in the Health Service: A problem for labour process analysis, in D. Knights and H. Willmott (eds.) *Gender and the Labour Process*, Hampshire: Gower Publishing Company Ltd.

Dutton, WH, Mackenzie, D, Shapiro, S and Peltu, M. (1995). Computer Power and Human Limits: Learning from IT and telecommunications disasters, Programme on Information and Communication Technology Policy Research Paper No. 33, Brunel University.

Engels, F. (2001). *Origins of the Family, Private Property and the State*. (Translator: Ernest Unterman), Tennessee: University Press of the Pacific.

Faulkner, W and Arnold, E. (eds.) (1985). *Smothered By Invention: Technology in women's lives*, London: Pluto Press.

Gerver, E. (1989). Computers and Gender, in T. Forrester (ed.) *Computers in the Human Context*, Oxford: Basil Blackwell.

Green, E, Owen, J and Pain, D. (eds.) (1993). *Gendered by Design: Information technology and office systems*, London: Taylor & Francis.

Grint, K and Gill, R. (eds.) (1995). *The Gender-Technology Relation: Contemporary theory and research*, London: Taylor & Francis.

Grundy, F. (1996). *Women and Computers*, Exeter: Intellect.

Henwood, F, Plumeridge, S and Stepulevage, L. (2001). A Tale of Two Cultures, in S. Wyatt, F. Henwood, N. Miller and P. Senker (eds.) *Technology and In/equality*, London: Routledge.

Howcroft, D and Wilson, M. (2003). Paradoxes of Participatory Practices: The Janus role of the systems developer, *Information and Organization* 13(1): 1–24.

Hughes, TP. (1983). *Networks of Power: Electrification in Western society, 1880–1930*, Baltimore, MD: John Hopkins University Press.

Karpf, A. (1987). Recent Feminist Approaches to Women and Technology, in M. McNeil (ed.) *Gender and Expertise*, London: Free Association Books.

Knights, D and Murray, F. (1994). *Managers Divided*, Chichester: John Wiley & Sons.

Knights, D and Willmott, H. (eds.) (1986). *Gender and the Labour Process*, Hampshire: Gower Publishing Company Ltd.

Lander, R and Adam, A. (1997). *Women in Computing*, Exeter: Intellect.

Latour, B. (1987). *Science in Action Milton Keynes*, Milton Keynes: Open University Press.

Law, J. (1987). Technology and Heterogeneous Engineering: The case of Portuguese expansion, in W. Bijker, T. Hughes and T. Pinch (eds.) *The Social Construction of Technological Systems*, London: MIT.

Ledwith, S and Colgan, F. (1996). *Women in Organisations: Challenging gender politics*, Basingstoke: Macmillan Press Ltd.

Liu, J and Wilson, D. (2001). *Developing Women in a Digital World*, Women in Management Review 16(8): 405–416.

Lloyd, G. (1984). *Man of Reason: Male and Female in Western philosophy*, London: Routledge.

Lukes, S. (1974). *Power: A radical view*, London: Macmillan.

MacKenzie, D and Wajcman, J. (eds.) (1985). *The Social Shaping of Technology*, Milton Keynes: Open University Press.

MacKinnon, A, Blomqvist, M and Vehvilainen, M. (1993). Gendering Computer Work: An international perspective, *AI and Society* 8: 280–294.

Maitland, A. (2001). A solution to the IT skills shortage, *Women in Computing, Financial Times*, 22 February.

Noble, D. (1984). *Forces of Production: A social history of industrial automation*, New York: Knopf.

Phillips, A and Taylor, B. (1980). Sex and Skill: Notes towards a feminist economics, *Feminist Review* 6: 79–88.

Pinch, TJ and Bijker, WE. (1987). The Social Construction of Facts and Artifacts or How the Sociology of Science and the Sociology of Technology Might Benefit One Another, in W.E. Bijker, T.P. Hughes and T.J. Pinch (eds.) *The Social Construction of Technological Systems*, Cambridge, MA: MIT Press.

Quicke, S. (2001). Where did all the IT girls go? The crisis in recruitment in the technology industry, *The Independent*, 19 November, p 9.

Quintas, P. (1996). Software By Design, in R. Mansell and R. Silverstone (eds.) *Communication By Design: The Politics of ICT's*, Milton Keynes: Open University Press.

Rasmussen, B and Hapnes, T. (1991). Excluding Women from the Technologies of the Future?, *Futures* **December**: 1107–1113.

Rubery, J and Fagan, C. (1994). Occupational Segregation: Plus ca change...?, in R. Lindley (ed.) *Labour Market Structures and Prospects for Women*, Manchester: Equal Opportunities.

Segal, L. (1994). *Is the Future Female? Troubled Thoughts on Contemporary Feminism*, (2nd ed) London: Virago Press.

Shwartz Cowan, R. (1985). How the Refrigerator Got Its Hum, in D. MacKenzie and J. Wajcman (eds.) *The Social Shaping of Technology*, Milton Keynes: Open University Press.

Smith, J. (1997). *Different for Girls: How culture creates women*, London: Chatto Press.

Snizek, W and Neil, C. (1992). Job characteristics, gender stereotypes and perceived gender discrimination in the workplace, *Organization Studies* **13**(3): 403–427.

Spencer, D. (2000). Braverman and the Contribution of Labour Process Analysis to the Critique of Capitalist Production – Twenty Five Years On, *Work, Employment and Society* **14**(2): 223–243.

Star, SL. (1995). The Politics of Formal Representations: Wizards, gurus and organisational complexity, in S.L. Star (ed.) *Ecologies of Knowledge: Work and politics in science and technology*, Albany: SUNY Press.

Strathern, M. (1980). No Nature, No Culture: The Hagen case, in C. MacCormack and M. Strathern (eds.) *Nature, Culture and Gender*, Cambridge: Cambridge University Press.

Trauth, E. (2002). Odd Girl Out: An individual differences perspective on women in the IT profession, *Information Technology and People* **15**(2): 98–118.

Van Zoonen, L. (1992). Feminist Theory and Information Technology, *Media, Culture and Society* **14**: 9–29.

Ward, H. (2001). 'Hewitt calls for more IT women', *Computer Weekly*, 18th October.

Wagner, I. (1993). Women's Voice: the case of nursing information systems, *AI and Society* **7**: 295–310.

Wajcman, J. (1991). *Feminism Confronts Technology*, Cambridge: Polity Press.

Wajcman, J. (1995). Feminist Theories of Technology, in S. Jasanoff, G.E. Markle, J.C. Petersen and T. Pinch (eds.) *Handbook of Science and Technology Studies*, London: Sage.

Wajcman, J. (2000). Reflections on Gender and Technology Studies: in what state is the art? *Social Studies of Science* **30**(3): 447–464.

Walby, S. (ed.). (1988). *Gender Segregation at Work*, Milton Keynes: Open University Press.

Walsham, G. (1993). *Interpreting Information Systems in Organisations*, Chichester: John Wiley & Sons.

Webster, J. (1990). *Office Automation: The labour process and women's work in Britain*, Hemel Hempstead: Harvester Wheatsheaf.

Webster, J. (1996). *Shaping Women's Work: Gender employment and information technology*, London: Longman.

Williams, R and Edge, D. (1996). The Social Shaping of Technology, *Research Policy* **25**: 865–899.

Wilson, M. (2002). Making Nursing Visible? Gender, Technology and the Care Plan as Script, *Information Technology and People* **15**(2): 139–158.

Wilson, M and Howcroft, D. (2002). Conceptualising Information Systems Failure: A social shaping approach, *European Journal of Information Systems* **11**(4): 236–250.